WE HOLD THESE TRUTHS

Dialectic

What Man Has Made of Man

How to Read a Book

How to Think About War and Peace

The Capitalist Manifesto (with Louis O. Kelso)

The Idea of Freedom

The Conditions of Philosophy

The Difference of Man and the Difference It Makes

The Time of Our Lives

The Common Sense of Politics

The American Testament (with William Gorman)

Some Questions About Language

Philosopher at Large

Reforming Education

Great Treasury of Western Thought (with Charles Van Doren)

Aristotle for Everybody

How to Think About God

Six Great Ideas

The Angels and Us

The Paideia Proposal

How to Speak/How to Listen

Paideia Problems and Possibilities

A Vision of the Future

The Paideia Program

Ten Philosophical Mistakes

A Guidebook to Learning

WE HOLD THESE TRUTHS

UNDERSTANDING THE IDEAS AND IDEALS OF THE CONSTITUTION

Mortimer J. Adler

Foreword by HARRY A. BLACKMUN
Associate Justice of the United States Supreme Court

With Annotated Appendices by WAYNE MOQUIN

COLLIER BOOKS
MACMILLAN PUBLISHING COMPANY
NEW YORK
COLLIER MACMILLAN PUBLISHERS
LONDON

Copyright © 1987 by Mortimer J. Adler

Collier Books
Macmillan Publishing Company
866 Third Avenue, New York, N.Y. 10022
Collier Macmillan Canada, Inc.

Library of Congress Cataloging-in-Publication Data
Adler, Mortimer Jerome, 1902–
We hold these truths.
Includes index.
1. United States—Constitutional law. I. Title.
KF4550.A725 1987b   342.73′029   87-9365
ISBN 0-02-064130-3 (pbk.)

Macmillan books are available at special discounts for bulk purchases for sales promotions, premiums, fund-raising, or educational use.
For details contact:

Special Sales Director
Macmillan Publishing Company
866 Third Avenue
New York, N.Y. 10022

First Collier Books Edition 1988

10 9 8 7 6 5 4 3 2 1

Printed in the United States of America

We Hold These Truths is also published in a hardcover edition by Macmillan Publishing Company.

To the Memory of
WILLIAM GORMAN

Contents

[vii]

PART THREE
The Preamble's Ideals

PART FOUR
The Emergent Ideal of Democracy

PART FIVE
Three Documents That Comprise the American Testament

APPENDICES
Annotated Excerpts from Historical Documents

Foreword

WHEN MORTIMER ADLER WRITES, his observations are always deserving of the fullest consideration. The reader will inevitably learn and profit from that writing. But when Dr. Adler writes about the Constitution of the United States at this bicentennial time, it properly may be said that one has nothing less than a duty to read and to learn.

This book sets forth bedrock knowledge about the government which we have structured and which has existed on this side of the Atlantic now for two hundred years. Familiarity with and understanding of the Constitution, our "blueprint" for government, and the amendments thereto—the most important ones of which are in terms of mandate, and in language that is broad and flexible, and that bends but does not break in the hot fire of experience—are basic to an understanding of ourselves as a people. The Constitution is what we live by in this nation. Too many of us know too little about it.

While this book is written by a most distinguished philosopher, and is naturally and admittedly philosophical in approach, it is readable and uncomplicated. That was the author's intention, and he has attained his goal. There is no excuse for not understanding the ideals of our Constitution.

Dr. Adler stresses the important, much of which ought to be obvious but so often is not, as, for example, that "citizenship is the primary political office under a constitutional government," that the Declaration of Independence, with all its magnificent pronouncements, did not bring this *nation* into existence in 1776, and that happiness, the pursuit of which is among the "unalienable" rights, "depends in part on our possession of moral virtue." I could go on, but one should make such exciting discoveries on his own.

Dr. Adler reminds us that, despite our proper reverence for the Constitution as amended to date, it is not perfect and thus falls short of attaining the ideal of democracy for which we strive and which is among the promises of the Declaration of Independence and of the Constitution's Preamble. He stresses the protection of inalienable human rights in the economic sphere, as well as in the political arena, as a condition for the equal enjoyment of liberty by all.

There may be those who disagree. And there will be those who disagree, at least in part, with his observations in the final chapter as to what "remains to be done." But in this chapter Dr. Adler acknowledges that he does not know all the answers and so proceeds interrogatively rather than declaratively.

This is good grist for serious thinking, and Dr. Adler makes us *think*. That is usually what he wants his writings to accomplish.

The book is needed and timely.

Harry A. Blackmun
Associate Justice
United States Supreme Court

Washington, D.C.
August 1986

PART ONE

Important Prefatory Considerations

CHAPTER 1

The Two Bicentennials

IN 1976 WE CELEBRATED what we called the bicentennial of the United States of America. But that is not what it was. The United States of America did not come into existence in 1776. What existed then were thirteen colonies of King George III who were at war with British troops on this continent. The fighting had begun almost a year before, but it was not until July 4, 1776, that the colonies declared their independence of Great Britain and gave their reasons for doing so.

What we celebrated on July 4, 1976, was the two hundredth anniversary of the promulgation of the Declaration of Independence. It was a bicentennial, indeed, but not of the United States of America, a single, sovereign nation, a federal republic.

The closing paragraph of the Declaration of Independence opens with these words: "We, therefore, the representatives of the United States of America, in general Congress assembled. . . ." The representatives assembled in the Continental Congress at Philadelphia did not represent a single nation which could then be designated by the proper name "The United States of America." They represented thirteen sovereign states. United they were in their resolution to fight together for their independence, but they were united in no other way.

Seven years later, in 1783, the thirteen colonies, now emerging from a military victory as independent, sovereign states, entered into an agreement or contract with one another to remain loosely united in peace as they had been in war. The army that had successfully fought that war was called "the continental army," not the army of the United States.

The loose union into which they entered for peaceful relationships was expounded in the "Articles of Confederation." The subheading of this document reveals that these articles did not form or constitute a single, sovereign nation, for it reads: "Articles of Confederation and Perpetual Union Between the States . . ." after which follows an enumeration of the names of the thirteen colonies in an order dictated by their geographical location from north to south.

In 1787, after the loose union formed by these thirteen sovereign states gave signs of ceasing to be perpetual, representatives of each state met once again in Philadelphia to form a more perfect union, one that had more likelihood of becoming perpetual and also of preserving peace on this continent.

The document framing and formulating that more perfect union was entitled "The Constitution of the United States of America." It was properly called a "constitution" for it did two things that a constitution should do.

In the first place, it did *constitute* a single, sovereign state, unlike the Articles of Confederation (and also unlike the Charter of the United Nations), which did no more than establish an alliance of a number of independent states, each of which remained sovereign in relation to all the others, as sovereign as each was before it agreed to become a member of the confederacy.

In the second place, it did what the Articles of Confederation (or the Charter of the United Nations) could not do: it established a government, outlined its purposes, limited its scope, indicated the several branches of that government, and defined the offices of each branch, saying how they shall be filled and how the authority and power vested in each shall be related to one another.

When we today use the words "United States of America," we are referring to the nation that is one of the many sovereign states that comprise the United Nations. But when, in 1776, the Declaration of Independence, in its concluding paragraph, introduced those who signed the Declaration by referring to them as "the representatives of the United States of America, in general Congress assembled" those same words—"United States of America"—had a different meaning.

The thirteen colonies of Great Britain on the North American continent were united in their determination to be independent of British rule. If they won their war for independence, they wished to establish themselves as thirteen sovereign states. As they were cooperatively engaged in that war under the auspices of their Continental Congress, they could properly refer to themselves as the united states of America, but not as the United States of America in the sense in which we now understand those words.

How, then, shall we interpret the opening lines of Lincoln's Gettysburg Address—"Four score and seven years ago our fathers brought forth on this continent a new nation"? What came into existence in 1776 was certainly not a new nation—that is, a new national state comparable to Great Britain, France, or Spain. What came into existence then was a *new people* who, through the Declaration, sought to justify in the eyes of the world their separation from the people of Great Britain and their right "to assume, among the powers of the earth, the separate and equal station to which the laws of nature and of nature's God entitle them."

In order to assume the station to which they thought they had a right, this new people had, first of all, to win a war. If they had not won that war, they could not have tried to perpetuate their independent status under the Articles of Confederation. Four years later, these two things having been accomplished, they could then try to form a more perfect union by drafting and adopting the Constitution of the United States, in the Preamble to which they refer to themselves as "We, the people of the United States. . . ."

The words "United States" occurs twice in the Preamble, first in that opening phrase, then in the closing, which says that we, the people "do ordain and establish this Constitution for the United States of America."

In its first occurrence, "United States" would have been more accurately written "united states," for the same reason that it should have been written that way in the last paragraph of the Declaration of Independence, because the nation now known as the United States of America did not exist in 1787 any more than it did in 1776.

In its second occurrence, "United States" should be interpreted as having a prospective reference. It refers to the nation or national state that would come into existence only after the document drafted by the Constitutional Convention during the summer of 1787 was ratified or adopted by three-quarters of the thirteen states to be united.

That did not occur until August of 1788. The remaining states fell in line somewhat later than that. George Washington did not take office as the first President of the United States until March of 1789; not until that year did the first Congress of the United States assemble; and not until then were there ambassadors from the United States to the courts of the European nations.

In political as in biological life there is a period of gestation between conception and birth. What we are celebrating in the year 1987 is the bicentennial of the conception, not the birth, of the new nation that only from 1789 on could be properly referred to as the United States of America.

The Constitution that was drafted in Philadelphia in 1787 and then sent to the Confederation Congress, meeting in New York, for transmittal to the thirteen states presented the conception of a government that was both national and federal. If that conception had failed to win a sufficient number of ratifying adoptions, the federal republic, thus conceived, would not have come into existence in 1789.

Since the Constitution established a federal union, not a unitary state, each state entering the union still retained some measure of individual sovereignty. The states surrendered only their power to make war and peace, to enter into alliances with one another or with foreign nations, to make treaties, and so on. They retained some measure of local or internal sovereignty over the citizens residing within their borders.

A dual sovereignty was thus established: one that was national, the sovereignty of the federal government; and thirteen local sovereignties, the sovereignty of each of the states adopting the Constitution. The citizens who made up the people of the United States also had a dual citizenship. They became citizens of the new United States but also remained citizens of Massachusetts, New York, Pennsylvania, Virginia, and the other states.

While the Declaration of Independence, as promulgated on July 4, 1776, did not bring this nation into existence or establish the government of the United States of America, it magnificently enunciated the fundamental principles of republican or constitutional government—principles that are not stated explicitly in the Constitution itself.

The Declaration was, therefore, in the most profound sense, a preface to the Constitution, more fundamental politically than the Constitution's own Preamble. Since the word "preface" lacks the dignity and weight that should be accorded the Declaration in relation to the Constitution, we should perhaps think of it as the architectural blueprint for the government of the United States.

This understanding of the relationship between the Declaration and the Constitution (and their related bicentennials) was expressed in a book published in 1976, written by me in collaboration with William Gorman, an associate at the Institute for Philosophical Research. That book, entitled *The American Testament*, was divided into three parts. The first dealt with the Declaration; the second with the Preamble to the Constitution; and the third with Lincoln's Gettysburg Address.

To call these three documents "the American testament" is to say that, together and in relation to one another, they are *like* the sacred scriptures of this nation.

From the first document, by the most careful interpretation and critical exegesis, we can derive the nation's basic articles of political faith.

From the second, together with the articles that follow the Preamble and their subsequent amendments, we can come to understand the elaboration of those articles of political faith in terms of governmental aims, governmental structures, and governmental policies.

An equally careful reading of the third gives us, in spite of Lincoln's incomparable brevity, a full, rich confirmation of our faith in government of the people, by the people, and for the people—the people who declared their independence, who formed a more perfect union, who resolved that that union would be perpetuated and that this nation would not perish from the earth. We are not only the heirs of those people, we *are* those people, and we are today engaged in celebrating our heritage.

Flag-waving, however sincere; public convocations, however well designed; and political oratory, however thoughtfully delivered, will not by themselves suffice to celebrate the event of this nation's conception and birth, its two centuries of development, the civil crisis it survived 125 years ago, and the long, prosperous, and progressive future for which we all hope.

As individual celebrants of this occasion, the personal obligation of every citizen of the United States is to understand as well as possible the three documents that are our American testament— words that should be piously revered even though they are not in a strict sense this country's holy scriptures.

To serve that purpose, I propose in this book to cover some of the same ground that Willian Gorman and I covered in *The American Testament*, which was the basis of a week-long seminar at the Aspen Institute for Humanistic Studies in 1975.* Though published in the year of the bicentennial celebration, the volume was not widely read or given much attention amidst all the flag-waving, fireworks, and pulpit-thumping. But understanding occurs as a private accomplishment, not a public event. It is something done in the quiet of one's own mind, with the solemnity of sober reflection.

While covering the same ground as *The American Testament*, this

---

*The participants in the Aspen Seminar, which served as a preparatory exercise in the drafting of *The American Testament*, included the following persons: Dumas Malone, Professor Emeritus of History at the University of Virginia and biographer of Thomas Jefferson; Edward Levi, former President of the University of Chicago and, at the time, Attorney General of the United States; James F. Hoge, then Editor of the Chicago *Sun-Times*; Seymour Topping, then Assistant Managing Editor of *The New York Times*; Bill Moyers of WNET-TV, New York; Douglass Cater, Senior Fellow of the Aspen Institute for Humanistic Studies; Phillips Talbot, then President of the Asia Society; Bethuel M. Webster of Webster and Sheffield, of New York City; and Elizabeth Paepcke, Trustee of the Aspen Institute for Humanistic Studies.

work goes much further in helping readers understand the uniqueness of the United States of America, and encourages them to look to its future as well as to its origin and development.

The dedication of this book to William Gorman expresses my debt to him as collaborator in the earlier effort as well as my hope that, were he alive today, he would gladly add his signature to mine as co-author. It might have been a better book had he participated in its production, but with such shortcomings as it may have, I trust that it does not fail to do for its readers what he and I set out to do to celebrate the first bicentennial.

I wish also to acknowledge my debt to two friends and associates—Theodore H. White and Father John Courtney Murray. Just before he died, Theodore White wrote a brief essay entitled "The American Idea." It was published posthumously in *The New York Times Magazine* (July 5, 1986). Many years ago, in 1960, Father Murray wrote a book entitled *We Hold These Truths*. Both anticipated some of the insights that I have sought to elaborate in this book.

I was tempted to adopt Teddy White's title for it, but I finally decided on Father Murray's because the truths in the Declaration of Independence, not all of which are self-evident, provide us with the overarching principles for understanding the ideals of the Constitution.

CHAPTER 2

A More Perfect Union

THE NOVELTY of the American Constitution does not consist in its being the first constitution ever proposed to a people for adoption, nor even in its being the first ever to be drafted. The idea of constitutional government, as radically contrasted with royal or despotic regimes, is as old as ancient Greece.

The line drawn by Plato to divide all forms of government into the legitimate and the illegitimate separated governments in which laws are supreme from governments in which the supremacy rests with men of power, ruling by might rather than by right. Following Plato, Aristotle defined a constitution as the fundamental law that conferred rightful authority, not just power or force, upon those who held the offices of government that the constitution established.

In addition, in one remarkable passage, Aristotle referred to those who first founded a state and called them the greatest of benefactors. Who did he have in mind?

We do not know with certitude, but it is a reasonable conjecture that he was thinking of Solon, who framed a constitution for Athens, and Lycurgus, who set one up for Sparta. Accounts of their innovative accomplishments are to be found in Plutarch's *Lives*, where their personal histories and achievements, as well as the states they constituted, are described.

What did Aristotle mean when he said these men—Solon and

Lycurgus—first founded a state? And what did he mean when he said we should regard them as the greatest of benefactors?

Egypt antedated Athens and Sparta by centuries. The kingdom of Persia existed at roughly the same time as Athens and Sparta. Why, then, did Aristotle assert that states did not exist before constitutions came into existence?

The answer lies in Aristotle's distinction between domestic and political government; in other words, between the government of a family and the government of a city, or *polis*.

In a family, the parents rule their children absolutely, without the children having any voice in the matter. They do so by virtue of their superiority as mature persons in relation to the immaturity of their offspring. Tribal rule, where the government is in the hands of the elders of the tribe, is the extension of parental rule to the larger group formed by the association of a number of families in a village or tribal community.

Even larger communities come into existence by the amalgamation of a number of tribes in a given locality. The kings who rule such communities do not do so by virtue of their superiority in age or wisdom, but rather by the superiority of the power they somehow manage to wield over others without giving those others any voice in the matter. The despotic kind of rule that is exercised by parents over very young children and by elders over the tribe is thus extended to a still larger population.

According to Aristotle, the community thus populated and governed should not be regarded as a state in the strict sense of that term because that kind of government—call it absolute, royal, or despotic—is appropriate for families and tribes but not for states. States do not come into existence until governments are constituted, until constitutions come into existence and communities larger in their populations than families or tribes are governed constitutionally.

That is why Aristotle thought that Solon in Athens and Lycurgus in Sparta can rightly be said to have first founded states by virtue of having given constitutions to those two communities. And his reason for saying that they should be regarded as the greatest of benefactors emerges as soon as we realize that, with the coming into existence of constitutions and constitutional governments, citizenship also comes into existence.

Before that, those who lived under the rule of the Pharaohs of ancient Egypt or under the dominion of the great kings of Persia were subjects, not citizens. When the Pharaohs or kings governed tyrannically as well as despotically, the people were no better than slaves under a master who ruled to serve his own interests, not benevolently, as good parents govern their children.

The invention of constitutions by the ancient Greeks stands out as one of the greatest advances in the history of societies, certainly as great as the invention of the wheel or the domestication of animals in the history of technology. Until that invention occurred, all communities consisted of human beings governed either as subjects or slaves. Citizenship did not exist anywhere.

Hence it is clear that our Founding Fathers, however remarkable their work in drafting the Constitution of the United States, did not invent the first constitution and, with it, citizenship. Nor did the French revolutionists a few years later when they overthrew the despotism of their Bourbon kings and created the first French republic, thereby giving the word "citizen" the revolutionary meaning it so rightly deserves.

The Constitution of the United States was not the first constitution ever to have been drafted by a group of men assembled in what they themselves called a Constitutional Convention, an assemblage that had as its express purpose the putting on paper of a written constitution.* Nor was the Constitution of the United States the first explicitly formulated constitution. In a treatise on Greek constitutions Aristotle described and discussed more than one hundred of them. His account of only one—the constitution of Athens—has survived.

Republics existed in the ancient world, in Rome as well as in

---

*Between 1776 and 1780, Virginia, Pennsylvania, Maryland, North Carolina, and Massachusetts held constitutional conventions.

Greece. In the modern world, constitutional government did not begin with its establishment in the United States in 1787. It began in England in 1215 with the Magna Carta, which was the first step in the long series of enactments that limited the power of English kings, increased the power of representative parliaments, and made those who voted for members of parliament self-governing citizens as well as subjects of the kings.

Constitutional government began on this continent as the result of a single political action. It did not begin that way in the British Isles. There it developed over centuries in which successive acts of Parliament turned a government that was at first completely royal or despotic into one that was both royal and constitutional and, finally, into one that is republican or completely constitutional in everything except the vestigial symbols that surround the throne. Though the legislative enactments that, cumulatively, comprise British constitutional law are all written laws, we do not speak of England as having a written constitution, probably because its constitution cannot be found in a single document formulated by a constitutional convention at one time. That is one of the unique things about the American event in 1787.

But it is not the only thing that is unique about it. The American Constitution created the first federal republic in the history of the world. The first objective or aim mentioned in its Preamble, a purpose distinctly different from all the other objectives thereafter mentioned, is "to form a more perfect union." Union of what? Of the thirteen sovereign states that, in the preceding five years, had been united under the Articles of Confederation.

What was more perfect about their union under the Constitution as compared with their union under the Articles of Confederation? The answer lies in one fact alone: Under the Articles of Confederation, each of the thirteen states retained its individual sovereignty, diminished not one whit by its entering into a confederacy with the other twelve. Under the Constitution, each of the thirteen states surrendered all its external sovereignty—that is, its sovereignty in relation to other American states as well as to foreign states in the arena of international affairs. They did, however, retain their internal sovereignty. Each remained a sovereign state in relation to the citizens of the United States who lived within that particular state, for those people were not only citizens of the United States, they were also citizens of the state in which they voted for the governors and for the representatives to the legislative assemblies.

A federal republic is thus seen to involve a plurality of sovereignties: on the one hand, the sovereignty of one national or federal government, and on the other hand, the sovereignty of each of the several federated states, be it thirteen as it was in 1787 or fifty as it is in 1987.

Under the Articles of Confederation, the citizens of New York or Virginia were just that and nothing more. When the Constitution replaced the Articles, the citizens of New York or Virginia became, in addition, citizens of the United States. In the period before the Civil War, most of them regarded themselves first as citizens of the particular state in which they lived, and second as citizens of the United States. Now most of us regard ourselves primarily as citizens of the United States and only secondarily as citizens of one of the fifty states. This change in attitude began several decades after the Civil War, and, since the turn of the century, it has spread to the point where it is now almost universal. The more perfect union has become ever more solidly perfect.

The response given so far as to what makes the union more perfect is correct but incomplete. To answer the question completely requires us to understand why that more perfect union is the indispensable condition of peace on this continent—civil peace as contrasted with civil war. If we do not understand this, we do not understand the prime motivation that brought the representatives of the thirteen sovereign states to Philadelphia to draft a constitution that would, first and foremost, unite them in a manner that would prevent their engaging in war with one another.

As long as they retained their external sovereignty vis-à-vis one another, they could also enter into treaties with each other, and a group of them could form an alliance to serve their common interests as against the common interests of the other states.

When treaties were violated or interests were infringed, one state or group of allied states could, if their conflict of interests became serious enough, resort to force by military means. The Articles of Confederation could not prevent this from happening; it could not prevent the state of war that always exists among states fully sovereign in their external as well as internal relations from turning into actual warfare.

What is properly called a state of war, as opposed to actual warfare, exists between any two sovereigns—sovereign princes or sovereign states—when, in serious conflict with one another, they cannot settle their differences amicably by negotiation. They have no way to resolve their conflict except by resort to force; and when that recourse is available, the state of war easily turns into actual warfare.

The record of events for the period 1783 to 1787 provides sufficient evidence of the fact that a state of war did exist between states, and could have erupted into actual warfare. New York and New Jersey, divided by the Hudson River, had serious conflicts of interest with respect to trade and other commercial matters, and similar conflicts of interest existed between other adjoining states. If diplomacy between the feuding states failed to resolve the conflict, what recourse was left but for them to engage in bloody warfare with one another?

We have additional evidence on the point under consideration. It consists in the explicit testimony to be found in the first nine of the *Federalist* papers. Written by Alexander Hamilton, James Madison, and John Jay, these papers, published in the *Independent Journal*, a New York periodical, attempted to persuade the citizens of New York State to vote for the adoption of the federal constitution.

The writers of those nine papers called attention to the intermittent but incessant warfare among the separate unfederated sovereign states of Europe. What could prevent the same thing from happening among the separate unfederated states on the eastern seaboard of this continent? Nothing, they answered, nothing except the more perfect union that would come into existence when the federal constitution was adopted and the separate states ceased to be unfederated by surrendering all their external sovereignty in relation to one another as well as in relation to other states abroad.

The overarching purpose of the men who assembled in Philadelphia was to preserve peace on this continent. That motivation was expressed in the opening words of the Constitution's Preamble: "We, the people of the United States, in order to form a more perfect union. . . ." The underlying reason for forming a more perfect union was, however, explicitly expressed in the first nine *Federalist* papers: peace on this continent.

The tensions that later developed between the northern and the southern states with regard to the institution of slavery gave early signs of threatening that peace and finally brought on the Civil War— not a civil war like Oliver Cromwell's war against King Charles I, but a war of secession that sought to dissolve the federal union.

Had the amendments to the Constitution that followed the victory of the northern states been an integral part of the Constitution itself, the Civil War might have been prevented; but it is also almost certain that an attempt to include the provisions made by those amendments would have disrupted the Convention and prevented it from finishing its work in concord.

In later chapters I shall return to a consideration of federal union for the sake of civil peace, which is one of the unique aspects of our Constitution. Equally unique is the Civil War or War of Secession, which the Constitution could not prevent and which attempted to dissolve the Union.

As Lincoln saw it, the North fought the South not to abolish slavery, but to preserve the Union. Nevertheless, the abolition of slavery, not by Lincoln's Emancipation Proclamation but by the post–Civil War amendments, removed the most serious conflict of interest that could threaten the Union's existence. Other amendments in subsequent years removed other obstacles to the Union's preservation by strengthening the power of the federal government vis-à-vis the rights of the federated states.

Earlier I called attention to the similarity between the Charter of the United Nations and the Articles of Confederation. The former does not, as the latter does not, create a union perfect enough to preserve peace among the states involved.

War between states thus united or confederated would be international war, not civil war. Strictly speaking, they could not be wars of secession (which is the accurate name for the War between the States in 1861–1865), because neither the Charter of the United Nations nor the Articles of Confederation created a federal union that can be dissolved by the secession of some of its members.

When international tensions in the contemporary world reach the breaking point and diplomatic conversations completely break down, the Charter of the United Nations will fail to prevent a third world war, just as the Articles of Confederation would have failed to prevent warfare between New York and New Jersey, or between other states in propinquity and with conflicting interests, had not the federal constitution replaced it with a more perfect union.

This is the lesson that a book published by Carl Van Doren in 1948 tried to teach. That was the year in which the Charter of the United Nations was being drafted in San Francisco. Van Doren's book was about the Constitutional Convention in Philadelphia in 1787. The title of his book attempted to relate what happened in Philadelphia to what was then happening in San Francisco. It was called *The Great Rehearsal*. But the lesson it tried to teach went unheeded. The rehearsal in Philadelphia did not produce the performance he had hoped it would produce on the stage in San Francisco.

CHAPTER 3

Every Citizen, Both Young and Old

THE AIM OF THIS BOOK is to set forth what every citizen, both young and old, should know about the ideas and ideals of the Constitution.

By "every citizen" I mean not only persons who are of an age to exercise the franchise that enables them to participate actively in political life. I include also those individuals who will become our future citizens—the young, who, when they come of age, will take on the responsibilities that the high office of citizenship puts on their shoulders.

Most Americans, I fear, do not know or appreciate the fact that citizenship is the primary political office under a constitutional government. In a republic, the citizens are the ruling class. They are the permanent and principal rulers. All other offices that are set up by the constitution are secondary.

The first and indispensable qualification for holding political office in any of the branches of government is to be a citizen. Officeholders, moreover, whether elected or selected, are citizens in office for a period of time, but all citizens are citizens for life. Officeholders, from the President down, are transient and instrumental rulers, unlike citizens in general who are permanent and principal rulers.

The distinction between the permanent status of citizenship and the transient or temporary character of government officials is obvious. But it may not be so obvious why I refer to citizens as the principal rulers and call government officials instrumental rulers. To understand this point it is necessary to realize that the government of the United States is not in Washington, not in the White House, not in the Capitol, which houses the Congress, nor in any or all the public office buildings in the District of Columbia.

The government of the United States resides in us—we, the people. What resides in Washington is the administration of our government. We recognize this, at least verbally, when we say, after a Presidential election, that we have changed one administration for another. That change leaves the government of the United States unchanged, because its principal rulers are also its permanent rulers, whereas its instrumental rulers—its administrative officials—are transient and temporary.

Administrative officials, from the President down, are the instruments by which we, the people, govern ourselves. They serve us in our capacity as self-governing citizens of the Republic. Lincoln never tired of saying that he conceived his role to be that of a servant of the people who elected him. The word "servant" in this connection does not carry any invidious connotations of inferiority or menial status. Rather, it signifies the performance of an important function, one carrying great responsibility, a responsibility officials are called upon to discharge while they are *serving a term* in public office.

I am sorry to say that most Americans think of themselves as the subjects of government and regard the administrators in public office as their rulers, instead of thinking of themselves as the ruling class and public officials as their servants—the instrumentalities for carrying out their will.

It is of the utmost importance to persuade the citizens of the United States, both young and old, that they have misconceived their role in the political life of this country. If they can be persuaded to overcome this misconception, and come to view themselves in the right light, they will understand that their high responsibility as citizens carries with it the obligation to understand the ideas and ideals of our constitutional government.

In earlier times, when much smaller societies than ours were ruled by princes, books were written to instruct princes in the art of governance. The education of the prince, both moral and intellectual, was of supreme importance if one had any expectation of obtaining good government from their benevolently despotic rule.

Now, when the people have replaced the prince, when they are the self-governing rulers of the Republic, how can we expect good government from them, or from the administrative officials whom they directly or indirectly choose to serve them, unless we think it supremely important that they, the citizens both young and old, be educated for the discharge of their responsibilities.

Preparation for the duties of citizenship is one of the three objectives of any sound system of public schooling in our society. Preparation for earning a living is another, and the third is preparation for discharging everyone's moral obligation to lead a good life and make as much of one's self as possible. Our present system of compulsory basic schooling, kindergarten through the twelfth grade, does not serve any of these objectives well.

The reasons why this is so and what must be done to remedy these grave deficiencies have been set forth in a series of books that have initiated much-needed reforms in our school system.* Here I will borrow from them only what is germane to the explanation of what must be accomplished educationally to make the future citizens of the United States better citizens than their elders.

I am going to state the educational objective in its minimal terms. The least to be expected of our future citizens (as well as all the rest of us) is that they will have read the three documents that are our political testament—the Declaration of Independence, the Constitution of the United States, and Lincoln's Gettysburg Address— and that their reading of these three documents will have eventuated in their understanding the ideas and ideals of our Republic. While much more might be added (and this book will try to provide some indication of what these additions should be), the primary concern here is the understanding of the ideas and ideals of the Constitution.

---

*The books are: *The Paideia Proposal* (New York: Macmillan Publishing Company, 1982), *Paideia Problems and Possibilities* (New York: Macmillan Publishing Company, 1983), and *The Paideia Program* (New York: Macmillan Publishing Company, 1984).

In the last four or five years, I have been engaged in the Paideia project to reform basic schooling in the United States. In the course of doing so I have had occasion to conduct many seminars with high school students in which the reading assigned for discussion was the Declaration of Independence. Taking part in the seminar resulted in their reading that document *for the first time.*

The discussions that followed revealed how little they *understood* the meaning of the Declaration's principal terms before the discussion began, and how much more remained to be done after the seminar was over to bring them to a level of understanding that, in my judgment, is the minimal requisite for intelligent citizenship in this country. The same can also be said with regard to the Constitution and the Gettysburg Address.

I am sure that the sampling of high school students I met in these seminars is representative of the general state of mind, and that a similar sampling of our college graduates would not change the picture.

Over the last thirty-five years, I have also conducted executive seminars under the auspices of the Aspen Institute for Humanistic Studies, in which the participants are graduates of our best colleges and universities and have reached positions of eminence in our society—the top echelons in industry, commercial establishments, journalism, the so-called learned professions, and government. Their understanding of the basic ideas in the Declaration and in the Preamble to the Constitution is not discernibly better than what I found among high school students.

On one very special occasion, I conducted a discussion of the Declaration with leading members of President John F. Kennedy's Cabinet and his political entourage. To my surprise and chagrin, the result was the same.

The inevitable conclusion that I draw from all these experiences is that there is work for this book to do. I am fully aware that I cannot hope it will succeed in achieving what its subtitle declares it seeks to do—to help *every* citizen, both young and old, understand the ideas and ideals of the Constitution. "Every" is a very large word, indeed. Reaching the minds of every American citizen lies beyond anyone's reasonable hope, but writing a book that is intended for every citizen is not an unreasonable undertaking.

Governed by that aim, the style and manner in which this book is written must be fashioned accordingly. Its message must be accessible—readable and intelligible—to high school students. If that can be achieved, it should also be accessible to everyone else.

Considering the extent of actual and functional illiteracy in this country, even that may be too much to hope for at the present time. Still, one must believe that something like the Paideia reform of basic schooling will succeed in the years that lie ahead and that, at some future time, an understanding of the fundamental principles that underlie the political life of this Republic will be the possession of every citizen of the United States.

CHAPTER 4

Should Know and Understand

I HAVE SAID that this book aims to provide citizens with what they should know about the ideas and ideals of the Constitution. But when it comes to ideas and ideals, knowledge is not enough. It must be illuminated by understanding; and, in addition to understanding the ideas and ideals of the Constitution, citizens should also have some knowledge of its history and development.

The difference between knowledge and understanding, between historical facts and philosophical ideas, cannot be stressed too heavily. During this bicentennial year there will undoubtedly be many books written by eminent scholars filled with knowledge about the Constitutional Convention in 1787, about the preceding years under the Articles of Confederation, about the debates between the Federalists and the Anti-Federalists who were for and against the ratification of the Constitution, about the development of the Constitution through a succession of amendments, about the decisions of the Supreme Court that advanced or altered our interpretations of constitutional law, and about changes in the social and political environment that have occasioned and influenced our constitutional history.

The eminent scholars who write these books will include historians, students of constitutional law and other jurists, sociologists, economists, political scientists, learned men of many sorts. I am not of that ilk. I am simply a philosopher and, with respect to such learning, a comparatively ignorant man.

As a philosopher, I am concerned with the understanding of ideas. It would be presumptuous of me to claim that this book will provide citizens with what they should know as matters of fact about the Constitution and its development. Indeed, I do not think that *every* citizen needs to know all the historical and other facts that scholarly books will supply on this occasion.

However, in addition to understanding the ideas and ideals of the Constitution, which I regard as a necessity for intelligent citizenship, I do think that it might be helpful if citizens were informed about the most relevant facts—that is, the most enlightening of the historical materials, knowledge of which lies in the background and scenic context of the ideas and ideals occupying the center of the stage.

That is why I have persuaded a longtime associate of mine in the work of the Institute for Philosophical Research and on the editorial staff of Encyclopaedia Britannica to collaborate with me in the production of this book. When, some years ago, I edited a twenty-volume set of the documentary materials that comprise the primary sources of American history—*The Annals of America*—Wayne Moquin, my present collaborator, made invaluable contributions to that work.

In the present instance, his contribution consists, as the title page of this book indicates, of four appendices. The first of these appendices draws materials from the records of the Constitutional Convention. The second has selections from the Federalist and Anti-Federalist papers. The third is comprised of selected commentaries on the Constitution drawn from *The Annals of America*. The fourth and last contains excerpts from decisions of the Supreme Court—passages that throw light on changing interpretations of the Constitution from the beginning to the present day. Each appendix includes notes by him, throwing light on the materials contained in that appendix.

The materials in these four appendices will not prove as readily accessible and intelligible as the contents of the main parts of this book—Parts Two, Three, and Four. These materials were written in earlier centuries, with a vocabulary and in a style that is no longer familiar to most readers today. In addition, they were not written for a large popular audience.

The few who were citizens in those earlier centuries possessed the same high level of literacy and the same skill in the liberal arts as the writers of these documentary materials. Their schooling was vastly superior in these respects to basic schooling and even college education in the United States today.

I have often remarked that the *Federalist* papers would probably not be regarded today by the editors of *The New York Times* as fit for publication on its Op Ed page because they would not be thought sufficiently accessible to its readership. The passages from Supreme Court decisions in the fourth appendix, even decisions handed down in the twentieth century, were not intended for general consumption.

With this warning about the appendices, I leave the readers of this book to pick and choose, to browse or scan rather than read carefully, and even, if they feel so inclined, to ignore the appendices entirely. Understanding the ideas and ideals of the Constitution is more important than knowing the historical facts that provide supporting evidence for understanding.

There are, however, three books that deal with the extraordinary events and transactions of the Constitutional Convention, books which are written in a style and manner that should be of great interest to the readers of this book.

I have already mentioned one of them—*The Great Rehearsal* by Carl Van Doren. Another is *Miracle at Philadelphia* by Catherine Drinker Bowen. The third book, more recently published, is *Witnesses at the Creation* by Richard B. Morris.

A few further words of explanation concerning the difference and relation between knowledge and understanding may be enlightening. Most Americans today confuse knowledge with information and fail to distinguish knowledge from understanding. Information comes to us in discrete bits, historical and scientific knowledge in some form of organization. Information is knowledge of matters of fact without any organizing scheme and without the light of any understanding of the facts known.

To know that something is true is knowledge simply, or bare

knowledge. A fact or truth (it does not make much difference which word you use) can be known simply or it can be understood as well as known. Clearly, understood truth is superior to truth simply known.

Consider, as an example, a truth declared self-evident in the Declaration of Independence: All human beings are by nature equal. (In stating this truth I have altered its wording in order to give it the self-evidence that Jefferson claimed for it.) For the moment, let us not question whether the statement is true or even whether it is self-evident. For the purpose at hand let us assume the statement to be true.

On that supposition, is it not clear that knowing this assumed truth—that is, taking it to be a matter of fact—is one thing and understanding why it is true is quite another? Most of us assert as matters of fact many things we do not understand. Those who have a great deal of bare knowledge may have in reality very little knowledge understood.

What is involved in understanding the truth that we are here considering? It derives from an understanding of the idea of equality. An understanding of that idea enables us to see why it can be truly said that all human beings are equal in the sense that, and only in the sense that, one person is neither more nor less human than another. Thus understood, the truth is self-evident.

The truth we have been considering is a philosophical truth, but what has just been said applies as well to historical truths and scientific truths. We can know them simply as matters of fact; or we can know them with an understanding of how underlying reasons or supporting evidence makes them true, and such understanding tells us why they are true.

So far we have seen how understanding relates to knowledge. But there is an understanding that goes beyond all knowledge, and that is our understanding of ideas and ideals. Knowledge is always knowledge of matters of fact. Ideas and ideals are not matters of fact and, therefore, are not, and cannot be, objects of knowledge.

If ideas and ideals are objects for our minds to think about (or if, more strictly speaking, they present to our minds intelligible objects for us to think about), then there must be some way other than knowing in which we use our minds. That other way is understanding.

Let me repeat the main point once more: We can use our ability to understand in two different connections. One is to use it in order to understand facts or truths that we know. The other goes beyond knowing, not only historical and scientific knowing, but also philosophical knowing. It consists in understanding ideas and ideals apart from all knowledge of matters of fact. Such understanding of ideas and ideals, or of the intelligible objects they place before our minds, is purely and exclusively philosophical.

To ask you, the readers of this book, to try to understand the ideas and ideals of the Constitution of the United States, an exercise certainly appropriate in this bicentennial year, is to ask you to do nothing less—or more—than embark on a philosophical undertaking.

CHAPTER 5

The Ideas and Ideals
of the Constitution

"IDEAS" AND "IDEALS" ARE TWO WORDS that look alike and sound alike, but have quite different meanings.

As I have already pointed out, ideas, or the intelligible objects they present to us, are objects to be understood. Ideals are objectives or goals to be sought, striven for, and realized by action on our part or on the part of organized society. All ideals germinate in ideas, but not all ideas give rise to ideals—only those that are ideas of goals we ought to seek or of means we ought to employ to attain them.

To put this another way, ideas divide into two sorts: those that are theoretical, and those that are practical. The latter are ideas that are relevant to action on our part; only they can become ideals for us. When or under what circumstances do they become ideals?

An end, objective, or goal that has been fully attained ceases to be an ideal. Once an ideal is fully realized, that realization removes it from the realm of ideals. Only those goals or objectives to which we aspire but which at a given time we have attained only to a certain extent, with some distance still to go for their complete realization, remain ideals for us.

A genuinely practicable idea is one that can be fully realized in fact—in practice and by action. What may be thought of as ideals but are in fact goals that cannot be fully realized are not genuine ideals at all; they are utopian fantasies. The line between genuine ideals and utopian fantasies may sometimes appear shadowy and hard to draw clearly. The distinction can be made only when we have a well-developed sense of what is possible and what is not. Genuine ideals belong to the realm of the possible. Utopian fantasies are dreams of the impossible.

All of us recognize the difference between the ideal and the real when we say in common speech that something or other—let us say dire poverty or destitution—should *ideally* be eliminated from our society, but *actually* (or in *reality*) we still fall far short of it. When we think of a completely just society, we think of one in which, *ideally*, all injustices have been eradicated. We are also quick to acknowledge that we have so far only remotely approximated this ideal in fact. If anyone thinks that a completely just society is impossible to achieve on earth, he or she would dismiss such a society as a utopian fantasy.

Almost all the underlying ideas of the Constitution are to be found in the second paragraph of the Declaration of Independence, in some phrases in Lincoln's Gettysburg Address, and here and there in the Constitution itself. They are the ideas of

> equality
> inalienable rights (or human rights)
> pursuit of happiness
> civil rights (to secure human rights)
> the consent of the governed
> the dissent of the governed

The Gettysburg Address throws light on the consent of the governed by stressing that constitutional government is government *of* the people, not just government *by* the people or government *for* the people.

Of the ideas so far mentioned, equality generates an ideal that we have not yet fully achieved. So does the idea of happiness and the idea of human rights. The phrase "we, the people" in the Preamble to the Constitution and the word "people" in Lincoln's government of, by, and for the people leads us to the idea of democracy, for the Greek roots of that word mean precisely that: government by the *demos*, or people. Once we have that idea in mind we can see that it is not just an idea, but also an ideal that is still far from being fully attained.

Turning to the Constitution's Preamble, we find there another set of ideas, a few of which are anticipated by words or phrases in the Declaration. They are the ideas of

> justice
> domestic tranquility (or civil peace)
> common defense (or national security)
> general welfare
> blessings of liberty

All of these ideas are also ideals, and they were all ideals in the eighteenth century at the inception of the Constitution. Some of them, especially justice and liberty, along with the ideals of equality and democracy, were realized to some degree by successive amendments to the Constitution, especially by the first ten amendments, known as the Bill of Rights, but also by the Thirteenth, Fourteenth, Fifteenth, Nineteenth, and Twenty-Fourth Amendments, all of which gradually turned our Republic into the beginnings of a democracy by extending suffrage and removing obstacles to the exercise of it. In these amendments we also find such phrases as "equal protection of the laws" and "due process of law" that evoke the idea—and the ideal—of a government of laws.

In Part Two of this book, we will be concerned mainly with the ideas to be found in the Declaration of Independence and in Lincoln's Gettysburg Address. At that point, I shall confine myself to considering them as ideas, postponing until later the consideration of them as ideals that our Republic must still aspire to realize more fully.

In Part Three, we will be concerned with the additional ideas to be found in the Constitution's Preamble, and I will also be concerned with them as ideals still on the road toward fulfillment.

Part Four will turn our attention to the slowly emergent idea of democracy in both its political and its economic aspects—an idea that made its first appearance in amendments to the Constitution and has only recently been recognized as an ideal that requires for its complete recognition the fullest possible realization of political and economic justice and, therewith, of liberty and equality. Therefore, in Part Four, we must also consider the obstacles to be overcome if a truly constitutional democracy and a truly democratic society are ever to come into existence in this nation and, perhaps, the world.

PART TWO

The Underlying Ideas in the Declaration

WHEN IN THE COURSE OF HUMAN EVENTS, it becomes necessary for one people to dissolve the political bands which have connected them with another, and to assume among the powers of the earth, the separate and equal station to which the laws of nature and of nature's God entitle them, a decent respect to the opinions of mankind requires that they should declare the causes which impel them to the separation.

We hold these truths to be self-evident, that all men are created equal; that they are endowed by their Creator with certain unalienable rights; that among these are life, liberty, and the pursuit of happiness. That to secure these rights, governments are instituted among men, deriving their just powers from the consent of the governed; that whenever any form of government becomes destructive of these ends, it is the right of the people to alter or to abolish it, and to institute new government, laying its foundation on such principles, and organizing its powers in such form, as to them shall seem most likely to effect their safety and happiness.

CHAPTER 6

Introduction:
Understanding the
Declaration as a Whole

THE UNDERLYING IDEAS of the Declaration are to be found in its second long paragraph, beginning with the words "We hold these truths to be self-evident." They are concerned with human equality, inalienable* rights, the pursuit of happiness, the consent of the governed, and the justification for overthrowing a government. We shall be concerned with understanding these ideas in the chapters to follow.

However, there are some things in the Declaration's initial and concluding paragraphs that deserve brief consideration before we give close attention to the five ideas just mentioned. Here are the words of the opening paragraph.

When in the course of human events, it becomes necessary for one people to dissolve the political bands which have connected them with another, and to assume among the powers of the earth, the separate and equal station to which the laws of nature and of nature's God entitle them, a decent respect to the opinions of mankind requires that they should declare the causes which impel them to the separation.

The pivotal idea enunciated here is that of a people having a distinct political status. We observed in Chapter 1 that the people of the thirteen colonies, in rebelling against British rule, understood

---

*The term "inalienable" is employed in narrative text for "unalienable" found in the original text.

themselves as a new people, separate from their British brethren overseas.

The fighting in which they were already engaged was more than a war of rebellion against what they regarded as despotism on the part of the British King and Parliament. It was a war to be fought for their independent status as a separate people—that is, a war to dissolve the political bands that tied them to the people of Great Britain. They asked the nations of Europe to look upon them as a political entity entitled to a separate and equal station among the peoples of the earth.

It is this appeal in the Declaration's opening paragraph that justified the celebration of the first bicentennial as the 200th anniversary of this nation's coming into existence. But it must be clearly understood that, in the fullest and most precise understanding of what a national state is, the United States of America as a national state did not come into being in 1776. What came into existence then was a separate people as a new political entity, and it was the harbinger of the new nation that would be born in 1789.

On what grounds did the colonists in 1776 claim to be *one* people even though they also belonged to thirteen quite distinct human groups, each with its own local loyalties? What constitutes the status of "peoplehood"? Just the fact that they spoke a common language, or the fact that most had emigrated from a common home and so shared common cultural and political traditions and a common body of laws?

Centuries earlier, Cicero, in his *De Republica*, had defined a people as "not any collection of human beings brought together in any sort of way, but an assemblage of them in large numbers associated in an agreement with respect to justice and a partnership for the common good." A multitude of persons forms a single people when they are united for a common purpose and are willing to cooperate in its pursuit. The establishment of a Continental Congress to which the thirteen colonies sent their representatives indicated that the separate populations of those colonies had become one people.

In the years immediately prior to 1776, committees of correspondence developed, first within each colony and then between colonies.

From such committees, and from the colonial assemblies, there issued calls for a first and then a second Continental Congress. This amounted to an initial affirmation that the Americans had become *one* people.

The resort to arms in 1775 occurred with the approbation of an all-colony-wide Congress. The Resolutions of Independence, issued on July 2, 1776, came from such a Congress. The final confirmation came two days later in the Declaration of Independence. Its closing paragraph referred to the persons who signed their names to it as representatives of the thirteen colonies "in general Congress assembled."

Now let us look at the final paragraph, certain words and phrases in which deserve close attention.

We, therefore, the representatives of the United States of America, in general Congress assembled, appealing to the Supreme Judge of the world for the rectitude of our intentions, do, in the name, and by authority of the good people of these colonies, solemnly publish and declare, that these united colonies are, and of right ought to be, free and independent States; that they are absolved from all allegiance to the British Crown, and that all political connection between them and the state of Great Britain is, and ought to be, totally dissolved; and that as free and independent States, they have full power to levy war, conclude peace, contract alliances, establish commerce, and to do all other acts and things which independent States may of right do. And for the support of this declaration, with a firm reliance on the protection of Divine Providence, we mutually pledge to each other our lives, our fortunes, and our sacred honor.

The signers of the Declaration speak of themselves as representatives of "the United States of America," but a few lines later they also say they are speaking in the name and by the authority of "the good people of these colonies" and then go on to say that "these united colonies are, and of right ought to be, free and independent States."

If these united colonies existed as free and independent states (in the plural), the words "the United States of America" could not have been understood by the signers of the Declaration to refer to a single political community.

This is confirmed by a passage a few lines further on. There we find it said that the thirteen colonies "as free and independent States . . . have full power to levy war, conclude peace, contract alliances, establish commerce, and to do all other acts and things which independent States may of right do." The powers enumerated are the very powers that any sovereign state claims its rights to exercise. Hence each of the thirteen colonies united in their struggle for independence regarded itself as a fully sovereign state.

It is precisely such sovereignty that was taken away from the thirteen independent states when they abandoned their loose confederacy and entered into a more perfect union by adopting the Constitution of the United States. According to that document, the power to levy war, conclude peace, contract alliances, establish commerce, and so on was taken away from the thirteen federated states and conferred solely upon the federal government—the government of the United States of America—which then came into being for the first time.

We now come to the part of the Declaration that is more than a declaration of independence on the part of the thirteen rebellious colonies. This part is a declaration of the political principles that underlie the Constitution of the United States.

To say that the Constitution, without all its amendments to come later, established a government that fully conformed to those underlying principles is to claim too much for it. Abraham Lincoln was at pains to remind us that the principles enunciated in the Declaration should be understood as a pledge to the future of ideals that would not be fully realized in the first fifty or even first hundred years of the Republic's existence.

Another statement by Lincoln confirms this insight. In 1859, he said:

All honor to Jefferson—to the man who, in the concrete pressure of struggle for national independence by a single people, had the coolness, forecast, and capacity to introduce into a merely revolutionary document, an abstract truth, applicable to all men and all times, and so to embalm it there that today and in all coming days it shall be a rebuke . . . to the very harbingers of re-appearing tyranny.

If we speak of the drafting of the Constitution—before its adoption or ratification—as the conception of the American republic and its government (a political community and political institutions yet to be born), then we can also talk about the political principles expressed in the Declaration as the germs generative of that conception.

With some slight excerpting, here is the second paragraph of the Declaration, containing all the words and phrases that we must now attempt to understand as clearly as possible.

We hold these truths to be self-evident, that all men are created equal; that they are endowed by their Creator with certain unalienable rights; that among these are life, liberty, and the pursuit of happiness. That to secure these rights, governments are instituted among men, deriving their just powers from the consent of the governed; that whenever any form of government becomes destructive of these ends, it is the right of the people to alter or to abolish it, and to institute new government, laying its foundation on such principles, and organizing its powers in such form, as to them shall seem most likely to effect their safety and happiness. Prudence, indeed, will dictate that governments long established should not be changed for light and transient causes and accordingly all experience hath shown, that mankind are more disposed to suffer, while evils are sufferable, than to right themselves by abolishing the forms to which they are accustomed. But when a long train of abuses and usurpations, pursuing invariably the same object, evinces a design to reduce them under absolute despotism, it is their right, it is their duty, to throw off such government, and to provide new guards for their future security. Such has been the patient sufferance of these colonies, and such is now the necessity which constrains them to alter their former systems of government. The history of the present King of Great Britain is a history of repeated injuries and usurpations, all having in direct object the establishment of an absolute tyranny over these states.

To prepare readers for the chapters that follow, in which the crucial ideas in the Declaration's second paragraph will each be treated at length, it may be useful to put down an explication of that paragraph as a whole.

The explication I propose will spell out as explicitly as possible what is said much more tersely and often more elliptically in the paragraph as written by Thomas Jefferson. As written by him, the paragraph has rhetorical power that was achieved by its extraordinary brevity and by all the things that were left unsaid—left implicit rather than spelled out.

All that I claim for my much more explicit rendering is that, in a straightforward and prosaic manner, it tries to state at much greater length in a logically explicit manner what is skipped over or only hinted at in a statement that, for good rhetorical reasons, is much briefer. My rendering is, of course, only one man's interpretation, submitted for whatever light it throws on the text before us.

1. We hold certain propositions to be true, true everywhere and at all times, capable of winning the assent of all reasonable men.

2. Among these at least one is self-evident because its truth is undeniable, a truth that is perceived as soon as its terms are understood, for when they are understood the opposite of what that proposition states is unthinkable.

3. That one is the proposition, here rephrased, that all human beings are by nature equal. None is more or less human than any other. All share or participate in the same specific nature, in virtue of which all have the same specific properties, though one human being may have these human characteristics or attributes to a higher or lower degree than another, in which respects they may be unequal.

4. We hold it to be true but not self-evident that all men are endowed with certain inalienable rights, rights inherent in their human nature and, therefore, equally inherent in all by virtue of their all having that same nature.

5. The inalienability of such inherent natural—or human—rights consists in their being rights that are not conferred upon persons by man-made laws and so cannot be rendered null and void by man-made laws, though they can be abrogated or transgressed by governments, the injustice of which consists in the violation of these rights.

6. Among these rights are life, liberty, and the pursuit of happiness. These three rights by no means exhaust all natural or human rights, but all the others that have so far been acknowledged, or that in the course of time remain to be discovered, implement these three principal rights.

7. Of these three principal rights, the primary one differs from

the rest by being concerned with an end or objective for the attainment of which the others serve as means. That one is the right of each person to pursue happiness—that is, to try to make a good human life for himself or herself. The most precise way of stating this truth is to say that our natural rights consist in our rights to life, liberty, and anything else that we need in order to pursue happiness—goods that the government of an organized society can confer upon us, or can aid and abet our efforts to obtain.

8. Governments have not always been instituted to secure or safeguard our possession of these rights, but that is one of the purposes for which they should be instituted, and they are just only insofar as they carry out this aim.

9. Another criterion of the justice of governments is that they derive their powers from the consent of the governed; in other words, the authority by which they exercise their powers has its source in a constitution voluntarily adopted by a people who have the right to govern themselves.

10. Whenever a government ceases to operate within its constitutional limitations and becomes despotic or tyrannical by treating the people as its subjects or slaves, the people are justified in trying to alter it by rectifying such injustice or, in the last resort, by overthrowing it and establishing in its place a government so constituted that it serves the objectives at which a just government should aim.

11. This drastic remedy is justified not by light and transient causes, but only by a long train of abuses or usurpations that manifest a settled tendency toward despotic or tyrannical rule.

12. When that occurs, the people are not only justified in overthrowing such government, but they also have the duty, the moral obligation, to do so in order to fulfill their moral obligation to make good lives for themselves.

While the foregoing twelve statements are an extended explication of the principles of government enunciated in the rhetorically superior second paragraph of the Declaration, they are by no means lengthy or detailed enough to provide us with a fully explicit and completely clear understanding of those principles.

This, I hope, can be achieved in the six chapters that follow.

CHAPTER 7

Human Equality

WE HAVE ALREADY OBSERVED what it means to say of any two objects under consideration that they are equal. It means that one of them is neither more nor less than another in an explicitly indicated respect.

To omit mentioning one or another respect in which two things are thought to be equal is to speak so unclearly and so inadequately that the statement cannot be either affirmed or denied, for the two things being considered may be equal in one respect and unequal in another.

Is there then any respect in which all human beings, without a single exception, can be declared equal? Yes, there is only one. It is that they are all human, all members of one species, called *homo sapiens*, and all having the same natural and thereby the same specific attributes that differentiate them from the members of all other species. In all other respects, any two human beings may be found unequal, one having more of a certain human attribute than another, either as the result of native endowment or of individual attainment.

When this is understood, it will be seen that there is no conflict or contradiction between saying (1) that all human beings are equal in respect of their common humanity, and (2) that all human beings are also unequal, one with another, in a wide variety of respects in which they differ as individual members of the human species.

Their equality lies in the fact that humans all belong to the same species, possessing the traits common to members of that species. Their inequality lies in their individual differences as members of that species. All being human, they are all persons, not things; and as persons they all equally have the dignity that inheres in their being persons. But each is not only a person, each is also a uniquely individual person.

Is it a self-evident truth that human equality exists as a matter of fact? What, as a matter of fact, are we asserting when we say that all human beings are equal in respect to their common humanity?

The Declaration asserts that all men are *created* equal. Lincoln, in the opening words of the Gettysburg Address, speaks of this nation being dedicated to that proposition. But that proposition is not self-evident, because it is not undeniable that God exists or that God created mankind along with other living organisms and everything else in the cosmos. These things may be true. They may be believed. But they can also be and have been disbelieved and denied; it is quite possible to think the opposite.

We can make the proposition self-evident by dropping the word "created" and rephrasing the statement as follows: All men are *by nature* equal. This reiterates what has already been said: Human equality consists in the fact that no human being is more or less human than another because all have the same specific nature by virtue of belonging to one and the same species. If they all have the same nature, then it cannot be denied that, in respect of having that nature, they are all equal; no one has more or less than another.

For a truth to be self-evident it must be beyond the shadow of a doubt. It must be undeniable simply because its opposite is impossible for us to think. Does any doubt lurk here that might make us reluctant to affirm human equality as a self-evident truth?

Yes, remarkable as it may seem, a doubt about the existence of human nature has appeared for the first time in our own century. It is not questioned that other species of animals have specific natures, each thereby having a set of common attributes that differentiate them. But in certain quarters of twentieth-century science and philosophy there has arisen the doubt—more than doubt, the denial—that the same can be said of the human species. It has been paradoxically said, for example, that "the nature of man is to have no nature."

I have attempted in another book* to expose the error in this view. Here I must be content simply to define that mistake without explaining how it came to be made.

The error consists in failing to recognize that the specifying or differentiating traits that constitute human nature are all potentialities or capacities for development. In different subgroups of the human race these potentialities or capacities receive different developments by the different ways in which the members of that subgroup are nurtured.

If one looks only to the widely differing nurtured developments of the common human potentialities or capacities, one will find no common set of traits in all human subgroups. It is only in the sameness of these potentialities or capacities that one can discern the common traits that constitute the human nature underlying all these divergent developments.

What has just been said of the human species cannot be said of any other species of living organism. The twentieth-century doubters or deniers of human nature should say not that there is no human nature, but that human nature is radically different from the natures of other animal species.

Another point remains to be clarified about the Declaration's assertion of human equality. The words used are not "all *human beings* are created equal," but rather "all *men*. . . ." To what does that word "men" refer?

We are sensitive today to the connotation of masculinity in the word "men." Knowing that many signers of the Declaration owned blacks as chattel slaves, we are also sensitive to the unexpressed adjective "white" in the eighteenth-century use of the word "men."

Such sensitivities lead many to charge the signers of the Declaration with hypocrisy if they pretended to assert that, when they said "all men," they meant "all human beings," not "all white males"

*See *Ten Philosophical Mistakes* (New York: Macmillan Publishing Company, 1985), Chapter 8, "Human Nature."

or even perhaps "some white males like ourselves who are men of property."

In the nineteenth century, Abraham Lincoln was confronted with such interpretations of the Declaration on the part of Senator Stephen Douglas, with whom he debated, and on the part of Chief Justice Roger Taney in the Dred Scott decision, with which he took issue. Lincoln insisted that the language of the Declaration should be interpreted as including all human beings without regard to sex or color or other traits that differentiate one group of human beings from another.

In a speech he delivered in Springfield, Illinois, in 1857, Lincoln pointed out that when it is understood that all human beings are equal not only in their common humanity but also in having by virtue of their common humanity the same human rights, it should not be thought that the signers of the Declaration were asserting "the obvious untruth that all were then actually enjoying that equality, nor yet that they [the signers] were about to confer it immediately upon them. In fact, they had no power to confer such a boon. They meant simply to declare the right, so that the enforcement of it might follow as fast as circumstances should permit."

In the same speech, Lincoln goes on to say

The assertion that "all men are created equal" was of no practical use in effecting our separation from Great Britain; and it was placed in the Declaration not for that but for its future use.

That reference to "its future use" turns our attention to the political significance of the truth concerning human equality. Human equality—the personal equality of men as men, or of human beings as human—is by no means the only equality with which we are concerned in our social lives. We are concerned with what, in contradistinction to *personal* equality, might be called *circumstantial* equality—that is, equality of conditions or results, equality of opportunity, and equality of treatment.

There is one very important difference between personal and circumstantial equality. Personal equality is either a fact or it is not. We say that human beings *are* equal as persons, not that they *should* or *ought* to be equal in that respect. With regard to circumstantial equality, we can speak both descriptively and prescriptively. On the one hand, we can say that in a given society at a certain time, all human beings *are* or *are not* politically or economically equal; and on the other hand, we can also say that whether or not they are, they should or ought to be. Under certain circumstances, they may not in fact be treated as equals, but those circumstances should be altered because they ought to be treated as equals.

The descriptive truth that, as a matter of fact, all human beings are by nature equal as persons underlies all prescriptions calling, as a matter of right, for equality of conditions, equality of opportunity, and equality of treatment.

That all human beings have the right to equal status as citizens with suffrage, that all have the right to equal treatment under the law, that all have the right to equal educational opportunity, that all have the right to a certain equality of economic conditions (to be haves rather than have-nots), together with all the prescriptive statements to which these rights lead, concerning what a just society ought to do about establishing circumstantial equality in these respects—these have their foundation in the truth that all human beings are by nature equal.

If that were not true, it would be impossible, in my judgment, to justify the demands for political and economic equality as ideals to be achieved. In the last 150 years, these demands have at last become dominant in our social life. *Égalité* together with *liberté* were fighting words in the French revolution. Liberty was one of the ideals mentioned in the Preamble to the Constitution, but not equality. In this country that must await a later epoch.

CHAPTER 8

Inalienable Rights

THE DECLARATION ASSERTS not only that all men are created equal
(equal as creatures in the eyes of their Creator) but also that they
are endowed by their Creator with certain inalienable rights.

We have already observed with respect to human equality that
the attribution of it to divine origin makes the proposition asserted
less than self-evidently true. It may still be true even if it is not self-
evident. It becomes self-evidently true and thus undeniable only if
we attribute the equality of all human beings to their equality as
human, as having the same specific nature, one individual being
neither more nor less human than another.

When we come to the assertion that they are endowed by their
Creator with certain inalienable rights, the same qualification applies. If instead of saying that these inalienable rights belong to
human beings by divine endowment, it had been said that they were
inherent in human nature, or that they were part of everyone's
natural endowment, one thing at least would become clear.

If all human beings are equal by virtue of their having the same
nature, and if they possess certain rights by virtue of their having
that nature, then it follows that they are all equally endowed with
those rights.

To assert that truth as a conclusion to which we are led by cogent
reasoning is to acknowledge that it is not a self-evident truth. Furthermore, if the rights under consideration are conceived as natural

or human rights, it becomes easier to explain what we mean when we call those rights "inalienable."

What is being denied by the negative statement that certain rights are *not* alienable? Human beings living in organized societies under civil government have many rights that are conferred upon them by the laws of the state, and sometimes by its constitution. These are usually called civil rights, legal rights, or constitutional rights. This indicates their source. It also indicates that these rights, which are conferred by constitutional provisions or by the positive enactment of man-made laws, can be revoked or nullified by the same power or authority that instituted them in the first place. They are *alienable* rights. The giver can take them away.

What the state does not give, it cannot take away. If human rights are natural rights, as opposed to those that are civil, constitutional, or legal, then their being rights by natural endowment makes them *inalienable* in the sense just indicated.

Their existence as natural endowments gives them moral authority even when they lack legal force or legal sanctions. Their moral authority imposes moral obligations, which may or may not be respected or fulfilled.

A given state or society may or may not, by its constitution and its laws, attempt to secure these rights or to enforce them. It may even do the very opposite. It may transgress or violate these inalienable natural or human rights. When it fails to enforce these rights or, worse, when it violates them, it is subject to condemnation on moral grounds as being unjust.

Later, in Chapter 10, we shall consider the question of how constitutional provisions or civil rights secure and enforce these human or natural rights. Right now we must deal with another question. If unjust governments can violate these human or natural rights, in what sense do they still remain inalienable? Are they not being taken away by such violations?

When a human right is not acknowledged by the state, or when it is not enforced or when it is violated by a government, it still exists. It retains its moral authority even though it is not enforced or has been transgressed. If these rights did not continue in existence in spite of such adverse circumstances, then we would have no basis for condemning as unjust a government that failed to enforce them or that trampled on them.

One question still remains concerning the inalienability of natural human rights. The Declaration mentions our inalienable right to life and to liberty. But when criminals are justly convicted and sentenced to terms in prison, are we not taking away their liberty? And when they are convicted of capital offenses for which death is the penalty, are we not taking away their lives? If so, how then do the rights in question still exist and remain inalienable?

It is easier to answer the question about imprisonment than it is to answer the question about the death penalty. Two points are involved in the answer.

First, the criminal by his antisocial conduct and by his violation of a just law has forfeited not the right, but the temporary exercise of it. His incarceration in prison does not completely remove his freedom of action, but it severely limits the exercise of that freedom for the period of imprisonment.

The right remains in existence both during imprisonment and after release from prison. If the prison warden attempted to make the prisoner his personal slave, that would be an act of injustice on his part, because enslavement would be a violation of the human right to the status of a free man. This human right belongs to those in a prison as well as those outside its walls.

When the criminal's term of imprisonment comes to an end, what is restored is not the individual's right to liberty (as if that had been taken away when he entered the prison), but only his fuller exercise of that right. It is the exercise of that right that is given back to him when he walks out of the prison gates, not the right itself, for that was never taken away or alienated.

When we come to capital punishment, we cannot deal with the question in the same way. The death penalty takes away more than the exercise of the right to life. It takes away life itself.

If that right is inalienable, it cannot be taken away by the state, nor can it be forfeited by the individual's misconduct. It is one thing to forfeit the exercise of a right and quite another to divest one's self of a right entirely. What cannot be taken away by another cannot be divested by one's self.

It would, therefore, appear to be the case that the death penalty is unjust as a violation of a natural human right. Nevertheless, capital punishment has been pragmatically justified as serving the welfare of society by functioning as a deterrent to the gravest of felonies. But its deterrent effect has been seriously questioned in the light of all the evidence available. Whatever deterrent effect the death penalty exerts might be equally possessed by another punitive treatment meted out for capital offenses—for example, life imprisonment with no possibility of parole, though with some alleviation of the harshness of prison life as a reward for good behavior.

For the time being, we are left with an unresolved issue between proponents and opponents of capital punishment. The substitution of life imprisonment for the death penalty might solve the problem.

We have so far considered briefly the rights to life and liberty and their inalienability. Much more remains to be said about them and about their sources in human nature itself, but they are not the only natural human rights. We must also look to the civil or legal rights, the enactment of which is requisite for securing and safeguarding whatever basic rights are recognized as inherent in human nature. Further still, we must ask whether what the Declaration calls a right—the right to overthrow a government that evinces a tendency toward despotism and tyranny—is a natural right or a civil right. If neither, why is it called a right?

Such matters and questions are reserved for treatment in the next three chapters.

CHAPTER 9

The Pursuit of Happiness

HAVING ASSERTED THE EXISTENCE of natural, human, and, therefore, inalienable rights, the Declaration goes on to say that among these rights are life, liberty, and the pursuit of happiness.

The phrase "among these" makes us immediately aware of the fact that the rights named do not exhaust those that are inherent in human nature. This leaves us with many questions to be answered.

What are these other rights? How do the rights mentioned and the others still to be named have their foundation or source in human nature? How, by examining our human nature, do we discover the inalienable rights we possess? What is the relation between our right to life, liberty, and other things, and our right to the pursuit of happiness?

That these questions remain to be answered plainly indicates that the Declaration's assertion about our natural rights is not a self-evident truth. It requires us to engage in reflective thought—in analysis and reasoning—which is never the case when we are presented with a truth that is self-evident.

The most important question to answer first is the one about the relation of all other human rights to the pursuit of happiness. Answering it will not only help us discover rights beyond the first two mentioned—life and liberty—but it will also enable us to discover the source in human nature of all such rights.

It was pointed out earlier (in Chapter 6) how Jefferson's brief and elliptical statement about life, liberty, and the pursuit of happiness can be made more explicit by expressing it as follows. Our right to pursue happiness differs from all the rest by being concerned with an end or objective for the attainment of which the others serve as means. In other words, all the others are rights to things that every human being needs in order to succeed in the effort to lead a decent human life.

That everyone desires happiness for himself or herself is an incontestable fact. In everyone's vocabulary, the word "happiness" stands for something always sought for its own sake and never as a means to anything beyond itself. No one can complete the sentence "I want happiness because I want . . ." as one can complete the sentence "I want wealth, or health, or freedom, or knowledge because I want to achieve happiness in this life." Any other object of desire of which we can think can always be thought of as a means to happiness, even when it is something that can also be thought of as something to be attained for its own sake.

There is one other connotation of the word "happiness" that makes it unique among all the words we use to name objects of desire. Happiness is not only an ultimate good to be sought for its own sake, and never as a means to anything beyond itself. It is also the one complete good; it is never a partial good, never one good among others—as wealth, or health, or freedom, or knowledge are partial goods—because possessing any one of them leaves many others to be possessed. When happiness is achieved, it leaves nothing more to be desired, for it involves the possession of all other goods.

This understanding of the special connotations of the word "happiness" as we generally use it is common to two quite distinct conceptions of happiness that have come down to us in the tradition of Western thought. One is the modern psychological conception of happiness as a feeling of contentment produced by the satisfaction we experience when we are able to fulfill whatever desires we happen to have at any moment in time. The other is the ancient ethical conception of happiness as a whole life well-lived because it is enriched by the cumulative possession of all the goods that a morally virtuous human being ought to desire.

The ethical conception of happiness includes the psychological conception. At any moment, a morally virtuous individual may feel contentment because he has the satisfaction of possessing goods that he ought to desire and that, in fact, he does desire at that moment. The reverse is not true.

The psychological conception of happiness is usually claimed by those who hold it to be the only conception, in which case happiness (or contentment) can be enjoyed by individuals regardless of whether the things they do in fact desire are goods they ought to desire. The morally vicious individual, no less than the morally virtuous individual, can enjoy the contentment (or happiness) of having his or her desires satisfied, whether the objects desired are rightly or wrongly desired.

This being the state of Western thought about happiness at the time the Declaration of Independence was drafted, we are compelled to ask which conception of happiness Thomas Jefferson had in mind when he spoke of our human right to pursue happiness. Two clues enable us to find the answer to this question.

One is the fact that Jefferson was acquainted with the thinking of his fellow-statesman, George Mason, who drafted the Virginia Declaration of Rights a month before the Declaration of Independence was written. It opened with the words:

That all men are by nature equally free and independent and have certain inherent rights . . . namely, the enjoyment of life and liberty, with the means of acquiring and possessing property, and pursuing and obtaining happiness and safety.

Almost a century earlier the English philosopher John Locke, in his *Second Treatise on Civil Government*, had asserted three natural rights: in one phrasing, "life, liberty, and property"; in another, "life, liberty, and estates." Mason retained property among the rights he enumerated, but his striking innovation was his addition of the right to pursue and obtain happiness.

With this before us, we must ask why Jefferson, in adopting Mason's innovation, retained the verb "pursue," and dropped the verb "obtain."

If, in using the word "happiness," Jefferson had the psychological rather than the ethical conception in mind, he would have had little or no reason for dropping the word "obtain," for it is quite possible for individuals to attain and enjoy happiness when it is conceived psychologically as a feeling of contentment produced by the satisfaction of the desires of the moment. But when happiness is conceived ethically as a whole life well-lived, then it cannot be enjoyed or attained at any moment during the course of one's life.

There is a further reason why Jefferson dropped the word "obtain," and this gives us our second clue to Jefferson's conception of happiness. On the ethical conception of happiness, one indispensable means to success in our pursuit of it is our possession of moral virtue—the settled habit or disposition of will to desire what we ought to desire. All the things we have a right to, such as the preservation of our lives and our freedom of action, are things not entirely within our own power. They depend on beneficent external circumstances. That being the case, a just government can secure our rights to them and safeguard our exercise of them. But whether or not we are morally virtuous lies almost wholly within our own power and totally beyond the power of any government, no matter how just it may be.

A just government can aid and abet our *pursuit* of happiness—our effort to make morally good lives for ourselves—but it cannot help us to obtain happiness, since that depends in part on our possession of moral virtue. Hence Jefferson's retention of "pursuit" and his elimination of "obtain" indicate his espousal of the ethical, not the psychological, conception of happiness.

That this is the case is confirmed by looking a little deeper into the desires that are operative in the pursuit of happiness, conceived psychologically as momentary contentment and conceived ethically as a morally good life, a whole life lived well.

One set of desires consists of wants human beings acquire in the course of their individual lives, conditioned by their temperaments, their nurture or upbringing, and their social environments. Such desires differ from person to person according to their individual differences and the differences in the circumstances of their lives.

Another set of desires consist of the needs that all human beings share in common because they are desires or appetites inherent in human nature itself. We normally speak of such desires as our natural needs. On the biological level, all of us need food, drink, sleep, and shelter of some sort. On the specifically human level, we need freedom and knowledge.

These generally acknowledged human needs, not exhaustively enumerated here, help us to understand the difference between our natural needs, desires inherent in our nature, and our individually acquired desires for the things we want, whether we need them or not.

We can want things that may appear good to us at the time we want them, but which at a later time turn out to be really bad for us and make us regret our wanting and getting them. But we never need anything that is really bad for us. We can want too much of something that is really good for us (such as too much food, too much sleep), but we never need too much of anything that is really good for us (such as too much freedom, too much knowledge).

What all this comes down to is that our needs are always right desires, desires for the real goods that we ought to desire, whereas our wants may be either right or wrong desires. They are wrong desires when we want things that are really bad for us or want in excess things that are really good for us.

Wants become right desires only when we want the things that we ought to desire, the things that are really good for us because we have a natural need for them. Some of the things that appear good to us when we want them are innocuous because getting them does not impair or frustrate our getting the real goods we need. But others are harmful because getting them interferes with our getting the goods we really need.

According to the psychological conception of happiness as contentment, individuals achieve happiness when they get what they want, regardless of whether what they want is something they also need and whether what they want is innocuous or harmful. Consider individuals who want power or domination over others and are willing to infringe on the freedom of others in order to satisfy their desires. How can a just government aid and abet their particular pursuit of happiness, to which they claim a natural right, by helping them get what they want without at the same time failing to secure and safeguard the right to freedom on the part of others?

If Jefferson had held the psychological conception of happiness, he could not have thought it possible for a government to aid and abet its pursuit by individuals whose wants bring them into conflict with the rights of others. This confirms the reasoning that led us to the conclusion that Jefferson held the ethical rather than the psychological conception of happiness when he asserted our natural right to pursue it and our natural right to obtain whatever real goods we need in order to make good lives for ourselves.

When happiness is conceived as the feeling of contentment produced by the satisfaction of our individual wants—our wrong as well as our right desires—then the pursuit of happiness is competitive. Its attainment by one individual may depend on the deprivation of it for another. Hence no government can attempt to aid and abet competing individuals in their pursuit of happiness. When happiness is so conceived, the right to pursue it cannot be secured for *all*.

However, when happiness is conceived as a whole life enriched by the cumulative possession of all the goods that human beings rightly desire because they are naturally needed, then the pursuit of happiness becomes cooperative rather than competitive. One individual's successful pursuit of it does not necessitate the frustration or failure of another's effort to achieve a morally good life. When happiness is so conceived, the right to pursue it can be secured for *all*.

The understanding we have now reached concerning the pursuit of happiness throws light on the source in human nature of all our natural rights. With one exception to be noted presently, all natural rights are founded on natural needs. We may be privileged to seek whatever we want and to get it, on condition, of course, that getting it involves no injury to others or to the general welfare. A privilege is one thing; a right is quite another. We do not have a right to things we may individually want, but only to the thing that we, along with everyone else, need in order to make good lives for ourselves in our pursuit of happiness.

The one exception mentioned above is our right to engage in the pursuit of happiness. Happiness, being an ultimate end and never a means, is not something needed. The means we must employ to pursue happiness are things we need. Our right to pursue happiness rests not on our needs, but on our moral obligation to make morally good lives for ourselves. If we were not under that obligation in the first place, we would not have a right to whatever is needed as means for the achievement of that end.

The moral obligation just stated is expressed by a prescription that is self-evidently true and, therefore, cannot be denied. When we understand the meaning of the words "ought" and "really good," we immediately recognize the truth of the prescriptive injunction that we *ought* to seek everything that is *really* good for us and that there is nothing else we *ought* to seek. We cannot think that we ought to seek what is really bad for us or that we ought not to seek what is really good for us.

Since happiness, ethically conceived, is the complete good of a whole life enriched by the cumulative possession of everything really good for us, the self-evident prescription just stated is equivalent to saying that we ought to seek happiness, that we are morally obliged to pursue it.

With the one exception of the right to pursue happiness, which rests on a prescriptive ought or moral obligation that we find inescapable, all other natural rights are concerned with the real goods we need in order to succeed in our pursuit of happiness. Apart from an inescapable moral obligation, on the one hand, and apart from our natural needs, on the other hand, I can think of no foundation for the rights we call natural, human, and inalienable.

A single qualification must be added. One thing we need as a means for the pursuit of happiness is moral virtue. But although we need it as an indispensable condition for success in leading a morally good life, it is an interior perfection that is almost wholly within our power to attain in some measure or degree.

No organized society or instituted government can confer moral virtue upon a human being or make him or her a person of good moral character. Therefore, although we need moral virtue as an indispensable means for achieving happiness, we do not have a right to it because a right that cannot be secured by devisable institutional enactments is devoid of political significance. Whatever rights we possess have the effect of imposing duties on others: on other individuals to respect them and on organized society and its government to help secure and safeguard them.

It is within the power of organized society and its government to provide human beings with the external conditions indispensable to the pursuit of happiness, facilitating but not ensuring its attainment. Among the real goods we need for a morally good life, the interior perfection of our character that is moral virtue is the only one within our power and subject to free choice on our part.

Our possession of all other goods—security of life and limb, freedom of action, political liberty, health, wealth, knowledge, to mention only some—depends to some degree on external circumstances beyond our control. These we have a right to, not only because we need them but also because it is within the power of organized society and its government either to facilitate or to ensure our possession of them.

What has just been said throws light on our right to liberty or freedom. That right applies to the two freedoms mentioned earlier: freedom of action, which consists in our being able to do as we wish within the limits set by just laws that prohibit us from injuring others; and political liberty, which consists in our being governed with our consent and with a voice in that government. There are other freedoms to which we do not have a right because they are in no way dependent on external circumstances within the control of organized society and its government.

One is the freedom of a free will—freedom of choice. Either we have that freedom as a natural endowment, or it is nonexistent. The same can be said of moral freedom—the freedom of being able to will as we ought, despite the pressure of our passions or emotions to act in a contrary fashion. Either we have such freedom through our acquisition of moral virtue and practical wisdom or it, too, is nonexistent.

Let me sum up what we have learned so far in our attempt to understand the Declaration's assertion that "among these [inalienable] rights are life, liberty, and the pursuit of happiness."

1. The primary right is the pursuit of happiness, having its foundation in our moral obligation to make good lives for ourselves.

2. The rights to life and liberty are subordinate rights because they are rights to means indispensable for the pursuit of happiness and also because security of life and limb, freedom of action, and political liberty are dependent on external circumstances that are within the power of an organized society and its government to control.

3. All other rights, those so far not mentioned or, if mentioned, not discussed, are also subordinate to the right to pursue happiness, either as supplementing the rights to life and liberty or as implementing these rights.

This last point calls for further comment. If the additional rights are supplementary, they have the same status as the rights they supplement. They, too, are natural rights, having their foundation in natural needs. But if the additional rights are not supplementary, but are implementations, they are then constitutional or civil rights, not natural rights.

Rights that implement natural rights are instrumental to the fulfillment of those rights. A few examples should clarify this point.

All human beings by nature desire to know. We have a natural need for knowledge. Under certain circumstances this need can be fulfilled without schooling or tutelage of any sort. However, schooling of one sort or another is certainly instrumental to the fulfillment of our need for knowledge. To whatever extent that is the case, we may have a right to schooling. While that is not a natural right, it may become a civil right when an organized society acknowledges it to be instrumental in the fulfillment of our natural right to knowledge.

Our natural right to life calls for the protection of our health as well as security of life and limb. Under certain circumstances, this may not involve the protection of the environment from spoliation by factors injurious to health. Under certain circumstances, it may not call for preventive medicine and medical care. Under different circumstances, such as those that exist today, the right to a healthy environment and to medical care may come to be regarded as necessary to implement our right to life. When that is acknowledged by an organized society, the instrumental civil rights may be legislatively enacted.

A further and fuller discussion of such instrumental civil rights will be found in the next chapter. Natural rights other than those mentioned in the Declaration will be treated in certain chapters of Parts Three and Four. What remains to be considered here is a question that may arise in the minds of readers with regard to the foundation of natural rights in natural needs. Animals other than man have natural needs. Why, then, do they not also have natural rights?

Those who tend to think that animals other than man have natural rights also think that all the differences between man and other animals are only differences in degree, not differences in kind.

A difference in degree is one in which the things being compared have the same properties, one having more, the other less, of whatever attributes they have in common. In sharp contrast, a difference in kind is one in which, of the things being compared, one has properties or attributes that are totally absent in the other. For example, a longer and shorter line differ only in the degree of their length; whereas a square and a circle differ in kind: one has angles, the other does not.

Those who hold that human beings and other animals differ in kind attribute to man attributes not possessed at all by brute animals. Only man has intellect capable of conceptual, as opposed to perceptual, thought. Because of this, only man has free will and the power of free choice. Because of these two natural endowments, human beings are persons. Brute animals lacking these endowments have natures different in kind, and are not persons.

Laws that permit the killing of animals and the use of them as beasts of burden as contrasted with laws that prohibit the murder and enslavement of human beings, or laws that permit the caging of animals in zoos as contrasted with laws that prohibit the unjust imprisonment of human beings, acknowledge the difference in kind between human beings who are persons and brute animals that are not persons.

Consequently, the presence of natural needs in brute animals does not give rise to their possession of natural rights. Only persons, having the moral obligation to make good lives for themselves by the use of their reason and by their exercise of free choice, have the right to life as a means to living well and a right to liberty of action as a means of carrying out the free choices they make in the pursuit of happiness.

The fact that we are morally obliged to treat brute animals as humanely as possible—to avoid the wanton and useless killing of them, to avoid submitting them to needless pain, to avoid the sadistic exploitation of them for our pleasure—should not be interpreted as an acknowledgment of their having natural rights to either life or liberty. We ought to treat them humanely even if we do not treat them as persons ought to be treated. Our moral obligation here is a matter of charity, not of justice, because it does not stem from the rights of brute animals.

Our need for freedom of action and our consequent right to it has its natural foundation in our natural endowment of free choice. Our need for political liberty and our consequent right to it has its natural foundation in our nature as political animals. There are other species of animals that, like us, are social or gregarious animals, with a natural need to live in groups or societies. But only man is a political animal; only man has a natural need to participate in government and, therefore, a right to do so as a citizen with suffrage.

CHAPTER 10

Securing Human Rights: Civil Rights

HAVING ASSERTED THAT HUMAN BEINGS are endowed with inalienable rights and having named some of these, the Declaration goes on to say that, in order to secure these rights, governments are instituted among men.

Two things strike us at once about this statement. One is the use of the word "are," having as it does the force of pointing to historical fact. With even a slight knowledge of political history, we know that many, perhaps most, governments have not served the purpose of securing human rights. On the contrary, despots and tyrants who have ruled by might rather than by right have trampled on the rights of those subject to their power.

The other thing that strikes us is the use of the word "secured." We have been told that these rights cannot be taken away from those who possess them because they are inherent in their human nature. Why, then, must they be secured?

With regard to the first point, our puzzlement is removed by substituting the words "should be" or "must be" for the word "are." We have no difficulty in understanding that one of the purposes of government, if it is justly instituted, should be the protection of human rights. The violation of such rights, or the neglect of them, is manifest injustice—the injustice to be found in tyrannical and despotic regimes.

Not only *should* just governments be instituted to protect these rights. It is, in addition, clear that they *must* be instituted if that purpose is to be served. Wherever they do not exist human beings are subject to tyrannical and despotic regimes imposed upon them by force. That is the difference between a government *imposed* by might and a government rightly *instituted*.

Our second puzzlement is removed by introducing such words as "protect" and "safeguard" to throw light on the meaning of "secure." *Cura* is the Latin root of the word "secure." Its English derivative is the word "care." Whatever we possess securely we have *without care*—without anxiety or worry about its loss. When our inalienable rights are protected and safeguarded by a justly instituted government that is just in the exercise of its powers, we enjoy our possession of those rights without care or apprehension.

The fact that human rights are inalienable does not prevent them from being abrogated or transgressed by tyrants and despots, or from being trampled upon by the violence of individual criminals or terrorist groups. Even when they are abrogated, transgressed, or trampled upon, we must remember that their continued existence provides our basis for crying out and fighting against the injustice that has been committed. Remembering this, we should have no difficulty in seeing that the inalienability of human rights does not remove the necessity of their being secured—protected and safeguarded by just constitutional provisions and the enactment of just laws.

The Declaration's statement about governments instituted to secure human rights echoes a formulation current in the Middle Ages: that governments should be of service to and for the sake of rights, not a power exercised beyond or outside rights. It would be wrong to suppose that this is the only purpose of governments. As we shall see when we come to the ideals expressed in the Preamble to our Constitution, governments may have other objectives as well. It would also be wrong to suppose that the protection and safeguarding of human rights is the only criterion by which the justice of a government is to be measured. This, too, we shall see later when we consider the establishment of justice as one of the objectives of government named in the Preamble.

All this being understood, we are left with the question: How does a government protect and safeguard the inalienable natural rights that, to be just, it should secure and serve? The answer is: by enacting and enforcing civil rights—rights that are instrumental in implementing natural rights.

This is not the place to go into all the prohibitions of criminal law that aim to prevent individuals or groups of individuals from disregarding or invading the natural rights of their fellow citizens. It should be sufficient to mention a few examples of such legislative enactments. The prohibition of murder and of violent assault and battery implements our right to life and our bodily health, which is adjunct thereto. The prohibition of kidnapping implements our right to liberty. In another body of positive law, the law of torts, the penalization of negligent conduct that endangers life and limb also implements our right to life.

However, such legislative enactments, while they do serve to protect and safeguard our natural rights, do not establish civil rights. For their establishment we must look to the provisions of the Constitution. As drafted in 1787 and adopted by the several states in 1788, the Constitution does not contain any clauses that establish civil rights for the protection of the two natural rights—the right to life and the right to liberty—named in the Declaration as serving our right to pursue happiness.

During the Constitutional Convention, an agitated debate occurred concerning the advisability of including a bill of rights in the Constitution itself. The proponents of that step did not succeed in getting a bill of rights included, but they won their point shortly after the Constitution was adopted when the first ten constitutional amendments were added.

Although these first ten amendments are usually called a "Bill of Rights," it is not clear from a careful reading of them that all tend in fact to establish civil rights that implement our natural rights to life and liberty. Let us look at the first ten amendments in order to discover, if we can, to what extent they can be interpreted as establishing civil rights that function instrumentally in this way.

Article One

Congress shall make no law respecting an establishment of religion, or prohibiting the free exercise thereof; or abridging the freedom of speech, or of the press; or the right of the people peaceably to assemble, and to petition the Government for a redress of grievances.

Article Two

A well-regulated militia being necessary to the security of a free State, the right of the people to keep and bear arms shall not be infringed.

Article Three

No soldier shall, in time of peace, be quartered in any house, without the consent of the owner, nor in time of war but in a manner to be prescribed by law.

Article Four

The right of the people to be secure in their persons, houses, papers, and effects, against unreasonable searches and seizures, shall not be violated, and no warrants shall issue, but upon probable cause, supported by oath or affirmation, and particularly describing the place to be searched, and the persons or things to be seized.

Article Five

No person shall be held to answer for a capital, or otherwise infamous crime, unless on a presentment or indictment of a Grand Jury, except in cases arising in the land or naval forces, or in the militia, when in actual service in time of war or public danger; nor shall any person be subject for the same offense to be twice put in jeopardy of life or limb; nor shall be compelled in any criminal case to be a witness against himself, nor be deprived of life, liberty, or property, without due process of law; nor shall private property be taken for public use, without just compensation.

Article Six

In all criminal prosecutions the accused shall enjoy the right to a speedy and public trial, by an impartial jury of the State and district wherein the crime shall have been committed, which district shall have been previously ascertained by law, and to be informed of the nature and cause of the accusation; to be confronted with the witnesses against him; to have compulsory process for obtaining witnesses in his favor, and to have the assistance of counsel for his defense.

Article Seven

In suits at common law, where the value in controversy shall exceed twenty dollars, the right of trial by jury shall be preserved, and no fact tried by a jury shall be otherwise reexamined in any court of the United States, than according to the rules of the common law.

Article Eight

Excessive bail shall not be required, nor excessive fines imposed, nor cruel and unusual punishments inflicted.

Article Nine

The enumeration in the Constitution of certain rights shall not be construed to deny or disparage others retained by the people.

Article Ten

The powers not delegated to the United States by the Constitution, nor prohibited by it to the States, are reserved to the States respectively, or to the people.

The First Amendment certainly establishes our right to a number of civil liberties that are involved in our exercise of the freedom of action to which we have a natural right.

The Fourth Amendment, prohibiting unreasonable or unwarranted searches and seizures, protects the political liberty of citizens from invasion by secret police action, the kind of paramilitary force used by governments that intimidate and coerce their subjects. Citizens cannot exercise their political liberty to dissent from the acts of government if they are threatened by or subject to unreasonable or unwarranted searches and seizures.

Clauses in the First Amendment also have the same effect: the right to freedom of speech and to the freedom of the press, the right of peaceable assembly, the right to petition for the redress of grievances—these are all civil rights that are enabling provisions for the exercise of political liberty as well as freedom of action.

The Fifth and Sixth Amendments, prohibiting Star Chamber proceedings whereby a despotic ruler can charge, convict, and imprison or execute subjects for crimes without due process of law, safeguard the right to life as well as the right to liberty.

It should be noted here that the due process clause mentions property as well as life and liberty. Mason, following Locke, included property along with life and liberty in his formulation of the Virginia Bill of Rights, but Jefferson, acquainted with both Locke's and Mason's views, made no mention in the Declaration of property as a natural right that needed protection.

Unquestionably, in the Anglo-American tradition, the possession and protection of property is a civil right. Whether we also have a natural right to property remains a question to be considered later when, in Part Three, we come to the ideals of the Constitution's Preamble.

Others may find in the Second and Third Amendments provisions that establish civil rights protective of either political liberty or freedom of action, considered as natural rights. As I see it, their significance comes largely from the experience of the colonists under British dominion: they were not allowed to keep and bear arms that might be used as weapons of insurrection, and the King's soldiers were quartered in their houses without their consent.

The Seventh Amendment, which extends the right to trial by jury from criminal to civil proceedings and establishes the common law as the law of the land, does not seem to me to be on a par with the earlier articles that clearly relate to our rights to life and liberty.

The Eighth Amendment's prohibition of excessive bail and, even more, its prohibition of cruel and unusual punishments serve the purpose of protecting individual freedom from the intimidations of duress. An individual's freedom of choice can never be taken away while he remains alive, but the extent to which the individual can exercise it and can put choices into action can certainly be diminished substantially by duress as well as by coercion and constraint. Coercion, constraint, and duress reduce the options with respect to which the individual can freely choose one or another.

The Ninth Amendment does not establish any specially formulated rights. Instead, it declares that the civil rights so far mentioned shall not be regarded as exhausting all the rights possessed by the people of the several states. Rights not enumerated in the preceding eight amendments should not be thought null and void because they have not been mentioned. The Tenth Amendment should be similarly interpreted.

The discussion so far has been limited to the natural rights of life and liberty as proclaimed in the Declaration, and to the civil rights for their protection established in the first eight amendments to the Constitution. The Declaration concedes that there are other things, in addition to life and liberty, to which we have a natural right because they are means we need for an effective pursuit of happiness. When we discover what these are, we can then look once more at the Constitution to see if later amendments to it establish civil rights that serve to protect these additional natural rights, as the first eight amendments function with respect to life and liberty.

CHAPTER 11

The Consent of the Governed

After saying that men have instituted governments in order to secure their rights, Jefferson adds that governments devised for this purpose derive their just powers from the consent of the governed.

Jefferson's compression again calls for a slightly more expanded statement to make clear what he meant: a government having just powers is a government by right, not might. Just powers have authority as well as force, and that authority derives from the consent of the governed.

The phrase "consent of the governed" comes down to Jefferson by way of John Locke, but the first use of it occurs in a debate that took place in Lord Cromwell's army between Cromwell and his son-in-law, Colonel Ireton, and a group called the Levellers.

Major Rainborough, representing the Levellers, expressed the view that "every man that is to live under a government ought first by his own *consent* to put himself under that government." A fellow Leveller, Sir John Wildman, added: "There is no person that is under a just government . . . unless he by his own free consent be put under that government."

The justice of a government, as we have already noted, can be measured in part by the extent to which it secures the natural rights of its people. That measure of justice does not derive from the consent of the governed. It is rather the just powers of a government that depend for their justice, and, consequently, for their authority, upon the consent of the governed.

In the preceding chapter we encountered the distinction between tyrannical and despotic governments imposed by might—by naked force—and governments rightly or justly instituted. The key to the difference between them lies in the contrast between the words "imposed" and "instituted." In governments *imposed* by might, the governed are involuntarily subject to the power exercised by their ruler. In governments *instituted*, the people themselves erect a government and confer upon it powers to which they voluntarily consent.

Framing and adopting a constitution is one way, although perhaps not the only way, in which a people who regard themselves as having the right to govern themselves can erect a government to serve that purpose.

What is a constitution? It is the framework of a government. It defines the offices of government and allocates to them certain governmental functions that each is expected to perform. It invests those offices (sometimes called the departments or branches of government) with the authority they need in order to perform these functions.

The officials of a constituted government—its officeholders—have no authority or power in their own persons. They have only such authority or power as the constitution confers upon the offices they hold. For officeholders to arrogate to themselves more power or authority than pertains to their offices amounts to usurpation on their part, and should be punishable by removal from office, by impeachment.

All these political ideas are implicit in the meaning of that single phrase "consent of the governed." Still more is there. Reference was made to the right of a people to govern itself. Whence comes this right?

It is implicit in the right to political liberty, that form of freedom which consists in being governed with one's own consent and with a voice in one's own government. Aristotle defined constitutional government as the government of freemen and equals, in which the citizens rule and are ruled in turn—that is, administering the law when they are citizens holding public office for a term of years and obeying it when, in or out of office, they are subject to the laws of the land, laws that they have had a voice in making.

The doctrine of the divine right of kings, to which loyalists in the American colonies appealed, attempted to make absolute rule government by right instead of government by might. One of those loyalists, Jonathan Boucher of Virginia, in an address delivered in 1775, rejected the notion that rightful government is derived from the consent of the governed. He said:

This popular notion that government was originally formed by the consent or by a compact of the people rests on, and is supported by, another similar notion, not less popular nor better founded. This other notion is that the whole human race is born equal; and that no man . . . can be made subject to another [except] by his own consent.

On the contrary, Boucher argued, kings and princes "so far from deriving their authority from any supposed consent or suffrage of men, . . . they receive their commission from Heaven; they receive it from God, the source and origin of all power."

Being a ruler by divine right, an absolute monarch, in Boucher's view, "is to be regarded and venerated as the vicegerent of God"— the representative of God on earth. The opposite view had been expressed centuries earlier by Thomas Aquinas in his Treatise on Law in the *Summa Theologica*.

The power to make laws, Aquinas wrote, "belongs either to the whole people or to someone who is the vicegerent of the whole people." While not denying that God is the ultimate source of all power, Aquinas maintained that God confers it upon a people able to govern themselves and that they, in turn, can confer it upon someone they appoint to perform this function as their vicegerent or representative.

As contrasted with the notion of the divine right of kings, the statement by Aquinas is an early expression of the notion of popular sovereignty. That notion is, in turn, inseparable from the idea with which we are here dealing: that a justly instituted government derives its authority, its just powers, from the consent of the governed.

Republican or constitutional government in ancient Rome was replaced by the absolute rule of emperors when the people gave the Emperor all authority and power. That was, of course, a legal fiction to cover up the seizure of absolute power by the Caesars.

The fiction pictured the transfer of authority from the people to the Emperor as a total and irrevocable transmission of authorized power. The people were thus supposed to have completely abdicated their sovereignty.

Constituting a government by the consent of the people does confer on government officials some of a people's power to govern themselves. This transmission of authority from the people to their representatives is, however, neither total nor irrevocable. Popular sovereignty still remains because officeholders are accountable to the citizens they represent and can be removed from office if they exceed the authority invested by the constitution in the offices they hold.

In Abraham Lincoln's famous statement—"government of the people, by the people, for the people"—it is the first phrase that expresses the notion that constitutional government derives its just powers from the consent of the governed. The word "of" in that phrase is misinterpreted when it is thought to mean that the people are subject to government. In that sense of the word "of," all governments, despotic as well as constitutional, are governments of the people—that is, the people are subject to its laws.

Only when the word "of" is interpreted to mean that the government *belongs* to the people, that it is voluntarily instituted by them, and has no more power or authority than that to which they have given their consent, do the words "government of the people" signify constitutional government.

The word "of" has this possessive meaning in such phrases as "the house of my friend" or "the hat of my aunt." Just as we can also say my friend's house or my aunt's hat, instead of saying government of the people, we can also say the people's government. Daniel Webster in his famous Reply to Hayne, a speech that Lincoln is known to have read, spoke of "the people's government, made for the people, made by the people, and answerable to the people."

Two questions remain to be considered. To whom does the phrase "the governed" refer when we speak of the consent of the governed? And how do those who give their consent give it?

In response to the first question, it should be immediately obvious that not all who are among the governed can or should be expected to give their consent. At no time are the people as a collectivity coextensive with the population. At any time, the population includes infants and children, to whom the phrase "below the age of consent" is applied. The population also includes temporarily resident aliens and persons hospitalized for mental deficiencies and disorders. All these members of the population are subject to the laws of the land and their human rights are also under protection by those laws.

In earlier centuries there were other disfranchised groups in the population who were among the governed but without suffrage—for example, women, blacks, individuals without sufficient property. They were, therefore, not members of the people who were governed with their own consent. It becomes necessary, then, to expand Jefferson's phrase "consent of the governed," replacing it by the statement that a government derives its just powers from the consent of all those who are politically in a position to give their consent. They are the *people* within the *population*—the enfranchised citizens of the republic.

The Declaration does not tell us who the people are. That we are left to discover by interpreting clauses in the Constitution and in its amendments that have to do with the qualifications for citizenship and with the extension of the suffrage. We will, therefore, return to this matter in later chapters dealing with the Constitution.

In response to the second question concerning the manner in which those who are in position to consent give it, we must distinguish the two principal ways in which consent can be given. One of these two ways was operative only in the years 1788 and 1789, when the people of the several states through their representatives voted yes or no on the question whether the Constitution that had been drafted in Philadelphia in 1787 and was now being submitted for their approval should be ratified and adopted.

That event occurred once and once only, although something like it was repeated many times thereafter when territories petitioned for the status of statehood in the federal union. On those occasions, the people of the territories who voted for statehood under the provisions of the Constitution were, in effect, giving their explicit consent to the Constitution itself. It is also the case that on occasions when citizens vote for an amendment to the Constitution, they are giving their explicit consent to the Constitution itself.

The consent of the people governed is explicitly given only in the manner described above. What about the minority who voted no on these occasions?

Since majority rule cannot become a regulative principle by the acquiesence of the majority, we must assume that all members of the people have unanimously accepted it. Unanimity, as Rousseau pointed out, is required for majority rule to become operative. It logically follows, then, that the minority who voted against adopting the Constitution, or voted against petitioning for statehood, gave their consent tacitly or implicitly when they retained their status as enfranchised citizens and acted politically in that capacity. In doing so, they tacitly acquiesced in the Constitution as the framework of a government in which they participated.

This applies to all who have become enfranchised citizens and have acted politically as such since the years 1788 and 1789. We have given our consent tacitly or implicitly, not explicitly.

Giving consent to government does not preclude dissent from government. Consenting citizens can become dissenting citizens on one occasion or another when they protest against the law or acts they deem unjust as violations of their natural rights or for other reasons. Such dissent remains clearly within the boundaries of consent as long as it is dissent by due process of law and employs constitutional or legal means for seeking the redress of grievances. The First Amendment to the Constitution gives consenting citizens the civil right "to petition the government for the redress of grievances," as well as rights to freedom of speech and freedom of the press.

This can be said another way. All those who do not explicitly withdraw their consent, including those who dissent within the boundaries of consent, can be regarded as implicitly or tacitly giving it. How, then, can anyone explicitly withdraw consent? In two ways: by emigrating to another country, or by taking up arms in violent insurrection. Civil disobedience that is nonviolent and accompanied by voluntary submission to the punishment allotted for such disobedience does not involve withdrawal of consent.

How the line should be drawn between such civil disobedience and the kind that becomes a mass political protest in which the resort to violence is latent will be considered in the next chapter when we will deal with the Declaration's statement about the right and duty to withdraw consent and overthrow an unjust government and replace it by another that will respect human rights and promote the pursuit of happiness by its people.

Some enfranchised citizens—currently too many as a matter of fact—do not exercise their rights or perform their duties as citizens. If we maintain that citizens give their consent tacitly when they act politically, must we then say that those who do not act as they should have tacitly withdrawn their consent? No. Although they do not act as citizens should, they nevertheless willingly accept all the benefits that government confers upon them. They can, therefore, be deemed to have given their tacit consent.

CHAPTER 12

The Dissent of the Governed

THE RIGHT OF THE PEOPLE to institute a government that secures their human rights would appear to have its foundation in their right to liberty; more specifically, that mode of freedom which is political liberty, the freedom of those who participate in popular sovereignty. According to the Declaration, a free people has another right: the right to alter or abolish any form of government that fails to protect or that violates their natural rights.

The second right, like the first, would appear to have its foundation in the same natural right, the right to liberty. But the two rights that derive from the right to liberty are not themselves natural rights. What can be said of all natural rights—that they arise from needs inherent in human nature—cannot be said of them. Nor are they, strictly speaking, civil rights, for they are not established by the provisions of a constitution, like the right to freedom of speech, or by legislative enactments. In what sense are they rights? Is it correct to call them rights?

The declaration of a right is often a short way of saying that certain action on the part of a people can be justified—that is, it can be regarded as in conformity with the principles of justice. On the basis of having the natural right to liberty, especially the freedom of self-government, a people is justified in setting up a government for themselves, to which they voluntarily give their consent.

It is equally clear that a people is justified in altering or abolishing any form of government that violates their right to liberty, as despotism does by reducing them to subjection under absolute rule. The Declaration's statement of this point, being so compressed, fails to spell out what its words suggest.

In the first place, we must note the difference between *altering* and *abolishing*. A constitutional government can be altered by amendments to its constitution; a despotic government cannot be altered in this way.

Constitutional defects that are altered by amendments may be either defects of omission or defects of commission. They are the former when a constitution fails to secure by its provisions certain rights that are, or come to be, acknowledged as natural rights. They are the latter when one or more articles of a constitution tend to abrogate known natural rights.

As we shall see in later chapters, our Constitution has been altered by amendments in order to remedy both sorts of defects. In addition, decisions of the Supreme Court, reviewing the acts of both state and federal governments, have provided remedies for the two sorts of defects.

To the extent that amendments to the Constitution have been adopted by popular mandate, they have been enacted with the consent of the governed. Altering our form of government in this way does not involve the withdrawal of consent.

Judicial decisions declaring certain acts of government unconstitutional have sometimes been occasioned by popular dissent that, in effect, petitions the government for a redress of grievances. When popular dissent proceeds in this way to bring about a rectification of injustice by due process of law, it, too, does not involve a withdrawal of consent.

Such popular dissent may involve acts of civil disobedience by a person or a group of persons who disobey a law and willingly accept the punishment assigned for its violation in order to call attention to the injustice of the law they think should be declared unconstitutional. Cases calling for the judicial review of such legislation have come to the Supreme Court in this way.

When does dissent from civil government or civil disobedience

involve a withdrawal of consent? If it does not do so when it seeks
to alter a constitutional government by due process of law and without violence, then the answer must be that it does so when the
actions taken seek to abolish one form of government and to replace
it with another.

The word "rebellion" does not appear in the Declaration of Independence. In common usage that word has the connotation of an
attempt to overthrow a government, and that is the meaning to be
found in the Declaration when it speaks of a people's right to "throw
off" a government that abrogates their rights and cannot be altered
by constitutional amendments and due process of law.

Despotic forms of government cannot be altered by constitutional
amendments and by due process of law. Being governments by might
or force, they can only be abolished or overthrown by resort to
might or force. Resort to force—acts of war—is implicit in the
etymology of the word "rebellion," the Latin root of which (*re-bellare*)
means return to the state of war, a state in which only force is
available to resolve conflicts.

A pronouncement by John Locke, with which Jefferson was acquainted, throws light on this point. Locke wrote:

Whosoever uses force without right . . . puts himself into a state of war
with those against whom he so uses it, and in that state all former ties are
canceled, all other rights cease, and every one has a right to defend himself,
and resist the aggressor.

The context in which the Declaration asserts the right of insurrection calls attention to a long train of abuses and usurpations on
the part of the British King and Parliament that manifest their design
to subject the American colonies to despotic rule. The colonists, the
Declaration says at a later point, "have petitioned for redress" and
their "repeated petitions have been answered only by repeated injury." In other words, the colonists had resorted to nonviolent means
of rectifying the injustices they thought had been inflicted on them.
Those attempts having failed, they were left with only one resort:
to take up arms and to use force to overthrow a despotic government.

According to the Declaration, the colonists were not only justified in using violent or forceful measures to overthrow the despotism to which they had been subjected; they were also under a moral obligation to do so. "It is their right, it is their duty," the Declaration asserts, "to throw off such government."

The right asserted, as we have seen, amounts to a justification of the act. But how shall we understand the duty, the moral obligation?

It would appear to stem from the moral obligation on the part of human beings to engage in the pursuit of happiness, to try to make morally good lives for themselves. Despotic government, abridging or abrogating the right to liberty as an indispensable means for the pursuit of happiness, prevents human beings from fulfilling their moral obligation to seek their ultimate good. It is, therefore, their duty to remove this obstacle.

Being justified in their effort to abolish or overthrow a despotic government that impairs their pursuit of happiness, the people, when successful in this effort, should not try to get along without any government, which would be a state of anarchy. They should, the Declaration tells us, "institute new government, laying its foundations on such principles, and organizing its powers in such form, as to them shall seem most likely to effect their safety and happiness."

The insurrection against despotism carried out by the colonists in their War of Independence was only the first step to be taken. The second step was taken five years after the war had been won, when the Constitutional Convention met in Philadelphia to set up a new form of government by drafting a Constitution and submitting it to the people for their adoption.

It should not go unremarked that the Declaration previsions this second step. Even more remarkable is the fact that, in doing so, it reflexively refers to the principles it has enunciated (the basic political ideas we have been considering) as providing the foundation for the new form of government to be instituted. It also speaks of organizing the powers of that new government in such a way that, when the Constitution is adopted, they will derive their authority from the consent of the governed.

We have reached the conclusion that only a despotic government justifies insurrection and even imposes on us a duty to rebel. With respect to constitutional government, what we are justified in doing and are also under a duty to do is not to abolish it by violent or forceful means, but rather to alter it by way of amendments and other lawful and nonviolent means.

In other words, the right and duty to overthrow a government applies only to the first step the colonists took on the road to setting up the Republic in which we live. Once the second step has been taken, enabling us to live under constitutional government, we have both the right and the duty as citizens to do what is necessary in order to rectify whatever injustices result from defects in our Constitution.

Understanding this leaves open for later consideration the problem of drawing the line between conditions that justify civil dissent within the boundaries of consent and conditions that justify the withdrawal of consent from a duly constituted government. It also postpones until later the question as to whether a completely just form of government should provide its people with adequate and sufficiently speedy means for civil dissent that seek to obtain redress for grievances or to remedy injustice within the boundaries of consent.

These matters will be taken up in Chapters 14 and 15, where we shall be concerned with two ideals stated as objectives of our government in the Preamble to its Constitution: to establish justice and to ensure domestic tranquility.

PART THREE

The Preamble's Ideals

We, the people of the United States, in order to form a more perfect union, establish justice, insure domestic tranquillity, provide for the common defense, promote the general welfare, and secure the blessings of liberty to ourselves and our posterity, do ordain and establish this Constitution for the United States of America.

CHAPTER 13

We, the People: Citizen-Constituents

LET US LOOK first at the opening and closing words of the Preamble: "We, the people of the United States, in order to form a more perfect union . . . do ordain and establish this Constitution for the United States of America."

The phrase "United States" occurs twice in the passage just quoted. In its first occurrence, it refers to the thirteen sovereign states united under the Articles of Confederation. In its second occurrence, it envisages a new sovereign state, both national and federal in character, which will come into existence for the first time if and when the Constitution proposed is ratified or adopted by the people of at least two-thirds of the thirteen colonies that had in 1783 become independent states.

All this is implied in the phrase "in order to form a more perfect union." The people of the thirteen states were already united by the Articles of Confederation. They had been united even before that by their successive joint efforts to seek redress of their grievances under British rule, and then to form a Continental Congress to direct their war for independence. But four years of experience of an imperfect union under the Articles of Confederation motivated their decision to set up a Constitutional Convention in order to form a more perfect union.

The difference between the imperfect union of the thirteen states under the Articles of Confederation and the more perfect union that

would be established if the Constitution proposed was adopted has
been sufficiently explained in Chapter 2. Only one thing needs to
be added here.

The ratification or adoption of the proposed Constitution would
not only *establish* a new sovereign state, the United States of America;
it would also *ordain* for that new political entity its framework of
government. The two would come into existence simultaneously,
for that new political entity could not become a reality until its
constituted government became actually operative. On this understanding of the matter, the United States of America came into
existence in 1789, not 1787.

We are left with a question about the three opening words: "We,
the people." Who make up *the people*?

It would obviously be wrong to suppose that those words referred
only to the delegates in Philadelphia who drafted the Constitution
and, by a majority of their number, approved it for submission to
the Confederation Congress then meeting in New York. If they were
the people who could have ordained the Constitution, it would not
have had to be submitted to anyone else for approval.

Nor were the members of the Confederation Congress the people
who had the power to ordain the Constitution as the fundamental
law of the land. When the approved draft came to them, it was their
duty to transmit it to the thirteen confederated states.

Those sovereign states had already allied themselves with one
another under the Articles of Confederation. It was by their action
as states that that confederacy had been established. To supplant
the Articles of Confederation by the Constitution of the United
States, the Constitution had to be ordained by the people of the
several states, not by the states as sovereign political entities.

In the years 1787–1789, the population of the thirteen states
amounted roughly to four million human beings. Did the phrase
"we, the people of the United States" refer to all four million?
Hardly. In that multitude there were many, undoubtedly a majority,
who could not have been among the people from whom approval of
the Constitution was to be sought.

A large part of the population was outside the pale of political

red in the operations of both con-
t. The essential point of the dis-
nderstand that in a constitutional
o the law, whereas in a despotic
bove the law.

ts that he enforces with whatever
e power he exercises is vested in
olds. He can change laws at will
coercive force.

ion of the United States to be the
distinguish it from the laws made
gislature's limited power to make
ch of government by the Consti-
s enact, not their legislature. Fur-
other officeholders are subject to
making.

m the chief magistrate down, can
hment for treason, for usurpation
nd misdemeanors. This fact alone
lawful government, for it makes
t to it. Despotic government, in
ecause the ruling individual, not

law—the supreme law of the land
not by their legislature—requires
of law itself.

ubject puts it concisely: A law is
mmon good, instituted by who-
to care for the community. That
n the Preamble when it speaks of
stitution to establish the United

ato recommended that every law
s purpose. Most written laws do
bles, but the Constitution does,

life. Some were infants or children, those who by reason of their immaturity were under the age of consent. A larger number consisted of those who, under the laws of the states in which they lived, had not for whatever reason been granted the status of enfranchised citizens.

The young disfranchised by their age, the women disfranchised by their gender, the blacks disfranchised by their enslavement, and a large number of white male adults disfranchised by their lack of sufficient property to pay a poll tax, made up that portion of the population who were not members of "the people." They were in fact an overwhelming majority.

When those persons who *were* among those in the several states who were capable of voting cast their ballots for or against the ratification of the Constitution, an affirmative majority prevailed in enough states to assure the ordination of the Constitution and the establishment of the United States of America. But what about the dissident minority? Can they, too, be construed as being among the people who constituted this nation and its federal form of government? Yes, on the ground that as voting citizens they had already accepted the principle of majority rule. Accordingly, all who exercised their suffrage as citizens had given their consent in advance to the outcome of the vote.

In our earlier consideration of the Declaration's statement that government derives its just powers from the consent of the governed, we saw that such consent was not to be sought from all who were governed—that is, the total population—but only from those who by their status as citizens with suffrage were in a position to give their consent. In other words, "the consent of the governed" means the consent of the enfranchised persons who comprised the people, not the consent of the total population.

That phrase in the Declaration calls for the establishment of constitutional government. Those who by their suffrage were in a position to give consent were not only the enfranchised citizens of a constitutional government, they were also its citizen-constituents, its constitution-ratifiers.

Those who drafted our Constitution did not invent constitutional

government, nor were they even the first to formulate a v
constitution. We owe that greatest of all political innovations
ancient Greeks—Solon in Athens and Lycurgus in Sparta-
first founded states by constituting them and thereby creat
status of citizenship.

These two things come into existence together: constitution;
ernment and citizenship. In societies that do not have constitu
governments, those who are governed, no matter how we
unconsenting subjects, ruled by force, no matter how gentle.
are not citizens who, by their consent, have acknowledged tl
thority of the government under which they live.

The idea of constitutional government involves a number
tions that need to be made fully explicit. One concerns the
powers of a government that derives its legitimate powers fro
consent of the people governed. Legitimate power has two f
authority and force.

Authority is not possessed by a government merely as a res
the submission of the governed to the power the government i;
to exert over the population. A government has genuine author
the right to govern—only when such authority is conferred
or transmitted to it, by acts of the people as its consenting co;
uents: their originating constitutive acts, their interim acts of
sent, and their periodically recurring electoral acts. While
authority is possessed and exercised by the officeholders or offi
in a constitutional government, it is held and exercised by the
dependence on the people who inalienably possess the right to
government.

When we acknowledge the authority of a just law, we hav
mind the fact that it elicits our voluntary compliance because c
justice. We do not obey it simply because it has coercive fo
which can be exercised against those who disobey the law. Gov
ment by coercive force alone is government by might. Only {
ernment that has authority as well as force at its disposal is govern
by right, which is to say legitimate government.

Whence comes this authority? Only from a constitution adop
by the consent of the people. Those who hold political offices un

or laws as well as men, are invo
stitutional or despotic governme
tinction is seen only when we u
government all men are subject
government the absolute ruler is

The despot makes laws by edi
might he personally possesses. T
his person, not in the office he
and is not himself subject to thei

In acknowledging the Constitu
fundamental law of the land, we
by legislative enactment. The le
laws is conferred upon that bran
tution—a law that they themselv
thermore, legislators as well as al
the laws they have had a voice in

In addition, all officeholders, fr
be removed from office by impea
of power, and for serious crimes
makes constitutional government
law supreme and all men subje
contrast, is lawless government
the law, is supreme.

Considering the Constitution as
enacted by the people themselves,
us to dwell briefly on the nature

A medieval statement on this
an ordination of reason for the c
soever has the authority and duty
word "ordination" finds an echo
the people as ordaining the Co
States of America.

In his dialogue on The Laws, F
should have a preamble stating
not have explicitly written prea

and though serving the common good is not mentioned as its controlling purpose, the five intermediate clauses in the Preamble to the Constitution specify objectives that are components of the common good. Those objectives as stated are to "establish justice, insure domestic tranquillity, provide for the common defense, promote the general welfare, and secure the blessings of liberty to ourselves and our posterity."

Before we consider these in relation to the common good, let us observe that a good can be common in two quite distinct ways. On the one hand, the word "common" signifies that certain goods are common because they are the same for all. On the other hand, it signifies that certain goods are common because they are shared or participated in by all.

The happiness which all human beings have an inalienable right to seek for themselves as individual persons is not an individual good, it is a common good. It is the same for all, since it consists in the enjoyment of all the real goods that everyone naturally needs. The fact that it is the same for all because the needs of our common nature are the same for all does not preclude individual differences in the pursuit of happiness, especially with regard to the satisfaction of individual wants that are not the same for all.

The domestic tranquility of a society, the justice of its laws, its self-defense or security, the general welfare, and the blessings of liberty—these, too, are common goods in the sense that they are goods shared by or participated in by all members of civil society or the political community.

In any society, especially in the most complex of all societies which is the state, government is necessary to effectuate the union of wills that brought the society into being in the first place. The government instituted for this purpose is well designed if its framework is so constructed that it is dedicated to objectives that the members of a society sought to achieve by associating for a common purpose. The Preamble to the Constitution as the framework of our government specifies those objectives.

Looking at the Preamble's statement of objectives in relation to the Declaration's comparable statement of the purpose for which human beings should institute governments, we must ask a number of questions.

The Declaration tells us that, in order to secure inalienable natural human rights, it is necessary for mankind to institute governments. As we have already observed, these rights are rights to all the goods that human beings naturally need in order to pursue happiness. Their happiness, or the conditions requisite for its effective pursuit, is the ultimate end to be served by a well-designed framework of government. Happiness is the ultimate common good. The various goods that are its component elements are subordinate common goods and indispensable means for achieving happiness.

Are all the subordinate common goods specified in the Preamble distinct from one another? That question will be addressed in the chapters to follow.

Is the enumeration of them in the Preamble exhaustive? Have some—one or more—been omitted? For example, equality? That question, too, will be considered later.

Is there some redundancy or overlapping to be found in this enumeration? With one exception, that would not seem to be the case. The one exception lies in the phrase "general welfare." It is sometimes understood to mean the general happiness or the happiness of all, in which case it ceases to be a subordinate good and becomes the ultimate good that is common by virtue of being the same for all.

The general welfare is also sometimes understood to mean the common good of the political community itself—the collection of common goods in which the members of the political community participate. If that were so, mentioning the general welfare would be redundant; it would merely sum up what is spelled out in the enumeration of the other objectives to be served by a government that aims at serving the common good.

We will return to the problem of what is meant by the general welfare clause in Chapter 17. Assuming for the moment that the general welfare can be understood as standing for a subordinate common good in which all members of the political community participate, we must ask about the relation of the five objectives to one another. While they may be distinct, they may not be independent if achieving one may not be possible unless one or more of the others is also achieved.

Are the several purposes harmonious with one another and so proportioned to one another that serving one does not detract from or impede the service of another?

Can the blessings of liberty, for example, be secured without establishing justice? Can justice be done without safe-guarding liberty? Or without promoting the general welfare? Can the general welfare be promoted without restricting liberty or without jeopardizing domestic tranquility? May providing for the common defense come into conflict with promoting the general welfare?

If the answers to these questions indicate that the several objectives mentioned in the Preamble are not only interdependent but may also come into conflict with one another, it could have been predicted from the outset that the constitutional history of the United States would be replete with evidence of difficult problems that either have been solved or still remain to be solved.

Implicit in the Preamble is the assertion that no society in which we would want to live can exist without justice, civil peace, self-defense, welfare, and liberty. This does not preclude the tensions that inevitably arise from inordinate efforts to achieve any one of these objectives at the expense of others.

The political life of our nation should be assessed not only by reference to the way in which we have implemented the purposes stated in the Preamble but also by reference to mistakes of policy that we have made in our attempts to resolve the tensions or conflicts that have arisen in our efforts to implement them.

To conclude this opening chapter about the ideals of the Preamble, it seems fitting to attempt a brief overview of the Constitution as a whole—as drafted and submitted, with no amendments added.

A constitution, Aristotle said centuries ago when written constitutions were novel political devices, consists in an arrangement of offices or magistracies, together with a statement of the powers vested in each. That describes the Constitution of the United States as a framework of government. But one thing more must be added. Our Constitution includes a statement of powers not granted the federal government and reserved either to the federated states or to the people themselves.

Article One establishes the legislative branch of government in a bicameral legislature consisting of a Senate and a House of Representatives. Its component sections first state the criteria of eligibility for holding office as a Senator or a Congressman, and it then goes on, in Section 8, to an enumeration of the powers to be exercised by the Senate and the House of Representatives. Almost all the objectives mentioned in the Preamble are covered in this section. Section 9 names things that the Congress does not have the power to do; Section 10, things that the several states are prohibited from doing.

Article Two establishes the executive branch of government, as consisting in a President and a Vice-President and other subordinate officials, and states the conditions of their eligibility for office and the manner in which they shall be elected. Section 2 enumerates the powers vested in the office of the President; Section 3 enumerates the duties of that office; and Section 4 provides for the removal from office of the President, Vice-President, and all civil officers on impeachment for and conviction of treason, bribery, or other high crimes and misdemeanors.

Article Three establishes the judicial branch of government in one Supreme Court and in a number of inferior courts. Section 2 states the scope of the jurisdiction to be exercised by federal courts—what cases in law and equity it is appropriate for these courts to adjudicate.

Article Four deals with the rights reserved to the several states and to be enjoyed by the citizens of these states. Section 3 provides for the admission of new states to the federal union. Section 4 guarantees to every state in the Union a republican form of government.

Article Five defines the process by which the Constitution can and shall be amended.

The main point of Article Six is its declaration that this Constitution and the laws of the United States that shall be made in pursuance thereof shall be the supreme law of the land, and that the judges in every state shall be bound thereby, anything in the constitution or laws of any state to the contrary notwithstanding.

Article Seven makes the ratification of the Constitution by nine of the thirteen states sufficient for the establishment of this Constitution between the states so ratifying the same.

CHAPTER 14

To Establish Justice

THE CLAUSE IN THE PREAMBLE to the Constitution calling for the establishment of justice is thrice anticipated in the Declaration of Independence.

The Declaration's espousal of inalienable—natural, human—rights lays down the first and most obvious demand for justice on the part of government. That doing justice is an overriding objective for governments to serve is made clear in other statements in the Declaration. Securing human rights is the supreme purpose for which governments should and must be instituted. A government's failure to secure these rights gives a people grounds for taking drastic steps to remedy the injustice being suffered.

A second and somewhat less direct consideration of justice is the remark in the Declaration that the powers exercised by a government are just only if they derive from the consent of the governed. As we have already seen in Chapter 11, the only government that derives its powers from the consent of the governed is constitutional government. In contrast, despotic government exercises purely arbitrary power over its subjects.

It cannot be this aspect of political justice that the framers of the Constitution had in mind when they called for the establishment of justice as one of the aims of the government they were constituting. The very fact that they were engaged in the process of creating a government that would become a reality only if it met with the approval and elicited the consent of the people assured the accomplishment of this one aspect of justice. If the Constitution was adopted, political justice would be served by the prevention of despotic domination.

However, while constitutional government is by its very nature just government, that does not mean that it is perfectly just. With regard to justice, it can be defective in a number of ways.

The Constitution itself, while establishing government with the consent of the governed, may be unjust in its provisions, either by way of commission or by way of omission. Providing for a legislative body to make laws by no means guarantees that the laws enacted by the legislature will be just. Nor does erecting a judicial system guarantee that the decisions of its courts will do justice in individual cases or that the operation of the system will provide effective remedies for the redress of injustice.

It is with this in mind that we can look to the Declaration for a third anticipation of the Preamble's commitment to the establishment of justice as one, if not the principal, aim of the government being constituted. It is the least direct or explicit of the three, but a moment's reflection will uncover its far-reaching significance.

The Declaration affirms that all human beings are equal in one fundamental respect. They are all equally human. What has this affirmation of human equality to do with justice?

The answer is to be found in the complaint we have all heard uttered by even very young children: that they are being treated unjustly or unfairly when one of their siblings receives treatment of which they themselves are deprived. Susie says to her parents, "You let Charlie do this. I should be allowed to do it, too."

The principle of justice to which appeal is being made is that equals should be treated equally, to which another clause must be attached: that unequals should be treated unequally in proportion to their inequality. This twofold principle of justice does not exhaust the essence of justice, as it is sometimes thought, but it does express the one aspect of justice that consists in fairness.

Two other aspects of justice are quite distinct from it: the justice that consists in securing human rights, and the justice that consists in serving the public good, the good of the community as a whole, usually referred to as the common good, common because it is a good shared by all members of the community.

It may come as a surprise, even as a shock, to some twentieth-century readers of the Preamble that equality—equality of treatment, equality of opportunity, equality of conditions—is not mentioned along with the blessings of liberty and the enjoyment of domestic tranquility as one of the major values to be served by the government being instituted. The rallying cry of the French revolution at almost the same time was to be liberty, equality, and fraternity. Why did our Founding Fathers make no reference to equality in the Preamble?

The answer cannot be that they gave no thought to equality. The Declaration removes any doubt on that score. The answer may lie in their recognition of the fact that in calling for the establishment of justice, they were also, implicitly if not explicitly, insisting that the government being instituted should attempt to establish as much equality as justice requires, not only the equal protection of the laws for all citizens but also equality of treatment in other respects, equality of conditions as well as equality of opportunity.

This answer finds strong confirmation in the controlling insight about America to be found in the observations about this country written by a young Frenchman, Alexis de Tocqueville, who visited these shores in the 1830s. What distinguished this newly constituted nation from all the European countries with which he was acquainted was its commitment to equality, even stronger than its commitment to liberty, a commitment to equality of conditions, not just to equality of opportunity. It was the first modern state that had no feudal past, the first in which there were no nobles. All were commoners.

De Tocqueville's insight concerning the innovation in human affairs that America was introducing into the world need not lead us to overlook the fact that many of our late eighteenth- and early nineteenth-century leaders were not as strongly devoted to equality for all as they were to liberty for themselves.

On the contrary, there were defenders of the institution of chattel slavery among them. In addition, statesmen such as Hamilton and Madison in the late eighteenth century and John C. Calhoun in the early nineteenth century thought that there was an irreconcilable conflict between liberty and equality. Equality before the law and equality of opportunity were compatible with the fostering of individual liberty and freedom of enterprise, but not attempts to impose an equality of conditions, political and economic.

I have elsewhere pointed out that these men were wrong in their fear about liberty being sacrificed for the sake of equality. There is no conflict whatsoever between the protection of liberty and the securing of equality when the service of these two fundamental values is regulated by justice. If no more individual liberty is asked for than justice allows, there can be no conflict between protecting all the freedom that is limited by considerations of justice and securing all the equality that is required, also by considerations of justice.

Libertarians, in their exclusive and excessive devotion to individual freedom, cry out for more liberty than anyone can use justly or without injury to others. Egalitarians, in their zeal for equality of treatment and of the conditions that justice requires because of human equality, overlook or even deny the inequality of treatment that justice also requires because of human inequalities.

Libertarians and egalitarians cannot help coming into conflict with one another. They have been at loggerheads throughout the history of this country. But that is a conflict between wrong extremes, not a conflict between liberty and equality as fundamental values, both of which must be regulated by justice to prevent them from becoming excessive and illicit.

I shall have more to say about the limitation of freedom by justice in Chapter 18. Here I wish only to repeat that no one who understands the aspect of justice that consists in a fair treatment of persons in whatever respects they are equal and unequal can fail to realize that the Preamble's call for the establishment of justice also calls, implicitly at least, for securing all the equalities and inequalities—of wealth, of honor, and even of political status—that justice requires.

Thus far we have considered three aspects of justice: (1) the securing of all inalienable or natural human rights; (2) the fairness involved in the equal treatment of equals and the unequal treatment of unequals in proportion to their inequality; and (3) the service of the public or common good, the good of the community as a whole.

Justice, looked at another way, gives rise to another threefold division: (1) the justice to be done by the state in relation to its people or by the government in relation to the governed; (2) the justice to be done with regard to the relation of one citizen or group of citizens to another citizen or group of citizens; and (3) the justice to be done by citizens in relation to the community as a whole and in service to its common good.

There are ancient and traditional names for this threefold division of justice. The justice of the state or of its government in relation to the people has been called distributive justice. This not only involves that aspect of justice which concerns securing human rights for all, it also involves an equal or unequal distribution of rewards and burdens according to the equality or inequality of the persons that should in all fairness receive them.

The justice to be done with regard to all transactions involving the relation of one individual or group of individuals to another individual or group of individuals has been called commutative justice. Here we may be concerned with protecting the legal, or even the natural, rights of one individual vis-à-vis another. We may also be concerned with considerations of equality in the exchanges that occur between individuals.

Whereas distributive justice consists in those measures by which the state or organized society renders to each person what is rightfully due that individual, commutative justice consists in one individual's rendering to another what is rightfully due that person. The rightfulness may derive either from a natural or from a civil right.

In order for human beings to live peacefully together in society and have peaceful commerce or dealings with one another, the rights and duties that are involved in commutative justice must be covered by the enactment of positive laws that prescribe or prohibit certain acts on the part of one individual in relation to another. In addition, a system of courts or judicial tribunals must be set up to render judgments in particular cases that fall under those laws. Sanctions have to be applied for the enforcement of the decisions rendered by those courts in the adjudication of disputes.

Hence, to establish justice, especially commutative justice, a constitution must provide for law-making or legislative bodies, for a judiciary or a system of judicial tribunals, and for agencies able to enforce the laws enacted and the decisions of courts. As for distributive justice, that is partly served by the provisions of the Constitution itself and by its amendments, but it may also be served by legislative enactments and by judicial decisions in accordance with those laws.

When we turn from commutative to contributive justice, we turn from the field of private to the field of public law. Contributive justice involves rights and wrongs other than those covered by the laws of property, contracts, torts, and so on. It also covers more than the wrongs prohibited by the criminal law.

On the positive side, contributive justice requires that an individual, in his or her relation to all others with whom that person is associated in organized society, should render to them what is owed them by virtue of their shared social objectives. Each individual owes all the rest whatever contribution he or she can make to the common good—the good that is common to all, the good of the society itself and the good life of its members.

Constitutional provisions, legislative enactments, and judicial decisions are the means for implementing the establishment of distributive and commutative justice. But with the possible exception of certain parts of the criminal law, contributive justice cannot be established by constitutional provisions, legal enactments, or judicial decisions.

Contributive justice is an aspect of moral virtue, which individuals either do or do not possess by the free choices they themselves make. The formation of moral virtue or the failure to form it is not a matter that can be controlled by legislatures, courts, or law enforcement agencies. If it were, crime and delinquency would be preventable; the treatment of criminals and delinquents would result in their reform and rehabilitation.

Our ancestors recognized that the task of establishing justice did not extend to this dimension of justice. They realized that contributive justice in the conduct of citizens must be left largely to impulses of moral virtue on their part; largely, but not entirely, for the law does prescribe some actions for the common good and prohibits some that are injurious to it.

The thrust of distributive justice is in the opposite direction to that of contributive justice. Distributive justice concerns that which is due the individual from organized society as a whole. It aims to assure that each individual shall have a fair share of the goods, economic as well as political, that only organized society can make available to all. Distributive justice is done when the distribution of these goods is fairly apportioned according to the twofold principle of equality: (1) treating equals equally, and (2) treating unequals unequally in proportion to their inequality.

So far so good, but one problem remains to be solved for which no solution appears to be provided in the Constitution or in its amendments. Without its solution, the Preamble's call for the establishment of justice cannot be fully realized.

The problem yet to be solved is a way of providing a remedy for the injustice of governmental acts, whether executive, legislative, or judicial. Let us consider legislative enactments first of all, either laws made by the federal government or laws made by the legislatures of the several states.

In the operation of legislative assemblies, majority rule prevails. It also prevails in referendums and plebiscites. But majorities can be wrong, both legislative and popular majorities. When they are wrong to the extent of serving their own interests at the cost of injuring minorities by violating their rights, the result is tyranny by the majority.

There is no legal cure for tyranny on the part of an absolute despot. The only recourse open to those who suffer from such tyranny is violent insurrection or, as happened in India, effective passive resistance. Insurrection was the remedy resorted to by the American colonists when the British government did not respond to their appeals for redress of their grievances.

However, there is a legal remedy for the tyranny of the majority in the operation of constitutional government. It is not the remedy proposed by James Madison in the tenth *Federalist* paper, nor by John Calhoun in his essay on constitutional government, nor even by John Stuart Mill in his treatise on *Representative Government*. All these proposals ultimately undermine the principle of majority rule itself while pretending only to prevent tyranny on the part of the majority.

The remedy that preserves the principle of majority rule while at the same time nullifying unjust laws approved by a legislative majority was found by our ancestors in the power of the Supreme Court to review the acts of government, executive as well as legislative, and to declare them unconstitutional and, therefore, null and void.

I say "found by our ancestors" to indicate that the power of judicial review was taken unto itself by the Supreme Court early in its history. It was not provided for in the Constitution itself or in any of its amendments. Once assumed, it was not, even at the outset, effectively challenged. In later years, it has gained general acceptance as if it were an integral provision of the Constitution.

Judicial review that results in nullifying laws or executive acts as unconstitutional may not always be rectifications of injustice because they violate inalienable human rights. But when that is the case, the injustice caused by the tyranny of a majority is corrected.

The clause in the Preamble that aims the Constitution in the direction of justice has, as we shall see in the chapters to follow, a close bearing on other aims of our Constitution as expressed in subsequent clauses of the Preamble: to ensure domestic tranquility, to promote the general welfare, and to secure the blessings of liberty. None of these other aims can be achieved without the establishment of justice.

However, there is one glaring exception, and that is the clause of the Preamble concerned with providing for the common defense or, as we currently speak, providing for our national security. That one aim can be accomplished without the establishment of justice; and, to our serious disquiet, we have found that at times it would seem to be the case that it cannot be accomplished without violations of or departures from justice.

CHAPTER 15

To Ensure Domestic Tranquility

THE WRITERS OF THE PREAMBLE were thoroughly aware of all the distresses and disorders to which the body politic is prone: crime, civil turmoil, and conflicts of every sort.

They were equally cognizant of the traditional affirmation that peace—civil peace—is an almost indispensable component of the common good. Without it, human beings associated in civil society to achieve a set of common purposes cannot accomplish them. They are debarred by civil strife from enjoying the advantages they seek by living together.

I have used the phrase "civil peace" where they used the phrase "domestic tranquillity." The substitution of the one for the other has its basis in an ancient definition of peace with which they were acquainted. St. Augustine defined peace as "the tranquility of order." They probably also knew that civil peace had been spoken of as "the work of justice," that its very existence depends not merely on the replacement of anarchy by government but also on its justice and the just enforcement of its laws.

The phrase "civil peace" as the equivalent of "domestic tranquillity" calls for a few words of further comment. In common parlance, when most of us speak of war and peace, we think of the international scene in which nations are engaged in diplomatic negotiations with one another. When that fails to resolve serious conflicts between them, they turn from diplomacy to warfare, employing all the weap-

ons of destruction available at the time. In consequence, we regard
nations as being at peace with one another at all times when they
are not actually engaged in the violent actions of warfare.

For a different conception of peace, we need only be reminded of
the fact that we also speak of riotous actions as disturbances of the
peace and of crimes as breaches of the peace. The peace we are then
considering is civil peace or domestic tranquility, not international
peace. Such peace is not to be identified with the mere absence of
fighting or violence, as we tend to identify international peace with
the mere absence of warfare. It is a positive, not a merely negative,
condition.

That positive condition consists in the possibility of resolving all
conflicts that may arise among the members of a civil society without
resort to violence. How? By the means that the machinery of government puts at the disposal of the people. They can settle their
differences by all the procedures afforded them by law. Civil peace,
in short, does not consist in the absence of serious conflicts among
the members of a society, but rather in the fact that there is a way
of resolving such conflicts without resort to violence.

When it is said that justice is a prime factor in the preservation
of peace, what is meant is that a justly constituted government
together with its enactment of just laws removes one of the causes
of civil dissension and strife. Those who regard themselves as suffering serious grievances as a result of unjust laws or injustice on
the part of the government under which they live always have recourse to violence open to them if they cannot get their grievances
redressed or rectified in any other way. When there are groups of
people suffering serious grievances for which they can find no remedies by legal means, the civil peace of that society becomes a fragile
thing that may not long endure.

Hence, to ensure domestic tranquility, what must be provided by
a constitution are adequate means of civil dissent—that is, dissent
from enacted laws and from the actions of government by legal
means, thus removing any need for resort to violent action for the
redress of serious grievances. When such means are either absent or
inadequate, mass political protests may arise. Violent disorder is

always latent in such movements, even when their leaders are committed to a policy of nonviolence.

Nonviolent civil dissent occurs through periodic resort to the polls, public assemblies, freedom of speech in all the media of communication, direct and indirect appeals to the courts. The inadequacy of such dissent is related to the amount of time required for the means to become effective or to the uncertainty of the result. How to make them more speedily effective is a problem no society has yet solved. Until it is solved, if it ever can be, domestic tranquility cannot be perfectly ensured in any society in which the establishment of justice remains imperfect.

There is, of course, another threat to domestic tranquility, and that is the ever-present criminal segment of the population, especially the existence of highly organized criminal groups. We are much more aware of this source of civil disorder than were the Founding Fathers. Organized crime is a very recent innovation, and even more recent are groups dedicated to the use of violence for political purposes.

Against such factors and forces that threaten our domestic tranquility, the prime, if not the only, agency that can be looked to for the preservation of civil peace is the police. The force that must be exercised by the police in the prevention of crime and the apprehension of criminals is radically different from the force employed by the criminal element in the population.

The criminal's use of force is unlawful violence. The force used in law enforcement agencies is by its very nature lawful and, therefore, nonviolent. It is authorized force. Violence is an unauthorized use of force.

However surprising and even incredible it may appear to many readers, it is a well-authenticated historical fact that the institution we know as a police force did not come into existence in this country until the second quarter of the nineteenth century. Until well after 1830, there were no uniformed police carrying weapons of enforcement in such cities as Boston, New York, or Philadelphia. What we now know as England's Metropolitan Police Force did not come into existence in London until around 1825.

The preservation of civil peace without the operation of a civil police force would appear to be unthinkable. Nevertheless, the existence of the one for the sake of the other is an innovation of very recent history.

The institution of a civil police force is still so new that it is far from being perfected in its operations. We are well aware that improperly trained and disciplined police may employ unauthorized means of law enforcement. They may resort to violent measures and themselves become a threat to civil liberty as well as civil peace.

To ensure domestic tranquility without encroaching upon liberties and without transgressing rights is a delicate assignment for the constitutional government of a society dedicated to freedom and justice. A constitutional government must see to it that law enforcement is itself lawful, its processes articulated in law and its conduct subject to steady, critical examination by the people, to whom the police are politically accountable.

CHAPTER 16

To Provide for
the Common Defense

ALTHOUGH WE TURN NOW from the Preamble's concern with domestic tranquility to its concern with the common defense, we are still considering matters of war and peace. In connection with domestic tranquility, the aspect of war under consideration was the strife of civil disorders and disturbances. Here it is international war—armed conflict involving sovereign states as the combatants.

As with war, so with peace the aspect of the subject also changes. Civil peace, as we observed, is not simply the negative condition that consists in the absence of fighting, bloodshed, and the destruction of property. It is rather that state of affairs in which even serious conflicts among the members of society can be resolved by legal means and the machinery of government so that there is no need to resort to force.

In sharp contrast, when peace prevails among sovereign states, it is a merely negative condition as contrasted with civil peace, which is positive. Sovereign states may not at the moment be engaged in actual warfare. But should diplomatic negotiations fail, should economic sanctions not prevail, should conversations completely break down, sovereign nations have no recourse except warfare to settle their differences if the conflict of interests is serious enough to require that drastic measure.

In all the other phrases of the Preamble, an ideal is held up as a controlling objective of the government being constituted: justice, peace, welfare, liberty. War is certainly not an ideal, nor is victory in warfare, although it may be necessary when a nation must resort to the awful arbitrament of war to serve its interests.

Is peace—the unstable condition of international peace—an ideal to be aimed at? Is it an element in the common good that a government should serve?

There can be no question that it is desirable and, as desirable, deserving of inclusion among the objectives of government, nor can there be any doubt about its being an element in the common good.

Individuals are better able to enjoy all the advantages conferred upon them by society, and hence are facilitated in the pursuit of their personal happiness, when the society in which they live is at peace with other nations and free from all the stresses and strains involved in warfare.

Why, then, should there be any hesitation in regarding the preservation of international peace as an ideal in the same sense that justice, domestic tranquility, the general welfare, and the blessings of liberty are ideals?

Before answering the question, let us note two things about the phrase "common defense." The word "common" here calls our attention to the fact that one of the significant changes in the replacement of the Articles of Confederation by a federal constitution is that the several states entering into the federal union no longer have the need to maintain military establishments for defense against foreign aggression. This will be done for them by the federal government.

The second point to be noted is that the maintenance of a military establishment by the federal government is said to be strictly for the purpose of defense, not for the sake of aggressive warfare of the kind in which sovereign princes, ambitious to aggrandize their domains by conquests, have in the past employed their armed forces. What the writers of the Preamble called the common defense we now call our national security. To be concerned with national security (defense against foreign aggression) is compatible with being a peace-loving nation—one that does not harbor any warlike intentions with regard to other states.

That being understood, why should any doubt remain about national security as a political ideal? One way of reaching for an answer to this question is to imagine a hypothetical state of affairs.

Imagine that the United States existed in total isolation from all other nations, untouchable by them as if there were a protective seal around it. Or imagine that it existed in a world in which somehow, by whatever means, perpetual peace prevailed—a world peace akin to civil peace, a state of affairs in which no recourse to military force was ever needed.

On either of these hypotheses, providing for national security would not be an objective of our national government. We would not have to maintain a military establishment of any kind, although we would still require civil police as an agency of law enforcement. In addition, we would not need a state department or a diplomatic corps, nor would we have to be concerned with questions of foreign policy.

If you will permit yourself to imagine either of the proposed hypotheses, how would you answer the question: Would the United States be better off *with* or *without* the need to provide for national security as an objective of its government? Before answering, pause long enough to consider whether the same question could conceivably be asked about the other objectives in the Preamble. Would the United States be better off if establishing justice, ensuring domestic tranquility, promoting the general welfare, and securing the blessings of liberty were not among the objectives of its government? It is questionable whether anyone would answer affirmatively.

However, as to the question about providing for national security, it does seem to me quite possible, and even likely, that the response could be that many advantages would be gained if national security did not have to be an objective of our government, certainly not the prime objective it has become today. Even if that response was not immediately unanimous, the reasons for it, when considered, might be so persuasive as to gain adherents.

What are those reasons? One was actually in the mind of the writers of the Preamble. In the light of all the historical evidence available to them, they realized that the maintenance of a standing army, whether for the purpose of defense against aggression or for the purpose of aggressive conquest, was a threat to liberty and to justice. "The liberties of Rome," James Madison declared, "proved the final victim to her military triumphs"; to which he added that the liberties of Europe "have, with few exceptions, been the price of her military establishments."

Alexander Hamilton argued in the same vein about the dangers implicit in standing armies "and the correspondent appendages of military establishments." In the eighth *Federalist* paper, he wrote:

Safety from external danger is the most powerful director of national conduct. Even the ardent love of liberty will, after a time, give way to its dictates. The violent destruction of life and property incident to war, the continual effort and alarm attendant on a state of continual danger, will compel nations the most attached to liberty to resort for repose and security to institutions which have a tendency to destroy their civil and political rights. To be more safe, they at length become willing to run the risk of being less free.

In another place he argued against the extreme unlikelihood of our needing "an army so large as seriously to menace the liberties of a great community." At that time, the geographical situation of the United States vis-à-vis Europe reduced, but did not remove, the threat of invasion by European powers.

In addition, our eighteenth-century ancestors thought they could put into the Constitution things that might further diminish the dangers implicit in a military establishment for the common defense. Not only would the new nation, because of its geographical distance from Europe, need only a small standing army, that military force would also be under civilian control by making the President its Commander-in-Chief. Furthermore, his use of that force would be checked by Congress.

Military appropriations, like other appropriations, must originate in the House of Representatives, the popular branch of Congress. Such appropriations could run for no more than two years, so that each new Congress was not only assured the opportunity but also placed under the necessity of reviewing afresh the military establishment.

Still other precautions were written into the Constitution. The President's selection of military officers was subject to senatorial confirmation. And, finally, the power to declare war was vested in the Congress, not the President.

In the debate that occurred concerning the ratification of the Constitution, the proponents argued that the checks provided to safeguard the use of military power by the President were adequate for the protection of liberty. Before going further, let us look at the actual wording of clauses in the Constitution to which this argument appealed.

Section 8 of Article One gives Congress the power to lay and collect taxes "to pay the debts and provide for the common defense and the general welfare of the United States." It also places in Congress the power "to declare war . . . make rules concerning captures on land and water" and "to raise and support armies, but no appropriation of money to that use shall be for a longer term than two years." In addition, it gives Congress the power "to provide and maintain a navy, to make rules for the government and regulation of the land and naval forces, to provide for calling forth the militia to execute the laws of the Union, suppress insurrections, and repel invasions."

Section 10 of the same article deprives the federating states of any power to engage in international affairs and denies them the right "to keep troops or ships of war in time of peace."

Section 2 of Article Two makes the President "Commander-in-Chief of the Army and Navy of the United States and of the militia of the several states when called into the actual service of the United States." It also gives him the power, "by and with the advice and consent of the Senate, to make treaties . . . and he shall nominate, and, by and with the advice of the Senate, shall appoint ambassadors, other public ministers and consuls. . . ."

Section 3 of Article Three declares that "treason against the United States shall consist only in levying war against them, or in adhering to their enemies, giving them aid and comfort." Obviously, supplying the nation's enemies with military or diplomatic secrets is covered by the phrase "giving them aid and comfort."

The Constitution drafted in 1787 did not fully contemplate the situation as it has developed in the course of this century under the pressures exerted by our involvement in two world wars.

Consider how far we have moved from a military presence comprising a small standing army, a small navy, and state militias to the present military establishment, huge in size and arsenal, globally stationed, biting deep into the nation's budget, affiliated with a substantial part of the nation's industrial power and with its scientific and technological research, raising issues of secrecy and using agencies of secret intelligence, and having immense impact not only on foreign policy but also on domestic politics.

Do the precautions written into the eighteenth-century Constitution against the dangers implicit in a military establishment now work as effectively as our Founding Fathers intended them to do?

The answer must take into account the enormous increase in the power of the Presidency vis-à-vis Congress in the sphere of foreign policy, in leading the nation by gradual steps into undeclared war, and in deploying our military might in order to serve our vital national interests without consulting Congress about them.

The device of dual political control over the military—by Congress as well as by the President—has not worked very impressively under an increase in the power of the presidency even as curtailed by the recently enacted War Powers Act. The role of the National Security Council, the Central Intelligence Agency, and the Joint Chiefs of Staff, with their large and independent bureacracies, could not have been foreseen by the framers of the Constitution.

During the debate over the ratification of the Constitution, James Madison wrote:

A standing force, therefore, is a dangerous, at the same time that it may be a necessary provision. On the smallest scale it has its inconveniences. On an extensive scale its consequences may be fatal. On any scale it is an object of laudable circumspection and precaution. A wise nation will combine all these considerations; and, whilst it does not rashly preclude itself from any resource which may become essential to its safety, will exert all its prudence in diminishing both the necessity and the danger of resorting to one which may be inauspicious to its liberties.

Reading these words, we are compelled to ask: Does the wisdom they express suffice to guide us in the exigencies that confront us today? Madison and other Founding Fathers were concerned mainly with the tension between providing for the common defense and securing the blessings of liberty. Our concerns are wider and deeper. With regard to all the other objectives mentioned in the Preamble, it can be said with reasonable assurance that they are harmonious and reciprocally supportive. The establishment of justice serves to ensure domestic tranquility, to promote the general welfare, and to secure the blessings of liberty. The promotion of the general welfare enlarges the enjoyment of freedom and strengthens civil peace by removing factors and conditions causative of crime. All these function together to create conditions of life that tend to facilitate the individual pursuit of happiness, which is the ultimate goal to be served by a just and benevolent government.

Providing for our national security is distinctly different from all the other objectives of government. Unless a nation can manage to survive under the anarchic condition of international affairs, its government cannot serve any of the other objectives that are ideals to be aimed at. Our national security is indispensable to our individual pursuit of happiness. Nevertheless, conflicts have arisen and will inevitably arise between providing for national security and safeguarding liberties and rights.

Liberty and other human rights have been infringed and even sacrificed in the service of that objective—sometimes justifiably, *but not always.* In our very recent past, we have witnessed serious disturbances of the peace that detracted from our domestic tranquility resulting from mass and often violent protests against our involvement in an undeclared war conducted for reasons of national security. The enormous drain on our national resources represented by the budgetary allotment for national defense greatly reduces what remains available for the promotion of the general welfare. The age-old conflict between guns and butter has reached staggering proportions in the political life of the nation.

With all this in mind, are we not persuaded that we would all be better off IF, *on either of the two hypotheses presented earlier in this chapter,* we did not have to include providing for national security as one of the objectives of our government?

That big IF requires us to remember the conditions hypothecated and to recognize that they are fantasies of the imagination beyond any chance of realization until the world is blessed with greater wisdom than it has so far managed to attain. That is not likely to occur in the immediately foreseeable future.

Whatever an ultimately wise solution of the problem might turn out to be, the present perilous state of world affairs places our national security high on the agenda of our government under any administration. We may wish that it were not so, but prudence dictates that it must be so until world civil peace is securely established.

CHAPTER 17

To Promote the General Welfare

OF THE FIVE PHRASES in the Preamble that state the objectives of the government being constituted, the one that calls for the promotion of the general welfare is the only one that raises certain perplexities about its meaning.

The eighteenth-century interpretation of what was meant by the general welfare was quite unsatisfactory for reasons that will presently become clear. In the discussions that took place in the years immediately after the Constitution was adopted, the dispute between James Madison and Thomas Jefferson, on the one hand, and Alexander Hamilton, on the other hand, went unresolved.

That discussion and dispute centered on the phrase "general welfare" in Section 8 of Article One and ignored its use in the Preamble. If attention had been paid to its occurrence in the Preamble, it would have been realized that any interpretation of the meaning of the phrase had to satisfy two requirements.

In the first place, like justice, domestic tranquility, common defense, and liberty, what the general welfare stood for had to be conceived as an element in the common or public good that the government was being created to serve directly, and the common good in turn conceived as a means to the pursuit of happiness—the ultimate end to be achieved by a just and benevolent government.

In the second place, as an element in the common or public good, the general welfare had to have a meaning distinct from the meanings attached to the other four elements. We can, therefore, dismiss at once certain interpretations of the phrase that can be immediately judged inappropriate because they fail to meet these two requirements.

If the general welfare of the country is regarded as being identical with its public or common good, then it cannot be conceived as one element in the common good distinct from all the others. On the contrary, as identical with the public good, it includes all the others.

Another interpretation is equally insupportable. The general welfare was thought at the time to be equivalent to the general happiness of the people, their general well-being. In one of his *Federalist* papers, Madison wrote that the general welfare stands for "the happiness of the people," and as "the real welfare of the great body of the people," he holds it up as the supreme objective of government. On this interpretation, the general welfare phrase does not belong in the Preamble at all.

A moment's digression is needed to clarify a double use of the phrase "common good." I think I have made this point before but it deserves repeating here.

A good can be common in two ways: (1) by being a good that is shared or participated in by many; and (2) by being a good that is the same for all who enjoy it.

In the first sense, the good of the organized community as a whole is a common good because all members in the community can participate in it. In the second sense, the personal happiness of each individual in the community is a common good because the essence of a morally good life is the same for all.

To keep them distinct, let us call the common good in the first sense the public common good, and the common good in the second sense the personal common good. With that clear, we can now recapitulate what has been said about the two wrong interpretations of the general welfare phrase as it is used in the Preamble.

It does not belong in the Preamble if the meaning given to it identifies it with the public common good, for in that case it is redundant. Nor does it belong there if the meaning identifies it with the personal common good, for in that case it states an objective no government can achieve. In neither case can it be an element co-ordinate with justice, domestic tranquility, the common defense, and liberty as the four other distinct elements in the public common good.

Before proposing an acceptable interpretation of "general welfare," let us examine the eighteenth-century discussion of it to see why that so far missed the mark. As I pointed out earlier, that discussion revolved entirely around the use of the phrase in Section 8 of Article One. Here is the part of that section which is relevant to our present concern.

. . . The Congress shall have power to lay and collect taxes, duties, imposts, and excises, to pay the debts and provide for the common defense and general welfare of the United States; but all duties, imposts, and excises shall be uniform throughout the United States;

To borrow money on the credit of the United States;

To regulate commerce with foreign nations and among the several States, and with the Indian tribes;

To establish an uniform rule of naturalization, and uniform laws on the subject of bankruptcies throughout the United States;

To coin money, regulate the value thereof, and of foreign coin, and fix the standard of weights and measures; . . .

To make all laws which shall be necessary and proper for carrying into execution the foregoing powers, and all other powers vested by this Constitution in the Government of the United States, or in any department or officer thereof.

The first clause in Section 8 gives Congress the power to lay and collect taxes and acquire other revenues. These Congress can then use to pay the nation's debts, and also to provide for the common defense and general welfare of the United States. There would appear to be no limit put on the amount that Congress can spend for the common defense and for the even broader purpose of promoting the general welfare of the nation, especially if the general welfare is thought to be identical with either the public or the personal common good.

This raised the issue about limited versus unlimited government, with Madison and Jefferson on one side, and Hamilton on the other.

Madison, a vigorous proponent of limited government, argued that the general welfare clause in the first paragraph of Section 8 had no specific meaning at all, and that the correct interpretation of that section should be that it limited the power of Congress to spend the money it was able to raise on the common defense in the first place, and then only on the other specific objectives enumerated in the paragraphs following the first paragraph of Section 8. If the general welfare clause had any meaning at all, it merely served as a covering term for the specific objectives enumerated in the paragraphs that followed.

In short, the first paragraph, according to Madison, did not give Congress a separate power to tax, spend, and act for the general welfare. The general welfare was simply an introductory heading to cover all the powers granted Congress as specified in the remaining paragraphs of Section 8.

The concluding paragraph of that section conferred on Congress an extensive scope of power by authorizing it "to make all laws which shall be necessary and proper for carrying into execution the foregoing powers, and all other powers vested by this Constitution in the Government of the United States." In Madison's view, to allow that concluding paragraph to confer on Congress the power to do anything that needed to be done on behalf of the general welfare with the general welfare left unspecified, amounted to giving Congress unlimited power.

Hamilton, as vigorous a proponent of a strong central government as Madison was an advocate of strictly limited government, advanced a diametrically opposite view. In his *Report on Manufactures*, written in 1791 when he was Secretary of the Treasury, he declared:

The National Legislature has express authority "to lay and collect taxes . . . and provide for the . . . general welfare." . . . These three qualifications excepted, the power to *raise money* is *plenary* and *indefinite*. . . . The phrase [general welfare] is as comprehensive as any that could have been used, because it was not fit that the constitutional authority of the Union to appropriate its revenues should have been restricted within narrower limits than the "general welfare," and because this necessarily embraces a vast variety of particulars, which are susceptible neither of specification nor of definition.

It is, therefore, of necessity, left to the discretion of the National Legislature to pronounce upon the objects, which concern the general welfare, and for which, under that description, an appropriation of money is requisite and proper.

Thomas Jefferson was so disturbed by this statement in Hamilton's report that he discussed it with George Washington, who was then President, saying that the people were compelled by it to consider whether they were living under a limited or an unlimited government.

Madison, writing to the Governor of Virginia, raised the same question. Did not Hamilton's commentary on the term "general welfare" radically alter the character of the government from one that had been strictly limited to definitely specified powers?

Madison succeeded in preventing Hamilton's *Report on Manufactures* from being acted on by Congress. But the issue about the general welfare clause, on which they took opposite sides, was for all intents and purposes left unresolved.

The issue, as I see it, was incorrectly stated at the time because of Madison's misuse of the term "limited government" and because Hamilton's opponents misinterpreted his espousal of a strong central government as if it called for unlimited government.

In the vocabulary of traditional political theory, the distinction between limited and unlimited government is identical with the distinction between constitutional and absolute or despotic government. A constitutional government is by its very nature always a limited government because the power exercised by its officeholders is limited to the authority conferred by the Constitution on the offices they hold. An absolute monarch, ruling despotically, is not an officeholder and is not subject to such limitations.

The authority conferred on any department of government by a constitution can involve a very extensive grant of powers and still not turn that government into an unlimited one. In other words, a constitutional government remains a limited government, strictly speaking, whether the powers with which it is endowed by the constitution are relatively restricted in extent or much more extensive. They are never totally unrestricted or unlimited.

The proponents of relatively restricted government often appeal to Jefferson's statement that "that government governs best which governs least." The opposite statement—"that government governs best which governs most"—might be construed as the slogan of the proponents of a government that intervenes much more extensively in the affairs, especially the economic affairs, of the country.

Neither statement or slogan goes to the heart of the matter. The question is how much governmental power and action is *needed* to satisfy all the purposes that government should serve if it is aimed, first and directly, at the public good, and then, indirectly, through serving the public good, the pursuit of happiness by its citizens, which is the ultimate objective of a just and benevolent government.

Hence, to the question of how much power should a limited or constitutional government possess, the answer is not as little as possible nor as much as possible, but rather as much as may be necessary in order for that government to discharge its obligations to the people.

That government governs best that governs most justly and most benevolently, whether in doing so the powers it exercises and the actions it undertakes are relatively slight or much more extensive. This means, in the words of Abraham Lincoln, that the government should do for the people whatever the people cannot do for themselves, either individually or collectively.

It is with this understanding of the role of government in the lives of the people that we can now assign a definite meaning to the phrase "general welfare"—one that justifies its conclusion among the Preamble's enumeration of five distinct elements in the public common good.

What is to be promoted is the general *economic* welfare of the nation and the participation in that general economic welfare by all members of the population. The introduction of the word "economic" as the qualifying adjective gives the general welfare phrase the specific meaning it needs for its inclusion, along with justice, domestic tranquility, common defense, and liberty, as an element in the public common good, while remaining quite distinct in meaning from the other four.

This would appear to be what Alexander Hamilton, as Secretary of the Treasury, had in mind when he commented on the general welfare in his report to Congress. In that report he was exclusively concerned with the economic prosperity of this country, which he thought depended on its ceasing to be mainly an agricultural economy and becoming largely an industrial one. However, there is no indication in the report of concern on his part with participation in that economic prosperity by all the people of the country.

The notion that the country's wealth should be so distributed that no one would go without a slice of the pie did not come to the fore until the third decade of the twentieth century. Until then, the promotion of the general welfare, even when understood as meaning the general *economic* welfare, did not call upon the government to take whatever steps might be necessary to see that no individuals or families were left out of the picture; or, in Franklin Roosevelt's memorable words, that there should be no forgotten men.

This twentieth-century interpretation of what is involved in promoting the general *economic* welfare turns our attention from those natural human rights that are purely political, like the right to political liberty, to other natural human rights that are economic rather than political. These other rights are not explicitly mentioned in the Declaration of Independence, but they are implicitly there when we understand the Declaration to be saying that among the inalienable rights that human beings possess are life, liberty, and whatever else they need for the pursuit of happiness.

Can there be any doubt that they need a sufficient amount of wealth in the form of those economic goods which supply them with the comforts and conveniences of life? When Aristotle defined happiness as a whole life lived in accordance with moral virtue, he was careful to point out that moral virtue is not enough for the pursuit of happiness. A moderate amount of wealth and of other external goods is also needed.

Becoming morally virtuous is almost wholly within the power of each person. Each individual succeeds or fails according to the free choices that individual makes. But acquiring sufficient wealth—the moderate amount that is needed for a decent life—is not wholly within the power of the individual. The individual's participation in the general economic welfare may, in many cases, depend on the government's doing for the people what the people cannot do for themselves, either individually or collectively.

Further treatment of the general economic welfare, at least as far as the twentieth-century understanding of what is required in order to promote everyone's participation in it, must be postponed until we come to the discussion of economic rights in Chapter 21. When economic rights are recognized, as they were not at the time the Constitution was drafted and ratified or in the century that followed, we cannot fail to see the very close connection between the establishment of justice and the promotion of the general welfare.

CHAPTER 18

To Secure the Blessings of Liberty

THE PREAMBLE ENDS with a rhetorical flourish. The Declaration was content to list liberty as one of the human rights that a just government should secure. The Preamble adds that it should secure not just the right to freedom but "the blessings of liberty for ourselves and our posterity."

Let us ponder for a moment the difference between rights and blessings. A blessing is a gift. We speak of the blessings of good fortune and of the blessed as those who have received special gifts from God. If liberty is a blessing, the only form of freedom that fits that description is the gift—either from God or from our natural endowment—of free will and the power of free choice.

That mode of freedom is certainly not within the power of the most just and benevolent government to secure. We either have it from other sources or we do not have it at all. But having it, if we do, is not irrelevant to the liberties that are within the power of a government to confer upon its citizens and to safeguard.

Without freedom of choice we would not be political animals, but merely instinctively gregarious ones, and our being political by nature is the basis for our natural right to political liberty. Our having the natural endowment of free will is also the basis for our right to individual freedom of action, the right to carry into execution the things we freely choose to do.

These two forms of freedom are the liberties with which the final phrase of the Preamble is concerned. Let us consider political liberty first.

As we have seen repeatedly in the course of the preceding chapters, we must conceive political liberty in the context of the fundamental distinction between constitutional and despotic government—that is, limited versus absolute government, a government of laws versus a government of men, a government by right versus a government by might. Political liberty comes into existence with the establishment of constitutional government and its creation of citizenship—that is, human beings governed with their own consent, as contrasted with those subject to arbitrary power.

Political liberty is more than freedom from arbitrary power—the capricious will of a despot who, whether he governs benevolently or tyrannically, imposes his own will by force upon those he rules. Freedom from arbitrary power is merely the negative aspect of political liberty. The positive aspect is self-government—being governed not only with one's own consent but also with a voice in government.

Citizens are self-governing in the sense that each is a participant in government along with his or her fellow citizens, especially when fundamental decisions are determined by the will of a majority of all whose voices have been heard. The adversely affected minority, by acquiescing in majority rule, have not been left out of the picture.

How is political liberty secured? First of all, by enfranchisement. Not all who live under constitutional government enjoy political liberty; it is possessed only by those upon whom the status of citizenship with suffrage has been conferred. Those not enfranchised as citizens are no more politically free than the subjects of a despot.

In the second place, participation in government by enfranchised citizens occurs in two ways: either *directly*, when they engage in referendums or plebiscites on important public issues or in the public discussion of them; or *indirectly*, when they elect those who are to represent them in legislative assemblies. Either way, citizens exercise a voice in the making of the laws under which they live and in the determination of policies that affect their lives.

In the republics of antiquity, the citizens participated directly in public affairs by meeting in the marketplace or forum and, after debate, taking a vote on the issues being considered. In modern republics such as ours, because of geographical extent and the size of population, republican government had to become a representative form of government. With that innovation arose a vexatious question about the role played by representatives in relation to the will of the electorate.

At one extreme, it has been thought that elected representatives should consult their own judgment and exercise their own choice in voting on issues before the legislative assembly. At the opposite extreme, it has been thought that they should be guided entirely by the view held by a majority of their constituents, provided they can discover what that is.

Neither of the extreme views is satisfactory. On the one hand, to give representatives total independence of the views held by their constituents deprives the citizens who elected them of a voice in the affairs under consideration and eliminates one aspect of their political freedom.

On the other hand, to require representatives to be entirely guided by the will of their constituents, or by the views held by a majority of them, is to reduce them to the status of emissaries rather than that of legislators. There are many matters that come before the legislature of a modern state on which the people's representatives, giving full time to the problems, can be much better informed and more expert in deliberation than the people themselves. It would, therefore, be ill-advised not to expect independent judgment and freedom of choice on the part of the people's representatives.

Somewhere in between the two extremes a middle ground can and must be found. Finding it results in a compromise that allows representatives to exercise their own judgment, while at the same time giving their constituents the opportunity to inform them of the views they hold and, ultimately, the power to remove them from office if they depart too radically and too obstinately from the position taken on important issues by the citizens they are supposed to represent.

What has just been said about the role of elected legislators in relation to their constituents applies as well to the role played by all other elected officers of government. They, too, are made responsible to their constituents by the power citizens exercise at the polls, such as removing them from office if their policies or actions are deemed unacceptable by the majorities who elected them.

Let us turn now to the other mode of freedom that should be secured not only for the citizens of a republic (who have by their suffrage political liberty) but also for those who are deprived of the franchise (and so lack political liberty) yet still have a natural, human right to individual freedom of action.

In what does such liberty consist? It consists in the freedom to do as one pleases or wishes, to carry out in action the choices that the individual has freely made.

To do everything one wishes? To act in any way one chooses? Hardly, for that would be complete, unlimited freedom. It would mean total autonomy for each individual. Each would be a law unto himself. Freedom of complete autonomy for all individuals is incompatible with their living together in society and deriving the benefits from doing so, among which is the security of each in being safeguarded from injury by others.

Cicero expressed this insight concisely when he said that "law is the foundation of the liberty we enjoy. We are all servants of the law in order that we can be free." John Locke expressed the same insight more fully. He wrote:

. . . Law, in its true notion, is not so much the limitation as the direction of a free and intelligent agent to his proper interest, and prescribes no farther than is for the general good of those under that law. Could they be happier without it, the law, as a useless thing, would of itself vanish; and that ill deserves the name of confinement which hedges us in only from bogs and precipices. So that however it may be mistaken, the end of law is not to abolish or restrain, but to preserve and enlarge freedom. For in all the states of created beings, capable of laws, where there is no law there is no freedom. For liberty is to be free from restraint and violence from others, which cannot be where there is no law. . . .

Just laws that restrain individuals from injuring others and, in doing so, also prevent them from infringing on the liberties of others do not themselves diminish anyone's freedom for two reasons.

In the first place, doing as one pleases if what one pleases to do is in violation of just laws is not liberty. It is license—a counterfeit of lawful freedom. When those with criminal intent are restrained from doing as they wish by fear of being apprehended and punished, they obey the law not because they acknowledge its justice, but only because they fear its coercive force.

In contrast, morally virtuous individuals with a proper understanding of what is just and unjust act lawfully by free choice on their part. That being the case, they have lost no liberty when, by free choice, they obey laws, the authority of which they acknowledge because of their justice. The coercive force of the law imposes no restraints upon them for they freely restrain themselves from violating just laws.

This is the second reason why restraints imposed by just laws upon individual freedom do not abolish any genuine liberties, but only the lawless freedom that is license rather than liberty. Those who think that law and liberty are opposed, so that the fewer the laws under which one lives the more liberties one enjoys, fail to recognize the distinction between liberty and license.

Those who espouse the doctrines of philosophical anarchism go even further. To maximize freedom, they would abolish government entirely and exempt everyone from the restraints imposed by laws. They are asking for the kind of complete autonomy that is incompatible with social life.

As Alexander Hamilton observed, if men were angels, no government would be necessary to restrain acts of license and to exercise coercive force for that purpose. But human beings are not angels, and so many individuals are not morally virtuous that they cannot be granted the complete autonomy the anarchist seeks.

All this being understood, we are still left with one problem about the relation of law to liberty. Once again, it is a statement by John Locke that throws light on the subject.

In addition to the freedom we enjoy when we voluntarily obey just laws, we should also have, according to Locke, the freedom to do as we please in all matters concerning which enacted laws neither prescribe nor prohibit action on our part.

How large should the sphere of such freedom be? The answer is that it should be circumscribed only by laws that are just—regulations of our conduct *for the sole purpose of preventing us from injuring others or the public common good*. Only laws that serve this purpose justly limit individual freedom of action, John Stuart Mill declared in his essay *On Liberty*. Restraints imposed upon individual freedom can be justified on no other ground than the prevention of injury to others or to the public good.

In contemporary life the most striking examples of mistakes and confusions about the point under consideration are to be found in the sphere of sexual conduct. Laws that attempt to restrain individuals from committing sexual acts that are deemed reprehensible either because they are sins in violation of the divine law or acts of vice in violation of the moral law fail to distinguish the proper sphere of man-made or civil law from that of divine and moral law.

One of the most eminent theologians, Thomas Aquinas, living in a society in which Christianity was the established religion, took great pains to emphasize the importance of restricting man-made law to the regulation of conduct on the part of individuals that affects the good of others or of society as a whole.

In his Treatise on Law in the *Summa Theologica*, he asked two questions about positive law—the laws made by civil governments. He asked, first, whether civil governments should make laws to prohibit every vicious or sinful act. He asked, second, whether they should make laws to prescribe all the actions that can be expected from virtuous and righteous individuals. To both questions, he responded with emphatic negatives. Civil law, the law of the state, enforced by its government, should extend, he said, only to those actions that affect the good of others and the good of the community.

According to the principle thus enunciated, there can be no crimes where there are no victims—where no individual is injured, nor society adversely affected. Sexual acts performed in private by consenting adults should not, therefore, be prohibited as criminal actions regardless of how sinful or unvirtuous they may be. Laws that attempt to prohibit such actions should be rejected as unjust because they are in violation of the human right to freedom in all matters that do not involve injury to others or to the public good.

To think otherwise is to confuse crimes with sins or with acts that are simply unvirtuous. A religious minority that arrogates to themselves the role of a moral majority may be offended by the knowledge that such sinful or immoral conduct is occurring in the community in which they live. But their being outraged by such knowledge does not constitute the kind of injury that the criminal law should attempt to prevent.

The opposite view leads to the most undesirable results. To think that laws should be made to prevent any group in the population from being outraged by actions on the part of others that they find morally reprehensible, or even aesthetically distasteful, would result in society's being overburdened with a mass of completely illegitimate legislation. It would also result in illegitimate restrictions of individual freedom.

One final comment is called for by a recent decision of the Supreme Court upholding a Georgia law making sodomy between consenting adults a crime. This fundamentally wrong decision is one example of many wrong decisions by the Court when its majority adopts a policy of strict interpretation of the Constitution.*

That policy constrains the Court to abide by the letter of the law and to ignore its spirit; worse, to try to abide by the intention of the laws' formulators; and, worst, to pay attention only to the words that are to be found in the Constitution's body and to ignore the words of the Preamble, as if that were no part of the Constitution itself but mere rhetoric. The words of the Preamble, echoing in part the language of the Declaration, breathe spirit into the rest of the Constitution.

---

*The Georgia sodomy law would also appear to be in violation of Section 1 of the Fourteenth Amendment, in which it is laid down that "No State shall make or enforce any law which abridges the privileges and immunities of citizens of the United States."

To ignore the Preamble is to disregard the ideals of the Constitution and the fundamental ideas and principles that it derives from the Declaration. In the Georgia case, it results in the majority's neglect of the right to individual liberty in all matters concerning which the law should neither prescribe nor prohibit because the exercise of freedom in these matters causes injury to no one.

The dissenting minority opinion in the Georgia case rightfully appealed to this principle. It had warrant for that appeal in a correct understanding of one of the Constitution's ideals as stated in the Preamble.

Strict justice, it has been said, often results in inequity. A strict interpretation of the Constitution as currently practiced often results in the acceptance of unjust laws.

CHAPTER 19

The Defects of the Eighteenth-Century Constitution

DID THE CONSTITUTION AS DRAFTED in 1787, ratified in 1788, and extended by the first ten amendments before the close of the eighteenth century fully realize the ideals set forth in its Preamble and give full effect to the ideas it inherited from the Declaration of Independence? If not, how far did it go in that direction?

To answer the first question negatively and the second by saying not nearly far enough is not to detract from the magnificence of the achievement that we see fit to celebrate in the current years. Perfection is not achieved on earth. It can never be closely approximated in one attempt.

What was achieved in the eighteenth century by American statesmen—a group of brilliant men unequaled since in this country's history—must be measured against the conditions and circumstances of the time in which they were living. Judged in that way, we can have nothing but high praise for what they then produced and handed down to succeeding generations as a basis for carrying their work forward.

There is only one way in which we can soberly assess how to give life to their ideas and how to realize the ideals they had in mind. To accomplish that we must recognize the defects in the Constitution they delivered to us who are alive many generations later.

Of the six objectives stated in the Preamble, the first—to form a more perfect union—was the one most completely realized by the adoption of the federal Constitution, which transformed a plurality of states into one: *E Pluribus Unum*. Let us consider the degree to which the Union was firm and solid before the Civil War and after it. Let us remember that Abraham Lincoln's controlling motive throughout those dire years was to preserve the Union. Thus we cannot fail to see that even that first objective was far from being consummated in the eighteenth century.

For largely the same reasons, domestic tranquility was more threatened in the early years of the Republic than in later periods. The seeds of strife between the states, and even within the states, which undermined civil peace were removed—some completely, some partly—by the resolution of the conflict between the states and by the amendments that followed thereupon.

In addition, as we noted earlier, the indispensable instrument for law enforcement in a republic—a civil police force, not the para-military force of a despotic regime—was a mid-nineteenth-century innovation. It is only in the twentieth century that we have recognized the necessity for perfecting its operations as well as the means that must be employed to do so.

When we come to the establishment of justice, which certainly involves the equal treatment of equals, we are confronted with one of the two great defects of the eighteenth-century Constitution. Liberty, not equality, was foremost in the minds of our Founding Fathers. They may not have forgotten that the one clearly self-evident truth proclaimed in the Declaration was the equality of all human beings by virtue of their common humanity, but the self-evidence of that truth did not overcome the strong prejudices against equality rampant at the time.

We encounter the other of the two great defects when we come to the Preamble's aim to promote the general welfare. As we observed in the chapter devoted to that subject, the general welfare, as a distinct component in the public common good, must be conceived as the economic welfare of the country as a whole and of its individuals. When the statesmen of the eighteenth century thought about inalienable human rights, they had only political rights in mind.

Not only those thinkers and leaders but also their nineteenth-century descendants were blind to the existence of economic rights in the inventory of inalienable human rights. They did not see that economic goods were needed by all to facilitate the pursuit of happiness, quite as much as were civil peace and political liberty. The recognition of economic rights as natural human rights did not occur until the twentieth century, and that recognition was not even partially implemented by legislation until the midpoint of this century.

We shall deal with the remedies that we have so far found for these two great defects in the next three chapters, where we will examine the emergent ideal of democracy and what remains to be done to realize it more fully.

Of the Preamble's objectives, two remain to be considered. It is certainly more difficult today to provide for the common defense than it was in the eighteenth century. It is also much more costly. That fact, together with the investment of our resources to promote economic welfare, has resulted in the financial crisis the country now faces. Does this call for a remedy that would involve changes in our Constitution?

Last, but not least, is the Preamble's dedication to securing the blessings—and the inalienable right—to liberty. Inalienable rights can be secured only by safeguarding them through the enforcement of civil rights, either through the provisions of the Constitution itself or through legislative enactments.

Certain provisions in the Constitution, taken together with the first ten amendments—the Bill of Rights—took some of the steps necessary to protect individual freedom. Suspension of the writ of habeas corpus was forbidden except in cases of rebellion or invasion; bills of attainder and ex post facto laws were prohibited; trial by jury was required; unreasonable searches and seizures were not allowed.

So far so good, but not nearly far enough to protect individual freedom from unjustifiable governmental interference or constraint. Even more inadequate was the constitutional recognition in the eighteenth century of the inalienable right of all human beings to political liberty—all with the sole exception of those justly excluded from suffrage because of infancy, insanity, or felony. We began to remedy this inadequacy with the post–Civil War amendments, and we have continued in the same direction with amendments adopted in the twentieth century, but we still have not gone the whole distance required to complete the job.

Of all the great ideas, and especially ones that project ideals to be realized, those that fall in the sphere of politics are most subject to change in relation to differing circumstances in successive periods of time.* To be deeply sensitive to the limitations of time and circumstance under which our Founding Fathers worked, one need only think of the subsequent developments in this country's life, and of the new institutions and the new problems that they did not contemplate and could not even imagine.

In the eighteenth century, there were few private corporations chartered by government; there were no labor unions having a status politically recognized; there was no public school system; there was no energy shortage; there was no threat to the healthfulness of the environment; there was no need for the Federal Reserve System.

In the eighteenth century, no one would have been able to imagine travel by any means other than by horse or foot on land or by boat on water; to imagine communication by any means other than by direct oral discourse or by the conveyance of handwriting or print on paper; to imagine the spread of industrialization from factories to farms; to imagine the economic interdependence of all the nations of the world; to imagine a national debt of staggering proportions; to imagine world wars and one that might result in a nuclear holocaust; to imagine the role that science and its technological applications might play in the operations of government, not only in providing for the common defense but also in promoting the general economic welfare.

---

*I have written a book about such ideas, which I entitled *A Vision of the Future* (New York: Macmillan Publishing Company, 1984) because the ideas treated therein are better understood today than in the past and can expect a still better understanding in the years to come.

PART FOUR

The Emergent Ideal
of Democracy

CHAPTER 20

From Liberty to Equality

THERE IS ONE POLITICAL IDEAL that does not make its appearance in the Constitution's Preamble. That is the ideal of democracy, the first step toward which was taken by the amendments adopted immediately after the Civil War.

But that was not the moment in history when the first step toward democracy occurred. That happened in England in 1647, almost 150 years before the Constitution was drafted. Before going into that event, let me comment on the words "republic" and "democracy" as used by our Founding Fathers, for that has a bearing on their devotion to liberty and their indifference to or denial of equality.

James Madison was right in insisting on the distinction between a republic and a democracy and also in maintaining that the Constitution's being submitted for adoption by the states set up a republic and not a democracy. But he was right on both points for the wrong reasons.

The governments of the Greek city-states in antiquity were certainly republics but never democracies, even when, as under Pericles in Athens in the fifth century B.C., men with very little property were admitted to citizenship. Even then that amounted to only about 30,000 individuals in a population of 120,000. Slaves, women, and artisans were disfranchised.

Although Pericles praised Athens as a government by the many, it was in fact government by the relatively few. In spite of that fact, compared with the ancient oligarchies in which citizenship was restricted to men of vast wealth, that few was larger than usual.

The mistake that Madison made was to think that the Greek city-states were democracies because the few who were citizens met in the marketplace or forum to debate and decide the political issues of the day. He incorrectly thought democracy involved direct participation by citizens in public affairs, as contrasted with indirect participation through elected representatives. As well as referring to the Greek city-states in antiquity as examples of democracy, he might have pointed to New England town meetings in his own century. Since the Constitution created a representative system of government, the result, according to Madison's view, was a republican form of government rather than a democracy.

Madison's mistake, shared by many of his associates in the Constitutional Convention, was egregious. He failed to recognize that every society under constitutional government, without any admixture of monarchical institutions, is a republic. Hence the Greek city-states, which had introduced constitutional republics into the world, were the very first republics in recorded history. He also failed to recognize that none of them, not even that of Pericles, was a democracy because the franchise was so severely limited. Direct participation versus participation through elected representatives has no bearing at all on the distinction between republics and democracies.

All constitutional democracies are republics, but not all republics are constitutional democracies. A republic exists when some members of the population enjoy political liberty by virtue of their being citizens with suffrage, even if these citizens make up a small majority of the population as was the case in all the ancient city-states as well as in eighteenth- and nineteenth-century America.

No republic, ours among them, becomes a democracy until universal suffrage is established, until all human beings, except the very few who are justly disfranchised for mental incompetence or felonious action, are accorded the equal political status of citizenship.

Only then do all equally enjoy political liberty and other forms of freedom that are theirs by natural right.

This nation began to become a democracy only in the twentieth century, with the institution of truly universal suffrage and with the equal possession of political liberty by all members of the population (with the few exceptions noted above). All the steps needed to bring that ideal to its fullest realization have not yet been taken.

In the political philosophy of the West, the initial espousal of the democratic ideal and the first affirmation of constitutional government as the ideal polity, the only perfectly just form of government, occurred as recently as 1863, with the publication of John Stuart Mill's great essay on *Representative Government*, the title of which, unfortunately, reverses Madison's error and identifies democracy with representative government.*

The definition of the democratic ideal stated above is inadequate in one respect. Equality with respect to suffrage—the enjoyment by all of the equal status of citizenship and the equal possession of political liberty—is not enough. For a republic to become a democracy it must extend the protection of inalienable human rights from the political to the economic sphere. This was intimated in an earlier chapter on the general welfare. It will be more fully discussed and defended in the chapter to follow.

The transition from a merely republican form of government to one that is a democratic republic is a transition from an exclusive concern with liberty to an additional concern with equality, or to an enlargement of the concern for liberty to a concern for the equal enjoyment of liberty by all. Indispensable to that transition is putting equality on a par with liberty among political ideals, and regarding both not only as secured but also as regulated by justice in its concern with human rights.

The reason why liberty rather than equality was the earlier of the

---

*For an explanation of why it took so long for the ideal of democracy to emerge in political theory, and for the reason why it will take still longer for that ideal to be fully realized, see Chapter 7 of my book *A Vision of the Future*.

two ideals can be easily explained. Constitutional government, by replacing despotic rule, brought political liberty into existence. It did so in ancient Greece. It did so again in the eighteenth century when the American colonies threw off the despotic imperial rule of Great Britain and, after winning their independence, adopted a republican form of government.

Hence our Founding Fathers, who framed a constitution and established a republic on this continent, were, first and last, proponents of liberty, with either no thought about an equality of conditions for all or, worse, with obstinate prejudices against it.

How, then, shall we interpret Alexis de Tocqueville's vision of American society as one committed to an equality of conditions as early as 1835, when his book *Democracy in America* was published? The brilliance of that vision stemmed primarily from its conception of the democratic ideal in terms of equality, not merely equality before the law or equality of opportunity, but an equality of conditions, economic and social as well as political.

Did that vision also stem from de Tocqueville's observation of the realities of American life in the 1830s? Was it a description of the American scene as it then actually existed, or was it rather a prophetic vision of what the United States would some day become because of tendencies deeply implicit in its origin as the first nation that had no feudal past to outlive?

Only one answer is possible. Although de Tocqueville was visiting America and writing about it in the wake of Jacksonian populism, his statements cannot be accepted as true descriptions of the actual state of affairs in this country at that time. For this vision of America to have any hold on the truth, his extraordinary book must be read as a prediction of a future state of affairs rather than as a description of institutions that then existed.

It should be added that the truth of this prediction rested on de Tocqueville's extraordinarily perceptive observations about tendencies and predilections in American life. De Tocqueville had the sagacity to see in them causes that would inevitably lead to the establishment of democracy in this country.

Some years later Lincoln had something of the same prophetic vision when he spoke of the Declaration of Independence as a pledge to the future rather than as a statement of political ideals capable of being realized at the time the Declaration was written. The first, and perhaps the only, self-evident truth in the Declaration's second paragraph asserts the equality of all human beings by virtue of their common humanity. If their common human nature is not only the basis of their being by nature equal but also of their inalienable natural rights, then it inexorably follows that all equally possess those rights.

All have an equal right to life, liberty, and whatever else anyone naturally needs for success in the pursuit of happiness. Should individuals be unable to secure for themselves whatever is thus needed, then a just government is called upon to secure for them their right to these goods.

I said at the beginning of this chapter that the first strivings toward the idea of democracy occurred in England in 1647. It occurred in Cromwell's army when a group of his officers, who called themselves the Levellers, appealed for an extension of the suffrage from the propertied class to the unpropertied working class of the country.

Supporting that appeal, Major Rainborough and Sir John Wildman declared that no man is politically free unless he is governed with his consent and also with a voice in government. In the event that Cromwell succeeded in deposing the despotic Stuart monarch, the Levellers demanded that, with the restoration of parliamentary government, the working poor as well as the landed rich should be in a position to enjoy the political liberty to which the Levellers claimed all men were entitled by natural right.

The Levellers did not prevail in their debate with Lord Cromwell and his son-in-law, Colonel Ireton. Nor did their revolutionary views have any effect on British political life until more than two centuries later when, in 1863, Parliament passed the second Reform Bill that extended the suffrage to the laboring masses of a recently industrialized England.

Only a few years later, after the end of the American Civil War, the United States took its first steps in the same direction by adopting the Thirteenth (1865), Fourteenth (1868), and Fifteenth (1870) Amendments.

The Thirteenth Amendment provided that

. . . Neither slavery nor involuntary servitude, except as a punishment for crime whereof the party shall have been duly convicted, shall exist within the United States, or any place subject to their jurisdiction.

The Fourteenth Amendment provided that

. . . All persons born or naturalized in the United States, and subject to the jurisdiction thereof, are citizens of the United States and of the State wherein they reside. No State shall make or enforce any law which shall abridge the privileges or immunities of citizens of the United States; nor shall any State deprive any person of life, liberty, or property, without due process of law; nor deny to any person within its jurisdiction the equal protection of the laws.

The Fifteenth Amendment provided that

. . . The right of citizens of the United States to vote shall not be denied or abridged by the United States or by any State on account of race, color, or previous condition of servitude.

Having abolished chattel slavery and conferred citizenship upon the blacks in the nineteenth century, the country waited until the second decade of the twentieth century to extend the franchise to the female half of the population. This occurred with the adoption of the Nineteenth Amendment in 1920, which provided that

The right of citizens of the United States to vote shall not be denied or abridged by the United States or by any State on account of sex.

The country waited still longer for the removal of a property qualification for the exercise of suffrage, which had disqualified from voting almost all the blacks and many of the poor whites in the southern states. This obstacle was removed in 1964 with the adoption of the Twenty-Fourth Amendment, which provided that

. . . The right of citizens of the United States to vote in any primary or other election for President or Vice-President, for electors for President or Vice-President, or for Senator or Representative in Congress, shall not be denied or abridged by the United States or any State by reason of failure to pay any poll tax or other tax.

The equality of conditions achieved by these successive amendments was purely political. Enjoyment of the equal status of citizenship by all human beings regardless of their gender, racial color, or possession of wealth established the almost-universal suffrage that justice requires in order to honor and secure the inalienable human right to political liberty.

This, however, is not enough for a full realization of the democratic ideal. Economic as well as political rights exist. They, too, are natural rights and have exactly the same basis in the natural needs of human beings in their pursuit of happiness and their attempts to achieve good and decent lives for themselves. Therefore, they, too, must be honored and secured by constitutional amendments if our Constitution is to become perfectly just.

The consideration of these matters belongs to the remaining chapters of this book. It seems fitting to conclude this chapter, in which the democratic ideal makes its first appearance, by quoting a letter written by de Tocqueville to a friend, telling him what he had in mind in writing *Democracy in America*.

To those for whom the word "democracy" is synonymous with disturbance, anarchy, spoliation, and murder, I have attempted to show that democracy may be reconciled with respect for property, with deference for rights, with safety to freedom, with reverence for religion; that, if democratic government fosters less than another some of the finer possibilities of the human spirit, it has its great and noble aspects; and that perhaps, after all, it is the will of God to bestow a lesser grade of happiness upon all men than to grant a greater share of it to a small number and to bring a few to the verge of perfection.

This passage should be accompanied by an equally remarkable passage from the closing pages of his book.

We may naturally believe that it is not the singular prosperity of the few, but the greater well-being of all that is most pleasing in the sight of the Creator and Preserver of men. What appears to me to be man's decline is, to His eye, advancement; what afflicts me is acceptable to Him. A state of equality is perhaps less elevated, but it is more just: and its justice constitutes its greatness and its beauty. I would strive, then, to raise myself to this point of the divine contemplation and thence to view and to judge the concerns of men.

CHAPTER 21

From Political
to Economic Rights

THE ISSUE RAISED BY THE LEVELLERS in Cromwell's army and on which they took an affirmative position, with Lord Cromwell and Colonel Ireton on the other side, can be stated succinctly as follows: Should those who are economically unequal be made politically equal?

Stated in eighteenth-century terms, it came to this: Should those who are propertyless, laboring wage-earners be given suffrage and thus made equal in political status with men of property, whose incomes derive from their landed estates?

In the last quarter of the nineteenth century and the first quarter of the twentieth, a remarkably different issue confronted England and the United States. By this time, in the United States, the franchise had been effectively extended to the wage-earning laborers, at least to white males, if not to emancipated blacks in the southern states where they were debarred from voting by poll taxes.

The issues then raised by economic reformers, such as Henry George in the United States and R. H. Tawney in England, can be stated as follows: Should those who are now politically equal as citizens with suffrage also be made economically equal through the recognition and securing of their economic rights?

On this issue, the economic reformers, often charged with being socialists, were opposed by conservatives such as William Graham Sumner who thought that attempts to establish an equality of eco-

nomic conditions and to acknowledge the existence of natural rights
in the economic sphere would infringe on or curtail individual freedom, especially freedom of enterprise.

In the background lay the dispute between Hamilton and Madison
about the general welfare clause, both in the Preamble and in the
Constitution itself. That dispute had still not been resolved by the
end of the eighteenth century, but it came to the fore and was
resolved in favor of Hamilton in the first half of the twentieth century. It might be more accurate to say that the twentieth-century
revolution, in its concern with the general economic welfare, went
further in the direction of economic equality and economic rights
than anything that Hamilton would have dreamed of, or could have
possibly accepted.

In a speech delivered in 1910, Theodore Roosevelt said:

> No man can be a good citizen unless he has a wage more than sufficient
> to cover the bare cost of living and hours of labor short enough so that after
> his day's work is done he will have time and energy to bear his share in the
> management of the community, to help in carrying the general load. We
> keep countless men from being good citizens by the conditions of life with
> which we surround them.

In that same speech, he also said that "the object of the government
is the welfare of the people," and that he was for "shaping the ends
of government to protect property as well as human welfare."

In 1912, Roosevelt ran for election on the Progressive party ticket.
He lost, but most of the political and economic reforms advanced
in his platform have since been enacted into law by one or both of
the two major political parties.

On the economic front, that platform contained planks calling for
the prohibition of child labor; minimum wage standards for working
women; the prohibition of night work for women and the establishment of an eight-hour-day for women and young persons; one day's
rest in seven for all wage-earners; the eight-hour day in continuous
twenty-four-hour industries; publicity as to wages, hours, and conditions of labor; standards of compensation for death by industrial
accident and injury and trade diseases; the protection of home life
against the hazards of sickness, irregular employment, and old age

through the adoption of a system of social insurance; and the development of the creative labor power of America by lifting the last load of illiteracy from American youth and by establishing continuation schools for industrial education under public control. This part of the platform ended with the statement that it favored "the organization of workers, men and women, as a means of protecting their interests and promoting their progress."

All that in the year 1912! It took the next forty years—mainly in the administrations of Woodrow Wilson, Franklin Roosevelt, and Harry Truman—for legislative enactments and Supreme Court decisions to move toward having more and more of the population participate in the general economic welfare, the goal that Theodore Roosevelt had in mind in 1912.

The impact of the Great Depression caused the Supreme Court in the years 1936–1937 to hand down a series of decisions that took Hamilton's side in his dispute with Madison about the power of Congress "to promote the general welfare." Various entitlements in the Social Security Act of 1935 were upheld by these decisions: unemployment compensation, old age pensions, and the like.

This movement toward the socialization of the economy or, in other words, toward the establishment of what has come to be called a "welfare state" because of its concern with the economic welfare of all its people, reached its climax in Franklin Roosevelt's message to Congress in 1944. In that speech, the President declared that "true individual freedom cannot exist without economic security and independence. . . . People who are hungry and out of a job are the stuff of which dictatorships are made. . . . In our day these economic truths have become accepted as self-evident. We have accepted, so to speak, a second Bill of Rights, under which a new basis of security and prosperity can be established for all."*

---

*The first Bill of Rights, all political, was enacted toward the end of the eighteenth century through the adoption of the first ten amendments. We had to wait until the mid-twentieth century for the proposal of a second, an economic, bill of rights. If economic as well as political rights are inalienable natural human rights, they must have always existed. They did not come into existence later than political rights. What happened later, under the influence of greatly changed circumstances and greatly advanced technology, was not the coming into existence of these economic rights, but the recognition that such rights existed.

Roosevelt then went on to enumerate the economic rights that he asked Congress to find ways of implementing. They include:

The right to a useful and remunerative job in the industries or shops or farms or mines of the nation;

The right to earn enough to provide adequate food and clothing and recreation;

The right of every farmer to raise and sell his products at a return which will give him and his family a decent living;

The right of every businessman, large and small, to trade in an atmosphere of freedom from unfair competition and domination by monopolies at home or abroad;

The right of every family to a decent home;

The right to adequate medical care and the opportunity to achieve and enjoy good health;

The right to adequate protection from the economic fears of old age, sickness, accident, and unemployment;

The right to a good education.

Economic rights, like political rights, are rights to goods that every human being needs in order to lead a decent human life and to succeed in the pursuit of happiness. In every case they must be goods that are not within the power of individuals to achieve for themselves, as their own moral virtue is. Therefore, a just and benevolent government must do whatever it can to help individuals obtain these goods in order to facilitate their pursuit of happiness.

However, our general understanding of economic goods is not as clear as our well-established understanding of political goods. We have long known that our political goods consist in peace, both at home and abroad, and in political liberty, together with the protection of individual freedom by the prevention of violence, criminal aggression, coercion, and intimidation.

These political goods are among the objectives stated in the Preamble of the Constitution and are also among the inalienable human rights stated in the Declaration. But one of those rights—the right to life—involves more than security of life and limb. It is a right not merely to subsist, but to live well in human terms. The right to a decent human life requires an adequate livelihood. This leads us at once to economic rights—rights to economic goods indispensable to the pursuit of happiness.

What are these economic goods? The error to be avoided is thinking of economic goods solely in terms of money. Money is artificial, not real wealth, which consists in the possession of the commodities we consume, the services we use, and the property from which we may derive income. Money is the economic equivalent of real wealth in the sense that its purchasing power enables us to buy the economic goods in which real wealth consists.

These economic goods include a decent supply of the means of subsistence; living and working conditions conducive to health; medical care; opportunities for access to the pleasures of sense, the pleasures of play, and aesthetic pleasures; opportunities for access to the goods of the mind through educational facilities in youth and in adult life; and enough free time from subsistence-work or toil, both in youth and in adult life, to take full advantage of these opportunities.*

I have said that the economic goods we need and to which we, therefore, have a right are needed for a decent human life as an ingredient in our pursuit of happiness. By using the word "decent," I stress the point that we require more than the quantity of real wealth necessary for bare subsistence. This brings us to the consideration of what is meant by economic equality.

In the preceding chapter, we had no difficulty in understanding what was meant by political equality. It is possessed by all who have the same political status—that of citizenship with suffrage—and who thereby have all the rights, privileges, and immunities appertaining to that status.

---

*The basic economic right is the right to a decent livelihood by whatever means it can be honestly obtained. The economic goods enumerated above are the essential ingredients of a decent livelihood. The rights listed in Franklin Roosevelt's message to Congress in 1944 are simply another way of describing the ingredients of a decent livelihood to which everyone has a natural, human right. Thus conceived, a decent livelihood involves the comforts and conveniences of life that are accessory to a successful pursuit of happiness.

Political inequality exists in a society when only some part of the population has the status of citizenship with suffrage and enjoys the political liberty which that status confers, while the rest of the population, disfranchised, does not have political liberty. Those people are subjects of a government to which they have not given their consent and in which they do not participate.

The politically unequal thus divide into the political *haves* and the political *have-nots*. Only a society in which all (with the few exceptions already noted) are political *haves* is one in which political equality exists.

This consideration of economic equality and political inequality gives us the model in terms of which we must conceive economic equality and inequality. The wrong conception that must be dismissed involves thinking of economic equality in terms of the possession of equal *amounts* of wealth. In a society in which all are economic *haves*, some may have more and some may have less, but all have *enough* wealth to supply them with the economic goods that anyone needs to lead a decent human life.

The recognition and securing of economic rights will establish a society in which economic equality is achieved by virtue of the fact that all its members, individuals or families, are economic *haves*, and none are economic *have-nots*—none are seriously deprived, by destitution or dire poverty, of that minimal supply of economic goods that everyone needs.

This conception of economic equality does not eliminate the economic inequality that exists among the *haves* between those who have *more* and those who have *less*. What justifies some in having more?

To answer this question, I turn once again to the political model. Though all who are citizens with suffrage enjoy equal political status, not all those who are political *haves* by virtue of having that status possess the same amount of political power. Those citizens who, by election or appointment, occupy public office for a term of years, exercise more political power than ordinary citizens. Their right to it derives from their duty to perform the functions of the political office they occupy.

In the economic sphere, differences in the contributions that individuals make to the production of wealth justify the distribution of more wealth to some than to others.* I said earlier that the right to liberty is not a right to unlimited freedom, not a right to complete autonomy, but rather a right to a limited freedom—only as much liberty as justice allows, no more than anyone can exercise justly and do so without injuring others or the public common good.

The right to equality, either political or economic, is similarly a limited right—a right to only as much equality as justice requires. This means that limited equality will always be accompanied by as much inequality as justice also requires.

In the economic sphere, as we have seen, the limited equality that justice requires consists in that state of affairs in which all are economic *haves* to the degree needed for the pursuit of happiness. The maxim of justice here is: to each and all according to their common human needs. The economic *inequality* that justice also requires consists in some having more wealth than anyone needs. The maxim of justice here is: to each according to his or her contribution.

Justice is also concerned with preventing the misuse of great wealth. Those who have much more wealth than anyone needs may use it to exert political pressures and exercise political powers that cannot be justified by any political function they perform, for they act as private citizens rather than as public officials.

The political liberty and the political participation of other private citizens is thus endangered, and the performance of their political duties by officeholders may be aborted or skewed by the undue influence exerted upon them by persons of great wealth in order to serve their private interests, not the public good.

How shall economic rights be secured? How shall the limited economic equality defined above be established?

There would appear to be two distinct ways in which this can be done. They are not incompatible and therefore they can be combined

---

*There are, of course, exceptions to this principle. Unjust distributions of wealth occur when they are not based either on economic need or on economic contribution.

to make a third way. One is by means of income-producing property; another is by means of the economic equivalents of property; and the third is by some combination of the first two.

Before we go any further, it is necessary to give some thought to income-producing property, for which another name is capital: the ownership of land or other instruments for the production of wealth.

John Locke, who influenced the thought of many of our Founding Fathers, in formulating the triad of basic natural rights, had said that they were either "life, liberty, and property" or "life, liberty, and estates." In the agricultural preindustrial economy of his day, the possession of landed estates was equivalent to the possession of income-producing property.

When, a little less than a hundred years later, George Mason drafted a Declaration of Rights for adoption by the Virginia Constitutional Convention in 1776, he proclaimed that "all men are by nature equally free . . . and have certain inherent rights," among which are "the enjoyment of life and liberty, with the means of acquiring and possessing property, and pursuing and obtaining happiness and safety."

Thomas Jefferson, as we know, in writing the Declaration of Independence, altered Mason's phrasing of our inherent human rights, substituting "the pursuit of happiness" for "the means of acquiring and possessing property" and eliminating the words "obtaining" and "safety."

These alterations were more than merely rhetorical. We must attribute to Jefferson a profound understanding of the fact that the possession of income-producing property implemented the right to life and to the pursuit of happiness. For a decent human life and for the pursuit of happiness, a sufficient supply of economic goods is needed. It is also needed for the exercise of political liberty.

This last point explains why our ancestors thought they were justified in limiting suffrage to men of sufficient property. Only those with landed estates or other income-producing property in the form of industrial capital had enough free time and other advantages, including schooling, to devote to public affairs and to engage in them intelligently.

This was not the case for individuals whose only income derived from the miserable pittances they received for their labors. For them, toil consumed the greater part of their waking lives from early childhood until the grave. They had neither the free time nor the other advantages required for a good use of the political liberty enjoyed by enfranchised citizens. To have conferred suffrage upon them under these circumstances would have jeopardized the conduct of public affairs.

Our ancestors failed to realize that those whom they felt justified in disfranchising by imposing a property qualification for suffrage were not unfit to be citizens by any natural inferiority to men of property, but rather by the economic deprivations they suffered as wage-earners, and by the way in which they were nurtured under the conditions of life that resulted from their being economic havenots.

It never occurred to our ancestors that if, as human beings, the poor and unpropertied had an equal right to political liberty along with the propertied rich, then they also had a right to the economic conditions that would have made it expedient as well as just to enfranchise them as citizens with suffrage.

As we have already observed, the way in which historic developments actually occurred involved extending the franchise to the laboring poor before it was prudent to do so because they had not yet been surrounded by conditions of life that enabled them to become good citizens and exercise their political liberty for the public good. For the sake of expediency as well as justice, it remained necessary to recognize the existence of economic rights and to secure them for the establishment of the economic as well as political equality that justice requires. Some progress in that direction has been made in this century and especially in recent years. But we must do much more, either by constitutional amendments or by legislative enactments, to establish economic equality and to secure economic rights.

Earlier I asked the question: How shall this be done? I answered by saying either by means of income-producing property or by its economic equivalent, or by some combination of the two. Now it is necessary to answer the further question: What are the economic equivalents of income-producing property?

Since the purchasing power of money is equivalent to the real wealth in goods and services that money can buy, receiving a living wage for one's labors is an economic equivalent of owning income-producing property in one or another form of capital. But a living wage is not the only economic equivalent. In addition to decent wages, those without income-producing property must also have some hold on the same economic goods that owners of income-producing property enjoy.

These include sufficient free time from toil to engage in public affairs; economic security throughout life and especially in its later years; adequate food and housing; access to adequate medical facilities for health care; adequate educational facilities for the cultivation of the mind; and even access to recreational facilities and other opportunities for a good use of free time in the pursuits of leisure.

All these economic goods can be secured for wage-earners by means of welfare legislation of the kind that was initiated at the time of the Great Depression by Franklin Roosevelt's New Deal. Of course, such welfare legislation had to be implemented fiscally by income and inheritance taxes. These were initiated in the administration of Woodrow Wilson; the revenues from these sources have been greatly increased since his day.

Economic independence is the one thing the economic equivalents of income-producing property, in the form of welfare entitlements and benefits, cannot provide wage-earners. Only individuals having sufficient income-producing property are persons of independent means. The possession of such economic independence by citizens with suffrage is certainly desirable, if not necessary, for the untrammeled and unfettered exercise of their political liberty.

Accordingly, the best solution of the problem of how to secure the economic rights and establish the economic equality that are the indispensable underpinnings of political democracy is by some combination of the two means for doing so: by every individual or family having a dual income, partly from the wages or salaries of labor, accompanied by some welfare benefits, and partly from the revenues earned by income-producing property through the ownership of equities in capital.

The ideal, of course, would be for incomes derived from wages or salaries combined with income derived from the ownership of capital to suffice for the possession of all the economic goods to which individuals have a right—the minimum needed for a decent human life, for the proper exercise of political liberty, and for an effective pursuit of happiness. Were that the case, some welfare entitlements and benefits could be eliminated and others might be greatly reduced.*

We are still far from even approximating the realization of the state of affairs in which all individuals have a measure of economic independence that only a relatively few have now. This means we are also far from realizing as fully as possible the recently emergent ideal of democracy. Some of the things that remain to be done will be considered in the next and final chapter of this book.

---

*Relevant in this connection is a book that Louis Kelso and I wrote in collaboration and published in 1958, entitled *The Capitalist Manifesto* (New York: Random House, 1958); and also a more recent book written by him and Patricia Hetter Kelso, entitled *Democracy and Economic Power* (Cambridge, Mass.: Ballinger Publishing Company, 1986).

CHAPTER 22

What Remains to Be Done?

To PROJECT ALL THE STEPS that should be taken to improve the Constitution by further amendments and more fully to realize the ideal of democracy in its economic as well as its political aspects would require me to pretend to wisdom I do not possess.

An even greater pretense to wisdom would be involved in attempting to describe the constitutional and legislative enactments needed to expedite the steps to be taken.

I therefore propose to proceed interrogatively by asking questions instead of proceeding declaratively as if I knew the answers. I dare not even claim to know all the questions that should be asked. I must be content with asking only those that, for the most part, come to mind from what has been said explicitly or implicitly in the preceding chapters.

Some of these questions have been prompted by reflections about our government occasioned by the Watergate crisis. Only some are concerned with increasing the justice of the Constitution and making it better serve the ideals in the Preamble. Others look to the effectiveness and efficiency of the government's operations. As background for all the questions asked, readers should recall what was said in Chapter 19 about novel circumstances and extraordinary innovations in the twentieth century, of which our eighteenth-century ancestors and even those in the nineteenth century could have had no inkling.

Two things, in my judgment, are essential to the effectiveness of constitutional government, with respect to its being a government of laws rather than a government of men. One is the authority vested in judicial tribunals to declare the acts of government or the acts of public officials unconstitutional. The other is the power to remove from public office those officials either who have acted unconstitutionally or who have violated other laws of the land. (The constitutional government of Great Britain is defective in these respects.)

It is questionable whether the constitutional devices of impeachment and conviction of officials impeached are the only ways to implement this power. We should also ask whether the privileges of officeholders should not be limited so that they are not unduly protected from proceedings aimed to remove them from office on sustained charges of unconstitutional or unlawful acts.

Whether the Constitution is at present perfectly just in the sense of safeguarding all human rights is, of course, highly questionable. It is, therefore, also questionable whether the present limitations on majority rule are enough to prevent it from becoming majority misrule involving injustice. Equally important is the question whether majority rule is in fact operative, unhindered and unfrustrated by such factors as undue influence of private or corporate wealth, social position, organized lobbies for special interests, and so on.

All the questions to be asked rest on the assumption that we are irrevocably committed to the presidential system of constitutional government and are not willing to replace it by the parliamentary system. That assumption requires us to reexamine the separation of powers and our system of checks and balances, which are supposed to make the rule of law effective. It also precludes us from asking whether it might not be a desirable innovation to have a head of state distinct from a chief of government, as is the case in other nations that have parliamentary systems of constitutional government.

The first group of questions look to making the rule of law more effective.

1. Should we introduce changes in the procedure for impeaching and convicting public officials aimed at making these procedures easier and speedier yet without introducing undue instability in the

administration of government? Should we, for example, substitute a congressional vote of no confidence for the impeachment of the President, leading to mandatory resignation?

2. Should we create one or more executive vice-presidents, as distinct from the one elected Vice-President who is successor to the President, these executive vice-presidents to be appointed by the President as members of his staff with the advice and consent of the Senate? Would not this type of organization have the advantage of replacing the rapidly growing White House staff with a set of public officials whose authority and power are constitutionally defined and limited, especially in relation to the officials who are members of the President's Cabinet and heads of departments in the executive branch of government?

3. Should we create a new constitutional office, that of Public Prosecutor, unattached to the Department of Justice (and thus independent of the executive branch of the government) who shall be an officer of the courts appointed in the same fashion as federal judges, that is, with the advice and consent of the Senate, and who shall be charged with the prosecution of public officials suspected of unconstitutional acts, with the further provision that no officeholder shall be immune from prosecution by reason of special privilege?

A second group of questions concern ways to make majority rule more effective.

1. Should we limit the President to a single six-year term in office in order to prevent the imbalance of power and opportunity that occurs in an electoral contest between an incumbent in that office and a contender for it?

2. Should we set severe limits to the public funding of all electoral campaigns as well as shorten the period of such campaigns to six or eight weeks at the most, thereby preventing the undue influence exerted by private wealth on the outcome of the electoral process, and also giving access to the electorate through television by public financing in a manner that assures candidates of equal time and equal opportunity?

3. Should we introduce changes in the nominating procedures for President and Vice-President by instituting a nationwide uniform system of primaries, with expenses involved in primary campaigns limited and controlled so that undue influence by private or corporate wealth is prevented? Should we also require that candidates for Vice-President be nominated through the primaries instead of leaving the nomination to the Presidential nominee? Or should the individual who receives the second largest number of votes in a nominating convention be automatically selected as candidate for the office of Vice-President?

4. Should we abolish the electoral college and elect the President and the Vice-President by a majority or a plurality of the popular vote?

A third group of questions looks to implementing the realization of the democratic ideal that has so recently become an objective of our Constitution.

1. Should we reconsider the innovations proposed by Theodore Roosevelt in 1912—namely, popular initiative, popular referendums or plebiscites, and popular recall from office of officials who have not been responsive to the majority of their constituents—in order to increase the participatory, as contrasted with the representative, aspect of our democracy? Some of these innovations have been adopted in particular states. Should all or some of them be adopted nationally by amendments to our Constitution?

2. Should we create a new constitutional office, that of Tribune of the People, whose duty it shall be to bring to the Supreme Court's attention cases involving the violation of inalienable human rights?

3. Should we attempt to develop new devices for civil dissent by dissident minorities that regard themselves as suffering serious grievances or injustices?

4. Should we attempt to enact a Bill of Economic Rights, as outlined by Franklin Roosevelt in 1944, in order to promote participation in the general economic welfare to a much greater extent than has so far been accomplished?

A fourth and final group of questions look to the further implementation of natural human rights.

1. Should we persist in the effort to get the Equal Rights amendment adopted, and to ensure the full equality that is due all persons regardless of their gender?

2. Should we abolish the death penalty for all capital offenses, replacing it with life imprisonment, permitting no release from prison on parole?

3. Should we introduce an amendment that prevents states from passing laws that make crimes out of actions that involve no victims, thus curtailing the exercise of individual freedom in matters not affected with the public interest and not resulting in injury to others?

It is possible that some readers of this book might answer all questions, or at least a large number of them, affirmatively. I must confess that my own answers would tend to be in the same direction.

Anyone who is in this position must face a further question. Can the changes called for be accomplished by further amendments to the Constitution, or must we consider setting up a second constitutional convention to draft a new constitution?

I wish I could unhesitantly recommend a second constitutional convention in light of novel conditions and innovations that exist today but did not exist in the preceding centuries and were not even imaginable or conceivable then.

I cannot do so for three reasons. The first is the prevalence in our day of single-issue politics that would prevent a constitutional convention from concentrating on the public common good instead of trying to serve the interests or prejudices of special groups in the population.

My second reason also has to do with the adverse effect on a constitutional convention of certain aspects of contemporary society. The first constitutional convention was conducted in secrecy. No word of the proceedings reached the public until the work was done and the document drafted was ready for submission to the states for ratification. If there were to be a second constitutional convention, it probably could not be conducted in the same way. Its daily sessions would be exposed to the disturbing glare of nationwide publicity, including television broadcasts of the proceedings. Considering the kind of response that this would probably elicit from the general public, and the level of citizenship we now have in this country, it is highly doubtful that a second convention could do its work in an atmosphere conducive to rational deliberation, cool reasoning, and farsighted as well as prudent judgment.

My third and final reason is the absence in our society today of statesmen or persons in public life of a caliber comparable to those who assembled in Philadelphia in 1787. Why, it may be asked, can we not find in a population so many times larger than the population of the thirteen original states a relatively small number who would be as qualified for the task as their predecessors?

I cannot give a satisfactory answer to this question except to say that the best minds in our much larger population do not go into politics as they did in the eighteenth century. Perhaps the much larger number of citizens in our present population are not nearly as well educated. Their minds are not as well cultivated and their characters not as well formed.

Even if a second constitutional convention were to assemble statesmen of a character comparable to those who met in Philadelphia in 1787, and even if that second convention could be conducted under circumstances favorable to a good result, the resulting constitution would not find a receptive and sympathetic audience among our present citizenry, to whom it would have to be submitted for adoption.

They would not have the kind of schooling that enabled them to understand its provisions and to appraise their worth. The vast majority would not even be able to read intelligently and critically the kind of arguments in favor of adopting the new constitution that were written by Alexander Hamilton, James Madison, and John Jay, and published in current periodicals in the years 1787 and 1788.

A radical reform of basic schooling in the United States would have to precede any attempt by whatever means to improve our system of government through improving its Constitution.

That is also an indispensable prerequisite for making the degree of democracy we have so far achieved prosper, work better, or, perhaps, even survive.

PART FIVE

Three Documents That Comprise the American Testament

PART FOUR

Three Documents
that Comprise the
American Testament

The Declaration of Independence

[THOMAS JEFFERSON]

A Declaration by the Representatives of the United States of America, in general Congress assembled, July 4, 1776

When in the course of human events, it becomes necessary for one people to dissolve the political bands which have connected them with another, and to assume among the powers of the earth, the separate and equal station to which the laws of nature and of nature's God entitle them, a decent respect to the opinions of mankind requires that they should declare the causes which impel them to the separation.

We hold these truths to be self-evident, that all men are created equal; that they are endowed by their Creator with certain unalienable rights; that among these are life, liberty, and the pursuit of happiness. That to secure these rights, governments are instituted among men, deriving their just powers from the consent of the governed; that whenever any form of government becomes destructive of these ends, it is the right of the people to alter or to abolish it, and to institute new government, laying its foundation on such principles, and organizing its powers in such form, as to them shall seem most likely to effect their safety and happiness. Prudence, indeed, will dictate that governments long established should not be changed for light and transient causes; and accordingly all experience hath shown, that mankind are more disposed to suffer, while evils are sufferable, than to right themselves by abolishing the forms to which they are accustomed. But when a long train of abuses and usurpations, pursuing invariably the same object, evinces a design to reduce them under absolute despotism, it is their right, it is their duty, to throw off such government, and to provide new guards for their future security. Such has been the patient sufferance of these colonies, and such is now the necessity which constrains them to alter their former systems of government. The history of the present King of Great Britain is a history of repeated injuries and usurpations, all having in direct object the establishment of an absolute tyranny over these states. To prove this, let facts be submitted to a candid world:

He has refused his assent to laws, the most wholesome and necessary for the public good.

He has forbidden his governors to pass laws of immediate and pressing importance, unless suspended in their operation till his assent should be obtained; and, when so suspended, he has utterly neglected to attend to them.

He has refused to pass other laws for the accommodation of large districts of people, unless those people would relinquish the right of representation in the legislature; a right inestimable to them, and formidable to tyrants only.

He has called together legislative bodies at places unusual, uncomfortable, and distant from the depository of their public records, for the sole purpose of fatiguing them into compliance with his measures.

He has dissolved representative houses repeatedly, for opposing, with manly firmness, his invasions on the rights of the people.

He has refused for a long time, after such dissolutions, to cause others to be elected; whereby the legislative powers, incapable of annihilation, have returned to the people at large for their exercise; the state remaining, in the meantime, exposed to all the dangers of invasion from without, and convulsions within.

He has endeavored to prevent the population of these States; for that purpose, obstructing the laws for naturalization of foreigners, refusing to pass others to encourage their migrations hither, and raising the conditions of new appropriations of lands.

He has obstructed the administration of justice, by refusing his assent to laws for establishing judiciary powers.

He has made judges dependent on his will alone, for the tenure of their offices, and the amount and payment of their salaries.

He has erected a multitude of new offices, and sent hither swarms of officers to harass our people, and eat out their substance.

He has kept among us, in times of peace, standing armies, without the consent of our legislatures.

He has affected to render the military independent of, and superior to, the civil power.

He has combined with others to subject us to a jurisdiction foreign to our Constitution, and unacknowledged by our laws; giving his assent to their acts of pretended legislation:

For quartering large bodies of armed troops among us:

For protecting them, by a mock trial, from punishment for any murders which they should commit on the inhabitants of these States:

For cutting off our trade with all parts of the world:

For imposing taxes on us without our consent:

For depriving us, in many cases, of the benefits of trial by jury:

For transporting us beyond seas to be tried for pretended offenses:

For abolishing the free system of English laws in a neighboring province, establishing therein an arbitrary government, and enlarging its boundaries so as to render it at once an example and fit instrument for introducing the same absolute rule into these colonies:

For taking away our charters, abolishing our most valuable laws, and altering fundamentally the forms of our governments:

For suspending our own legislatures, and declaring themselves invested with power to legislate for us in all cases whatsoever.

He has abdicated government here, by declaring us out of his protection, and waging war against us.

He has plundered our seas, ravaged our coasts, burnt our towns, and destroyed the lives of our people.

He is, at this time, transporting large armies of foreign mercenaries to complete the works of death, desolation, and tyranny, already begun, with circumstances of cruelty and perfidy scarcely paralleled in the most barbarous ages, and totally unworthy the head of a civilized nation.

He has constrained our fellow-citizens taken captive on the high seas to bear arms against their country, to become the executioners of their friends and brethren, or to fall themselves by their hands.

He has excited domestic insurrections amongst us, and has endeavored to bring on the inhabitants of our frontiers, the merciless Indian savages, whose known rule of warfare is an undistinguished destruction of all ages, sexes, and conditions.

In every stage of these oppressions, we have petitioned for redress, in the most humble terms; our repeated petitions have been answered only by repeated injury. A prince, whose character is thus marked by every act which may define a tyrant, is unfit to be the ruler of a free people.

Nor have we been wanting in attentions to our British brethren. We have warned them from time to time of attempts by their legislature to extend an unwarrantable jurisdiction over us. We have reminded them of the circumstances of our emigration and settlement here. We have appealed to their native justice and magnanimity, and we have conjured them, by the ties of our common kindred, to disavow these usurpations, which would inevitably interrupt our connections and correspondence. They, too, have been deaf to the voice of justice and of consanguinity. We must, therefore, acquiesce in the necessity which denounces our separation, and hold them, as we hold the rest of mankind, enemies in war, in peace, friends.

We, therefore, the representatives of the United States of America, in general Congress assembled, appealing to the Supreme Judge of the world for the rectitude of our intentions, do, in the name, and by authority of the good people of these colonies, solemnly publish and declare, that these united colonies are, and of right ought to be, free and independent States; that they are absolved from all allegiance to the British Crown, and that all political connection between them and the state of Great Britain is, and ought to be, totally dissolved;

and that as free and independent States, they have full power to levy war, conclude peace, contract alliances, establish commerce, and to do all other acts and things which independent States may of right do. And for the support of this declaration, with a firm reliance on the protection of Divine Providence, we mutually pledge to each other our lives, our fortunes, and our sacred honor.

The Constitution of the United States of America

SEPTEMBER 17, 1787

WE, THE PEOPLE OF THE UNITED STATES, IN ORDER TO FORM A MORE PERFECT UNION, ESTABLISH JUSTICE, INSURE DOMESTIC TRANQUILLITY, PROVIDE FOR THE COMMON DEFENSE, PROMOTE THE GENERAL WELFARE, AND SECURE THE BLESSINGS OF LIBERTY TO OURSELVES AND OUR POSTERITY, DO ORDAIN AND ESTABLISH THIS CONSTITUTION FOR THE UNITED STATES OF AMERICA.

Article One

SECTION 1. All legislative powers herein granted shall be vested in a Congress of the United States, which shall consist of a Senate and House of Representatives.

SECTION 2. The House of Representatives shall be composed of members chosen every second year by the people of the several States, and the electors in each State shall have the qualifications requisite for electors of the most numerous branch of the State legislature.

No person shall be a Representative who shall not have attained to the age of twenty-five years, and been seven years a citizen of the United States, and who shall not, when elected, be an inhabitant of that State in which he shall be chosen.

Representatives and direct taxes shall be apportioned among the several States which may be included within this Union, according to their respective numbers, which shall be determined by adding to the whole number of free persons, including those bound to service for a term of years, and excluding Indians not taxed, three-fifths of all other persons. The actual enumeration shall be made within three years after the first meeting of the Congress of the United States, and within every subsequent term of ten years, in such manner as they shall by law direct. The number of Representatives shall not exceed one for every thirty thousand, but each State shall have at least one Representative; and until such enumeration shall be made, the State of *New Hampshire* shall be entitled to choose three, *Massachusetts* eight, *Rhode Island and Providence Plantations* one, *Connecticut* five, *New York* six, *New Jersey* four, *Pennsylvania* eight, *Delaware* one, *Maryland* six, *Virginia* ten, *North Carolina* five, *South Carolina* five, and *Georgia* three.

When vacancies happen in the representation from any State, the executive authority thereof shall issue writs of election to fill such vacancies.

The House of Representatives shall choose their Speaker and other officers, and shall have the sole power of impeachment.

SECTION 3. The Senate of the United States shall be composed of two Senators from each State, chosen by the legislature thereof, for six years; and each Senator shall have one vote.

Immediately after they shall be assembled in consequence of the first election, they shall be divided as equally as may be into three classes. The seats of the Senators of the first class shall be vacated at the expiration of the second year, of the second class, at the expiration of the fourth year, and of the third class, at the expiration of the sixth year, so that one-third may be chosen every second year; and if vacancies happen by resignation or otherwise during the recess of the legislature of any State, the executive thereof may make temporary appointments until the next meeting of the legislature, which shall then fill such vacancies.

No person shall be a Senator who shall not have attained to the age of thirty years, and been nine years a citizen of the United States, and who shall not, when elected, be an inhabitant of that State for which he shall be chosen.

The Vice-President of the United States shall be President of the Senate, but shall have no vote, unless they be equally divided.

The Senate shall choose their other officers, and also a President pro tempore in the absence of the Vice-President, or when he shall exercise the office of President of the United States.

The Senate shall have the sole power to try all impeachments. When sitting for that purpose, they shall be on oath or affirmation. When the President of the United States is tried, the Chief Justice shall preside: and no person shall be convicted without the concurrence of two-thirds of the members present.

Judgment in cases of impeachment shall not extend further than to removal from office, and disqualification to hold and enjoy any office of honor, trust, or profit under the United States; but the party convicted shall, nevertheless, be liable and subject to indictment, trial, judgment, and punishment, according to law.

SECTION 4. The times, places, and manner of holding elections for Senators and Representatives shall be prescribed in each State by the legislature thereof; but the Congress may at any time by law make or alter such regulations, except as to the places of choosing Senators.

The Congress shall assemble at least once in every year, and such meeting shall be on the first Monday in December, unless they shall by law appoint a different day.

SECTION 5. Each house shall be the judge of the elections, returns, and qualifications of its own members, and a majority of each shall constitute a quorum to do business; but a smaller number may adjourn from day to day, and may be authorized to compel the attendance of absent members, in such manner, and under such penalties, as each house may provide.

Each house may determine the rules of its proceedings, punish its members for disorderly behavior, and, with the concurrence of two-thirds, expel a member.

Each house shall keep a journal of its proceedings, and from time to time publish the same, excepting such parts as may in their judgment require secrecy, and the yeas and nays of the members of either house on any question shall, at the desire of one-fifth of those present, be entered on the journal.

Neither house, during the session of Congress, shall, without the consent of the other, adjourn for more than three days, nor to any other place than that in which the two houses shall be sitting.

SECTION 6. The Senators and Representatives shall receive a compensation for their services, to be ascertained by law and paid out of the Treasury of the United States. They shall, in all cases except treason, felony, and breach of the peace, be privileged from arrest during their attendance at the session of their respective houses, and in going to and returning from the same; and for any speech or debate in either house they shall not be questioned in any other place.

No Senator or Representative shall, during the time for which he was elected, be appointed to any civil office under the authority of the United States, which shall have been created, or the emoluments whereof shall have been increased during such time: and no person holding any office under the United States shall be a member of either house during his continuance in office.

SECTION 7. All bills for raising revenue shall originate in the House of Representatives; but the Senate may propose or concur with amendments as on other bills.

Every bill which shall have passed the House of Representatives and the Senate shall, before it become a law, be presented to the President of the United States; if he approve he shall sign it, but if not he shall return it, with his objections, to that house in which it shall have originated, who shall enter the objections at large on their journal and proceed to reconsider it. If after such reconsideration two-thirds of that house shall agree to pass the bill, it shall be sent, together with the objections, to the other house, by which it shall likewise be reconsidered, and if approved by two-thirds of that house it shall become a law. But in all such cases the votes of both houses shall be determined by yeas and nays, and the names of the persons voting for and against the bill shall be entered on the journal of each house respectively. If any bill shall not be returned by the President within ten days (Sundays excepted) after it shall have been presented to him, the same shall be a law, in like manner as if he had signed it, unless the Congress by their adjournment prevent its return, in which case it shall not be a law.

Every order, resolution, or vote to which the concurrence of the Senate and House of Representatives may be necessary (except on a question of adjournment) shall be presented to the President of the United States; and before the same shall take effect, shall be approved by him, or being disapproved by him, shall be repassed by two-thirds of the Senate and House of Representatives, according to the rules and limitations prescribed in the case of a bill.

Section 8. The Congress shall have power to lay and collect taxes, duties, imposts, and excises, to pay the debts and provide for the common defense and general welfare of the United States; but all duties, imposts, and excises shall be uniform throughout the United States;

To borrow money on the credit of the United States;

To regulate commerce with foreign nations and among the several States, and with the Indian tribes;

To establish an uniform rule of naturalization, and uniform laws on the subject of bankruptcies throughout the United States;

To coin money, regulate the value thereof, and of foreign coin, and fix the standard of weights and measures;

To provide for the punishment of counterfeiting the securities and current coin of the United States;

To establish post-offices and post-roads;

To promote the progress of science and useful arts by securing for limited times to authors and inventors the exclusive right to their respective writings and discoveries;

To constitute tribunals inferior to the Supreme Court;

To define and punish piracies and felonies committed on the high seas and offenses against the law of nations;

To declare war, grant letters of marque and reprisal, and make rules concerning captures on land and water;

To raise and support armies, but no appropriation of money to that use shall be for a longer term than two years;

To provide and maintain a navy;

To make rules for the government and regulation of the land and naval forces;

To provide for calling forth the militia to execute the laws of the Union, suppress insurrections, and repel invasions;

To provide for organizing, arming, and disciplining the militia, and for governing such part of them as may be employed in the service of the United States, reserving to the States respectively the appointment of the officers, and the authority of training the militia according to the discipline prescribed by Congress;

To exercise exclusive legislation in all cases whatsoever over such district (not exceeding ten miles square) as may, by cession of particular States and the acceptance of Congress, become the seat of the Government of the United States, and to exercise like authority over all places purchased by the consent of the legislature of the State in which the same shall be, for the erection of forts, magazines, arsenals, dockyards, and other needful buildings; and

To make all laws which shall be necessary and proper for carrying into execution the foregoing powers, and all other powers vested by this Constitution in the Government of the United States, or in any department or officer thereof.

SECTION 9. The migration or importation of such persons as any of the States now existing shall think proper to admit shall not be prohibited by the Congress prior to the year one thousand eight hundred and eight, but a tax or duty may be imposed on such importation, not exceeding ten dollars for each person.

The privilege of the writ of habeas corpus shall not be suspended, unless when in cases of rebellion or invasion the public safety may require it.

No bill of attainder or ex post facto law shall be passed.

No capitation or other direct tax shall be laid, unless in proportion to the census or enumeration hereinbefore directed to be taken.

No tax or duty shall be laid on articles exported from any State.

No preference shall be given by any regulation of commerce or revenue to the ports of one State over those of another; nor shall vessels bound to or from one State be obliged to enter, clear, or pay duties in another.

No money shall be drawn from the Treasury but in consequence of appropriations made by law; and a regular statement and account of the receipts and expenditures of all public money shall be published from time to time.

No title of nobility shall be granted by the United States; and no person holding any office of profit or trust under them shall, without the consent of the Congress, accept of any present, emolument, office, or title, of any kind whatever, from any king, prince, or foreign state.

SECTION 10. No State shall enter into any treaty, alliance, or confederation; grant letters of marque and reprisal; coin money; emit bills of credit; make anything but gold and silver coin a tender in payment of debts; pass any bill of attainder, ex post facto law, or law impairing the obligation of contracts, or grant any title of nobility.

No State shall, without the consent of Congress, lay any imposts or duties on imports or exports, except what may be absolutely necessary for executing its inspection laws; and the net produce of all duties and imposts, laid by any State on imports or exports, shall be for the use of the Treasury of the United States; and all such laws shall be subject to the revision and control of the Congress.

No State shall, without the consent of Congress, lay any duty of tonnage, keep troops or ships of war in time of peace, enter into any agreement or compact with another State or with a foreign power, or engage in war, unless actually invaded or in such imminent danger as will not admit of delay.

Article Two

SECTION 1. The executive power shall be vested in a President of the United States of America. He shall hold his office during the term of four years, and together with the Vice-President, chosen for the same term, be elected as follows:

Each State shall appoint, in such manner as the legislature thereof may direct, a number of electors, equal to the whole number of Senators and Representatives to which the State may be entitled in the Congress; but no Senator or Representative, or person holding an office of trust or profit under the United States, shall be appointed an elector.

[The electors shall meet in their respective States and vote by ballot for two persons, of whom one at least shall not be an inhabitant of the same State with themselves. And they shall make a list of all the persons voted for, and of the number of votes for each; which list they shall sign and certify, and transmit sealed to the seat of the Government of the United States, directed to the President of the Senate. The President of the Senate shall, in the presence of the Senate and House of Representatives, open all the certificates, and the votes shall then be counted. The person having the greatest number of votes shall be the President, if such number be a majority of the whole number of electors appointed; and if there be more than one who have such majority, and have an equal number of votes, then the House of Representatives shall immediately choose by ballot one of them for President; and if no person have a majority, then from the five highest on the list the said House shall in like manner choose the President. But in choosing the President the votes shall be taken by States, the representation from each State having one vote; a quorum for this purpose shall consist of a member or members from two-thirds of the States, and a majority of all the States shall be necessary to a choice. In every case, after the choice of the President, the person having the greatest number of votes of the electors shall be the Vice-President. But if there should remain two or more who have equal votes, the Senate shall choose from them by ballot the Vice-President.]*

The Congress may determine the time of choosing the electors and the day on which they shall give their votes, which day shall be the same throughout the United States.

No person except a natural-born citizen, or a citizen of the United

*This procedure was changed by the Twelfth Amendment.

States at the time of the adoption of this Constitution, shall be eligible to the office of President; neither shall any person be eligible to that office who shall not have attained to the age of thirty-five years, and been fourteen years a resident within the United States.

In case of the removal of the President from office, or of his death, resignation, or inability to discharge the powers and duties of the said office, the same shall devolve on the Vice-President, and the Congress may by law provide for the case of removal, death, resignation, or inability, both of the President and Vice-President, declaring what officer shall then act as President, and such officer shall act accordingly until the disability be removed or a President shall be elected.

The President shall, at stated times, receive for his services a compensation, which shall neither be increased nor diminished during the period for which he shall have been elected, and he shall not receive within that period any other emolument from the United States or any of them.

Before he enter on the execution of his office he shall take the following oath or affirmation:

"I do solemnly swear (or affirm) that I will faithfully execute the office of President of the United States, and will to the best of my ability preserve, protect, and defend the Constitution of the United States."

SECTION 2. The President shall be Commander-in-Chief of the Army and Navy of the United States, and of the militia of the several States when called into the actual service of the United States; he may require the opinion, in writing, of the principal officer in each of the executive departments, upon any subject relating to the duties of their respective offices, and he shall have power to grant reprieves and pardons for offenses against the United States, except in cases of impeachment.

He shall have power, by and with the advice and consent of the Senate, to make treaties, provided two-thirds of the Senators present concur; and he shall nominate, and, by and with the advice and consent of the Senate, shall appoint ambassadors, other public ministers and consuls, judges of the Supreme Court, and all other officers of the United States, whose appointments are not herein otherwise provided for, and which shall be established by law; but the Congress may by law vest the appointment of such inferior officers, as they think proper, in the President alone, in the courts of law, or in the heads of departments.

The President shall have power to fill up all vacancies that may happen during the recess of the Senate, by granting commissions which shall expire at the end of their next session.

SECTION 3. He shall from time to time give to the Congress information of the state of the Union, and recommend to their consideration such measures as he shall judge necessary and expedient; he may, on extraordinary occasions, convene both houses, or either of them, and in case of disagreement between them with respect to the time of adjournment, he may adjourn them to such time as he shall think proper; he shall receive ambassadors and other public ministers; he shall take care that the laws be faithfully executed, and shall commission all the officers of the United States.

SECTION 4. The President, Vice-President, and all civil officers of the United States shall be removed from office on impeachment for and conviction of treason, bribery, or other high crimes and misdemeanors.

Article Three

SECTION 1. The judicial power of the United States shall be vested in one Supreme Court, and in such inferior courts as the Congress may from time to time ordain and establish. The judges, both of the Supreme and inferior courts, shall hold their offices during good behavior, and shall, at stated times, receive for their services a compensation which shall not be diminished during their continuance in office.

SECTION 2. The judicial power shall extend to all cases, in law and equity, arising under this Constitution, the laws of the United States, and treaties made, or which shall be made, under their authority; to all cases affecting ambassadors, other public ministers and consuls; to all cases of admiralty and maritime jurisdiction; to controversies to which the United States shall be a party; to controversies between two or more States; between a State and citizens of another State; between citizens of different States; between citizens of the same State claiming lands under grants of different States, and between a State, or the citizens thereof, and foreign states, citizens, or subjects.

In all cases affecting ambassadors, other public ministers and consuls, and those in which a State shall be party, the Supreme Court shall have original jurisdiction. In all the other cases before mentioned the Supreme Court shall have appellate jurisdiction, both as to law and fact, with such exceptions and under such regulations as the Congress shall make.

The trial of all crimes, except in cases of impeachment, shall be by jury; and such trial shall be held in the State where the said crimes shall have been committed; but when not committed within any State, the trial shall be at such place or places as the Congress may by law have directed.

SECTION 3. Treason against the United States shall consist only in levying war against them, or in adhering to their enemies, giving them aid and comfort. No person shall be convicted of treason unless on the testimony of two witnesses to the same overt act, or on confession in open court.

The Congress shall have power to declare the punishment of treason, but no attainder of treason shall work corruption of blood or forfeiture except during the life of the person attainted.

Article Four

SECTION 1. Full faith and credit shall be given in each State to the public acts, records, and judicial proceedings of every other State. And the Congress may by general laws prescribe the manner in which such acts, records, and proceedings shall be proved, and the effect thereof.

SECTION 2. The citizens of each State shall be entitled to all privileges and immunities of citizens in the several States.

A person charged in any State with treason, felony, or other crime, who shall flee from justice, and be found in another State, shall, on demand of the executive authority of the State from which he fled, be delivered up, to be removed to the State having jurisdiction of the crime.

No person held to service or labor in one State, under the laws thereof, escaping into another, shall, in consequence of any law or regulation therein, be discharged from such service or labor, but shall be delivered up on claim of the party to whom such service or labor may be due.

SECTION 3. New States may be admitted by the Congress into this Union; but no new State shall be formed or erected within the jurisdiction of any other State; nor any State be formed by the junction of two or more States or parts of States, without the consent of the legislatures of the States concerned as well as of the Congress.

The Congress shall have power to dispose of and make all needful rules and regulations respecting the territory or other property belonging to the United States; and nothing in this Constitution shall be so construed as to prejudice any claims of the United States or of any particular State.

SECTION 4. The United States shall guarantee to every State in this Union a republican form of government, and shall protect each of them against invasion, and on application of the legislature, or of the executive (when the legislature cannot be convened), against domestic violence.

Article Five

THE Congress, whenever two-thirds of both houses shall deem it necessary, shall propose amendments to this Constitution, or, on the application of the legislatures of two-thirds of the several States, shall call a convention for proposing amendments, which, in either case, shall be valid to all intents and purposes, as part of this Constitution, when ratified by the legislatures of three-fourths of the several States, or by conventions in three-fourths thereof, as the one or the other mode of ratification may be proposed by the Congress; provided that no amendment which may be made prior to the year one thousand eight hundred and eight shall in any manner affect the first and fourth Clauses in the Ninth Section of the first Article; and that no State, without its consent, shall be deprived of its equal suffrage in the Senate.

Article Six

ALL debts contracted and engagements entered into, before the adoption of this Constitution, shall be as valid against the United States under this Constitution, as under the Confederation.

This Constitution and the laws of the United States which shall be made in pursuance thereof and all treaties made, or which shall be made, under the authority of the United States, shall be the supreme law of the land; and the judges in every State shall be bound thereby, anything in the Constitution or laws of any State to the contrary notwithstanding.

The Senators and Representatives before mentioned, and the members of the several State legislatures, and all executive and judicial officers, both of the United States and of the several States, shall be bound by oath or affirmation, to support this Constitution; but no religious test shall ever be required as a qualification to any office or public trust under the United States.

Article Seven

THE ratification of the conventions of nine States shall be sufficient for the establishment of this Constitution between the States so ratifying the same.

DONE in convention by the unanimous consent of the States present the seventeenth day of September in the year of our Lord one thousand seven hundred and eighty-seven and of the independence of the United States of America the twelfth, in witness whereof we have hereunto subscribed our names.

G⁰ WASHINGTON—*Presidt*
and deputy from Virginia

Attest:
WILLIAM JACKSON, *Secretary*

AMENDMENTS

Article One

CONGRESS shall make no law respecting an establishment of religion, or prohibiting the free exercise thereof; or abridging the freedom of speech, or of the press; or the right of the people peaceably to assemble, and to petition the Government for a redress of grievances.

Article Two

A well-regulated militia being necessary to the security of a free State, the right of the people to keep and bear arms shall not be infringed.

Article Three

No soldier shall, in time of peace, be quartered in any house, without the consent of the owner, nor in time of war but in a manner to be prescribed by law.

Article Four

THE right of the people to be secure in their persons, houses, papers, and effects, against unreasonable searches and seizures, shall not be violated, and no warrants shall issue, but upon probable cause, supported by oath or affirmation, and particularly describing the place to be searched, and the persons or things to be seized.

Article Five

No person shall be held to answer for a capital, or otherwise infamous crime, unless on a presentment or indictment of a Grand Jury, except in cases arising in the land or naval forces, or in the militia, when in actual service in time of war or public danger; nor shall any person be subject for the same offense to be twice put in jeopardy of life or limb; nor shall be compelled in any criminal case to be a witness against himself, nor be deprived of life, liberty, or property, without due process of law; nor shall private property be taken for public use, without just compensation.

Article Six

IN all criminal prosecutions the accused shall enjoy the right to a speedy and public trial, by an impartial jury of the State and district wherein the crime shall have been committed, which district shall have been previously ascertained by law, and to be informed of the nature and cause of the accusation; to be confronted with the witnesses against him; to have compulsory process for obtaining witnesses in his favor, and to have the assistance of counsel for his defense.

Article Seven

IN suits at common law, where the value in controversy shall exceed twenty dollars, the right of trial by jury shall be preserved, and no fact tried by a jury shall be otherwise reexamined in any court of the United States, than according to the rules of the common law.

Article Eight

EXCESSIVE bail shall not be required, nor excessive fines imposed, nor cruel and unusual punishments inflicted.

Article Nine

THE enumeration in the Constitution of certain rights shall not be construed to deny or disparage others retained by the people.

Article Ten

THE powers not delegated to the United States by the Constitution, nor prohibited by it to the States, are reserved to the States respectively, or to the people.

Article Eleven

THE judicial power of the United States shall not be construed to extend to any suit in law or equity, commenced or prosecuted against one of the United States by citizens of another State, or by citizens or subjects of any foreign state.

Article Twelve

THE electors shall meet in their respective States, and vote by ballot for President and Vice-President, one of whom, at least, shall not be an inhabitant of the same State with themselves; they shall name in their ballots the person voted for as President, and in distinct ballots the person voted for as Vice-President, and they shall make distinct lists of all persons voted for as President and of all persons voted for as Vice-President, and of the number of votes for each, which lists they shall sign and certify, and transmit sealed to the seat of the Government of the United States, directed to the Pres-

ident of the Senate; the President of the Senate shall, in the presence
of the Senate and House of Representatives, open all the certificates
and the votes shall then be counted; the person having the greatest
number of votes for President shall be the President, if such number
be a majority of the whole number of electors appointed; and if no
person have such majority, then from the persons having the highest
numbers not exceeding three on the list of those voted for as President, the House of Representatives shall choose immediately, by
ballot, the President. But in choosing the President the votes shall
be taken by States, the representation from each State having one
vote; a quorum for this purpose shall consist of a member-or members
from two-thirds of the States, and a majority of all the States shall
be necessary to a choice. And if the House of Representatives shall
not choose a President whenever the right of choice shall devolve
upon them, before the fourth day of March next following, then the
Vice-President shall act as President, as in the case of the death or
other constitutional disability of the President. The person having
the greatest number of votes as Vice-President shall be the Vice-
President, if such number be a majority of the whole number of
electors appointed, and if no person have a majority, then from the
two highest numbers on the list, the Senate shall choose the Vice-
President; a quorum for the purpose shall consist of two-thirds of
the whole number of Senators, and a majority of the whole number
shall be necessary to a choice. But no person constitutionally inel-
igible to the office of President shall be eligible to that of Vice-
President of the United States.

Article Thirteen

SECTION 1. Neither slavery nor involuntary servitude, except as a
punishment for crime whereof the party shall have been duly convicted, shall exist within the United States, or any place subject to
their jurisdiction.

SECTION 2. Congress shall have power to enforce this article by
appropriate legislation.

Article Fourteen

SECTION 1. All persons born or naturalized in the United States, and subject to the jurisdiction thereof, are citizens of the United States and of the State wherein they reside. No State shall make or enforce any law which shall abridge the privileges or immunities of citizens of the United States; nor shall any State deprive any person of life, liberty, or property, without due process of law; nor deny to any person within its jurisdiction the equal protection of the laws.

SECTION 2. Representatives shall be apportioned among the several States according to their respective numbers, counting the whole number of persons in each State, excluding Indians not taxed. But when the right to vote at any election for the choice of electors for President and Vice-President of the United States, Representatives in Congress, the executive and judicial officers of a State, or the members of the legislature thereof, is denied to any of the male inhabitants of such State, being twenty-one years of age, and citizens of the United States, or in any way abridged, except for participation in rebellion, or other crime the basis of representation therein shall be reduced in the proportion which the number of such male citizens shall bear to the whole number of male citizens twenty-one years of age in such State.

SECTION 3. No person shall be a Senator or Representative in Congress, or elector of President and Vice-President, or hold any office, civil or military, under the United States, or under any State, who, having previously taken an oath as a member of Congress, or as an officer of the United States, or as a member of any State legislature, or as an executive or judicial officer of any State, to support the Constitution of the United States, shall have engaged in insurrection or rebellion against the same, or given aid or comfort to the enemies thereof. But Congress may, by a vote of two-thirds of each House, remove such disability.

SECTION 4. The validity of the public debt of the United States, authorized by law, including debts incurred for payment of pensions and bounties for services in suppressing insurrection or rebellion, shall not be questioned. But neither the United States nor any State shall assume or pay any debt or obligation incurred in aid of insurrection or rebellion against the United States, or any claim for the loss or emancipation of any slave; but all such debts, obligations and claims shall be held illegal and void.

SECTION 5. The Congress shall have power to enforce, by appropriate legislation, the provisions of this article.

Article Fifteen

SECTION 1. The right of citizens of the United States to vote shall not be denied or abridged by the United States or by any State on account of race, color, or previous condition of servitude.

SECTION 2. The Congress shall have power to enforce this article by appropriate legislation.

Article Sixteen

THE Congress shall have power to lay and collect taxes on incomes, from whatever source derived, without apportionment among the several States, and without regard to any census or enumeration.

Article Seventeen

THE Senate of the United States shall be composed of two Senators from each State, elected by the people thereof, for six years; and each Senator shall have one vote. The electors in each State shall have the qualifications requisite for electors of the most numerous branch of the State legislatures.

When vacancies happen in the representation of any State in the Senate, the executive authority of such State shall issue writs of election to fill such vacancies: *Provided*, That the Legislature of any State may empower the executive thereof to make temporary appointments until the people fill the vacancies by election as the legislature may direct.

This amendment shall not be so construed as to affect the election or term of any Senator chosen before it becomes valid as part of the Constitution.

Article Eighteen

SECTION 1. After one year from the ratification of this article the manufacture, sale, or transportation of intoxicating liquors within, the importation thereof into, or the exportation thereof from the United States and all territory subject to the jurisdiction thereof for beverage purposes is hereby prohibited.

SECTION 2. The Congress and the several States shall have concurrent power to enforce this article by appropriate legislation.

SECTION 3. This article shall be inoperative unless it shall have been ratified as an amendment to the Constitution by the legislatures of the several States, as provided in the Constitution, within seven years from the date of the submission hereof to the States by the Congress.

Article Nineteen

THE right of citizens of the United States to vote shall not be denied or abridged by the United States or by any State on account of sex.

Congress shall have power to enforce this article by appropriate legislation.

Article Twenty

SECTION 1. The terms of the President and Vice-President shall end at noon on the twentieth day of January, and the terms of Senators and Representatives at noon on the third day of January, of the years in which such terms would have ended if this article had not been ratified; and the terms of their successors shall then begin.

SECTION 2. The Congress shall assemble at least once in every year, and such meeting shall begin at noon on the third day of January, unless they shall by law appoint a different day.

SECTION 3. If, at the time fixed for the beginning of the term of the President, the President elect shall have died, the Vice-President elect shall become President. If a President shall not have been chosen before the time fixed for the beginning of his term, or if the President elect shall have failed to qualify, then the Vice-President elect shall act as President until a President shall have qualified; and the Congress may by law provide for the case wherein neither a President elect nor a Vice-President elect shall have qualified, declaring who shall then act as President, or the manner in which one who is to act shall be selected, and such person shall act accordingly until a President or Vice-President shall have qualified.

SECTION 4. The Congress may by law provide for the case of the death of any of the persons from whom the House of Representatives may choose a President whenever the right of choice shall have devolved upon them, and for the case of the death of any of the persons from whom the Senate may choose a Vice-President whenever the right of choice shall have devolved upon them.

SECTION 5. Sections 1 and 2 shall take effect on the fifteenth day of October following the ratification of this article.

SECTION 6. This article shall be inoperative unless it shall have been ratified as an amendment to the Constitution by the legislatures of three-fourths of the several States within seven years from the date of its submission.

Article Twenty-One

SECTION 1. The eighteenth article of amendment to the Constitution of the United States is hereby repealed.

SECTION 2. The transportation or importation into any State, territory, or possession of the United States for delivery or use therein of intoxicating liquors, in violation of the laws thereof, is hereby prohibited.

SECTION 3. This article shall be inoperative unless it shall have been ratified as an amendment to the Constitution by conventions in the several States, as provided in the Constitution, within seven years from the date of the submission hereof to the States by the Congress.

Article Twenty-Two

SECTION 1. No person shall be elected to the office of the President more than twice, and no person who has held the office of President, or acted as President, for more than two years of a term to which some other person was elected President shall be elected to the office of the President more than once. But this Article shall not apply to any person holding the office of President when this Article was proposed by the Congress, and shall not prevent any person who may be holding the office of President, or acting as President, during the term within which this Article becomes operative from holding the office of President or acting as President during the remainder of such term.

SECTION 2. This article shall be inoperative unless it shall have been ratified as an amendment to the Constitution by the legislatures of three-fourths of the several States within seven years from the date of its submission to the States by the Congress.

Article Twenty-Three

SECTION 1. The District constituting the seat of Government of the United States shall appoint in such manner as the Congress may direct:

A number of electors of President and Vice-President equal to the whole number of Senators and Representatives in Congress to which the District would be entitled if it were a State, but in no event more than the least populous State; they shall be in addition to those appointed by the States, but they shall be considered, for the purposes of the election of President and Vice-President, to be electors appointed by a State; and they shall meet in the District and perform such duties as provided by the twelfth article of amendment.

SECTION 2. The Congress shall have power to enforce this article by appropriate legislation.

Article Twenty-Four

SECTION 1. The right of citizens of the United States to vote in any primary or other election for President or Vice-President, for electors for President or Vice-President, or for Senator or Representative in Congress, shall not be denied or abridged by the United States or any State by reason of failure to pay any poll tax or other tax.

SECTION 2. The Congress shall have power to enforce this article by appropriate legislation.

Article Twenty-Five

SECTION 1. In case of the removal of the President from office or of his death or resignation, the Vice-President shall become President.

SECTION 2. Whenever there is a vacancy in the office of the Vice-President, the President shall nominate a Vice-President who shall take office upon confirmation by a majority vote of both Houses of Congress.

SECTION 3. Whenever the President transmits to the President pro tempore of the Senate and the Speaker of the House of Representatives his written declaration that he is unable to discharge the powers and duties of his office, and until he transmits to them a written declaration to the contrary, such powers and duties shall be discharged by the Vice-President as Acting President.

SECTION 4. Whenever the Vice-President and a majority of either the principal officers of the executive departments or of such other body as Congress may by law provide, transmit to the President pro tempore of the Senate and the Speaker of the House of Representatives their written declaration that the President is unable to discharge the powers and duties of his office, the Vice-President shall immediately assume the powers and duties of the office as Acting President.

Thereafter, when the President transmits to the President pro tempore of the Senate and the Speaker of the House of Representatives his written declaration that no inability exists, he shall resume the powers and duties of his office unless the Vice-President and a majority of either the principal officers of the executive department or of such other body as Congress may by law provide, transmit within four days to the President pro tempore of the Senate and the Speaker of the House of Representatives their written declaration that the President is unable to discharge the powers and duties of his office. Thereupon Congress shall decide the issue, assembling within forty-eight hours for that purpose if not in session. If the Congress, within twenty-one days after receipt of the latter written declaration, or, if Congress is not in session, within twenty-one days after Congress is required to assemble, determines by two-thirds vote of both Houses that the President is unable to discharge the powers and duties of his office, the Vice-President shall continue to discharge the same as Acting President; otherwise, the President shall resume the powers and duties of his office.

Article Twenty-Six

SECTION 1. The right of citizens of the United States, who are eighteen years of age or older, to vote shall not be denied or abridged by the United States or any state on account of age.

SECTION 2. The Congress shall have power to enforce this article by appropriate legislation.

The Gettysburg Address

[Abraham Lincoln]

FOUR SCORE AND SEVEN YEARS ago our fathers brought forth on this continent a new nation, conceived in liberty and dedicated to the proposition that all men are created equal.

Now we are engaged in a great civil war, testing whether that nation, or any nation so conceived and so dedicated, can long endure. We are met on a great battlefield of that war. We have come to dedicate a portion of that field as a final resting place for those who here gave their lives that that nation might live. It is altogether fitting and proper that we should do this.

But, in a larger sense, we cannot dedicate—we cannot consecrate—we cannot hallow—this ground. The brave men, living and dead, who struggled here have consecrated it far above our poor power to add or detract. The world will little note nor long remember what we say here, but it can never forget what they did here. It is for us the living, rather, to be dedicated here to the unfinished work which they who fought here have thus far so nobly advanced.

It is rather for us to be here dedicated to the great task remaining before us—that from these honored dead we take increased devotion to that cause for which they gave the last full measure of devotion; that we here highly resolve that these dead shall not have died in vain; that this nation, under God, shall have a new birth of freedom; and that government of the people, by the people, for the people shall not perish from the earth.

APPENDICES

Annotated Excerpts
from
Historical Documents

The Constitutional Convention of 1787

THE CONVENTION MET from May 14 until September 17, 1787. The most complete record of the sessions was kept by James Madison, although his notes were not published until 1840. During the sessions no reports of the debates were released to the public so as not to prejudice the ratification process. While we now take the result of the Convention's work for granted, the outcome was never certain. The Convention did not convene with a mandate to draw up a new frame of government but to rework the Articles of Confederation. Strong differences of opinion existed among the delegates, and they were freely expressed.

The comments reprinted below represent only some of the issues that were touched upon: the small-state, large-state controversy; direct or indirect representation; protection of human rights; the legitimate objects of government; the real purpose of the Convention; the need for a bill of rights; the admission of new states to the Union; and whether the Congress should have two houses or only one.

The delegates quoted here are, in order of appearance:

Roger Sherman of Connecticut
George Mason of Virginia
James Madison of Virginia
John Dickinson of Delaware
William Paterson of New Jersey

Alexander Hamilton of New York
Elbridge Gerry of Massachusetts
Benjamin Franklin of Pennsylvania

Their statements are in chronological order, not in order of subject matter.

MR. SHERMAN [Conn.]: If it were in view to abolish the state governments, the elections ought to be by the people. If the state governments are to be continued, it is necessary, in order to preserve harmony between the national and state governments, that the elections to the former should be made by the latter. The right of participating in the national government would be sufficiently secured to the people by their election of the state legislatures. The objects of the Union, he thought, were few: (1) defense against foreign danger: (2) against internal disputes and a resort to force; (3) treaties with foreign nations; (4) regulating foreign commerce and drawing revenue from it. These, and perhaps a few lesser objects, alone rendered a confederation of the states necessary. All other matters, civil and criminal, would be much better in the hands of the states. The people are more happy in small than large states. States may indeed be too small, as Rhode Island, and thereby be too subject to faction. Some others were perhaps too large, the powers of government not being able to pervade them. He was for giving the general government power to legislate and execute within a defined province.

COLONEL MASON [Va.]: Under the existing Confederacy, Congress represent the *states*, not the *people* of the states; their acts operate on the *states*, not on the individuals. The case will be changed in the new plan of government. The people will be represented; they ought therefore to choose the representatives. The requisites in actual representation are that the representatives should sympathize with their constituents, should think as they think and feel as they feel, and that, for these purposes, [they] should even be residents among them. Much, he said, had been alleged against democratic elections. He admitted that much might be said; but it was to be considered that no government was free from imperfections and evils and that improper elections, in many instances, were inseparable from republican governments. But compare these with the advantage of this form in favor of the rights of the people, in favor of human nature. He was persuaded there was a better chance for proper elections by the people, if divided into large districts, than by the state legislatures. Paper money had been issued by the latter when the former were against it. Was it to be supposed that the state legislatures then would not send to the national legislature patrons of such projects if the choice depended on them?

MR. MADISON [Va.] considered an election of one branch, at least, of the legislature by the people immediately as a clear principle of free government, and that this mode, under proper regulations, had the additional advantage of securing better representatives as well as of avoiding too great an agency of the state governments in the general one. He differed from the member from Connecticut (Mr. Sherman) in thinking the objects mentioned to be all the principal ones that required a national government. Those were certainly important and necessary objects; but he combined with them the necessity of providing more effectually for the security of private rights and the steady dispensation of justice.

Interferences with these were evils which had more, perhaps, than any-thing else produced this Convention. Was it to be supposed that republican liberty would long exist under the abuses of it practised in some of the states? The gentleman (Mr. Sherman) had admitted that, in a very small state, faction and oppression would prevail. It was to be inferred then that, wherever these prevailed, the state was too small. Had they not prevailed in the largest as well as the smallest—though less than in the smallest; and were we not thence admonished to enlarge the sphere as far as the nature of the government would admit? This was the only defense against the inconveniencies of democracy consistent with the democratic form of gov-ernment.

All civilized societies would be divided into different sects, factions, and interests, as they happened to consist of rich and poor, debtors and creditors, the landed, the manufacturing, the commercial interests, the inhabitants of this district or that district, the followers of this political leader or that political leader, the disciples of this religious sect or that religious sect. In all cases where a majority are united by a common interest or passion, the rights of the minority are in danger. What motives are to restrain them? A prudent regard to the maxim that honesty is the best policy is found by experience to be as little regarded by bodies of men as by individuals. Respect for character is always diminished in proportion to the number among whom the blame or praise is to be divided.

Conscience, the only remaining tie, is known to be inadequate in indi-viduals; in large numbers, little is to be expected from it. Besides, religion itself may become a motive to persecution and oppression. These observations are verified by the histories of every country, ancient and modern. . . . Why was America so justly apprehensive of parliamentary injustice? Because Great Britain had a separate interest, real or supposed, and, if her authority had been admitted, could have pursued that interest at our expense.

We have seen the mere distinction of color made, in the most enlightened period of time, a ground of the most oppressive dominion ever exercised by man over man. What has been the source of those unjust laws complained of among ourselves? Has it not been the real or supposed interest of the major number? Debtors have defrauded their creditors. The landed interest has borne hard on the mercantile interest. The holders of one species of property have thrown a disproportion of taxes on the holders of another species.

The lesson we are to draw from the whole is that where a majority are united by a common sentiment, and have an opportunity, the rights of the minor party become insecure. In a republican government the majority, if united, have always an opportunity. The only remedy is to enlarge the sphere and thereby divide the community into so great a number of interests and parties that, in the first place, a majority will not be likely at the same moment to have a common interest separate from that of the whole or of the minority; and, in the second place, that, in case they should have such an interest, they may not be apt to unite in the pursuit of it. It was incumbent on us then to try this remedy, and with that view to frame a republican system on such a scale and in such a form as will control all the evils which have been experienced.

MR. DICKINSON [Del.] considered it as essential that one branch of the legislature should be drawn immediately from the people and as expedient that the other should be chosen by the legislatures of the states. This combination of the state governments with the national government was as politic as it was unavoidable. In the formation of the Senate, we ought to carry it through such a refining process as will assimilate it as near as may be to the House of Lords in England. . . .

MR. PATERSON [N.J.]: . . . If the sovereignty of the states is to be maintained, the representatives must be drawn immediately from the states, not from the people; and we have no power to vary the idea of equal sovereignty. The only expedient that will cure the difficulty is that of throwing the states into hotchpot. To say that this is impracticable will not make it so. Let it be tried, and we shall see whether the citizens of Massachusetts, Pennsylvania, and Vermont accede to it. It will be objected that coercion will be impracticable. But will it be more so in one plan than the other? Its efficacy will depend on the quantum of power collected, not on its being drawn from the states or from the individuals; and according to his plan it may be exerted on individuals as well as according that of Mr. Randolph.

A distinct executive and judiciary also were equally provided by his plan. It is urged that two branches in the legislature are necessary. Why? For the purpose of a check. But the reason of the precaution is not applicable to this case. Within a particular state, where party heats prevail, such a check may be necessary. In such a body as Congress, it is less necessary, and, besides, the delegations of the different states are checks on each other. Do the people at large complain of Congress? No. What they wish is that Congress may have more power. If the power now proposed be not enough, the people hereafter will make additions to it. With proper powers, Congress will act with more energy and wisdom than the proposed national legislature; being fewer in number, and more secreted and refined by the mode of election. . . .

Mr. Hamilton [N.Y.] had been hitherto silent on the business before the Convention, partly from respect to others whose superior abilities, age, and experience rendered him unwilling to bring forward ideas dissimilar to theirs, and partly from his delicate situation with respect to his own state,. to whose sentiments as expressed by his colleagues he could by no means accede. The crisis, however, which now marked our affairs was too serious to permit any scruples whatever to prevail over the duty imposed on every man to contribute his efforts for the public safety and happiness. He was obliged, therefore, to declare himself unfriendly to both plans.

He was particularly opposed to that from New Jersey, being fully convinced that no amendment of the Confederation leaving the states in possession of their sovereignty could possibly answer the purpose. On the other hand, he confessed he was much discouraged by the amazing extent of the country in expecting the desired blessings from any general sovereignty that could be substituted. As to the powers of the Convention, he thought the doubts stated on that subject had arisen from distinctions and reasonings too subtle. A *federal* government he conceived to mean an association of independent communities into one. . . .

Two sovereignties cannot coexist within the same limits. Giving powers to Congress must eventuate in a bad government or in no government. The plan of New Jersey, therefore, will not do. What then is to be done? Here he was embarrassed. The extent of the country to be governed, discouraged him. . . . In every community where industry is encouraged, there will be a division of it into the few and the many. Hence, separate interests will arise. There will be debtors and creditors, etc. Give all power to the many, they will oppress the few. Give all power to the few, they will oppress the many. Both, therefore, ought to have power that each may defend itself against the other. . . .

MR. GERRY [Mass.] wished, before the question should be put, that the attention of the House might be turned to the dangers apprehended from Western states. He was for admitting them on liberal terms, but not for putting ourselves into their hands. They will, if they acquire power, like all men, abuse it. They will oppress commerce and drain our wealth into the Western country. To guard against these consequences, he thought it necessary to limit the number of new states to be admitted into the Union in such a manner that they should never be able to outnumber the Atlantic states. He accordingly moved that in order to secure the liberties of the states already confederated, the number of representatives in the first branch of the states which shall hereafter be established shall never exceed in number the representatives from such of the states as shall accede to this Confederation. . . .

MR. MADISON: In all cases where the general government is to act on the people, let the people be represented and the votes be proportional. In all cases where the government is to act on the states as such, in like manner as Congress now act on them, let the states be represented and the votes be equal.

This was the true ground of compromise, if there was any ground at all; but he denied that there was any ground. He called for a single instance in which the general government was not to operate on the people individually. The practicability of making laws, with coercive sanctions, for the states as political bodies had been exploded on all hands. He observed that the people of the large states would in some way or other secure to themselves a weight proportioned to the importance accruing from their superior numbers. If they could not effect it by a proportional representation in the government, they would probably accede to no government which did not in great measure depend for its efficacy on their voluntary cooperation; in which case they would indirectly secure their object. . . .

MR. WILSON: That the states ought to be preserved he admitted. But does it follow that an equality of votes is necessary for the purpose? Is there any reason to suppose that if their preservation should depend more on the large than on the small states the security of the states against the general government would be diminished? Are the large states less attached to their existence, more likely to commit suicide, than the small? An equal vote, then, is not necessary as far as he can conceive; and is liable, among other objections, to this insuperable one: The great fault of the existing Confederacy is its inactivity.

It has never been a complaint against Congress that they governed overmuch. The complaint has been that they have governed too little. To remedy this defect we were sent here. Shall we effect the cure by establishing an equality of votes as is proposed? No, this very equality carries us directly to Congress—to the system which it is our duty to rectify. The small states cannot, indeed, act by virtue of this equality, but they may control the government as they have done in Congress. This very measure is here prosecuted by a minority of the people of America. Is, then, the object of the Convention likely to be accomplished in this way? Will not our constituents say—We sent you to form an efficient government and you have given us one more complex indeed, but having all the weakness of the former government. . . .

THE CLOSING DAY, SEPTEMBER 17

DR. FRANKLIN [PA.] rose with a speech in his hand, which he had reduced to writing for his own convenience, and which Mr. Wilson read in the words following:

Mr. President, I confess that there are several parts of this Constitution which I do not at present approve, but I am not sure I shall never approve them. For having lived long, I have experienced many instances of being obliged, by better information or fuller consideration, to change opinions, even on important subjects, which I once thought right but found to be otherwise. It is therefore that the older I grow the more apt I am to doubt my own judgment and to pay more respect to the judgment of others. Most men, indeed, as well as most sects in religion, think themselves in possession of all truth, and that wherever others differ from them it is so far error. Steele, a Protestant, in a dedication, tells the Pope that the only difference between our churches in their opinions of the certainty of their doctrines is [that] the Church of Rome is infallible and the Church of England is never in the wrong. But though many private persons think almost as highly of their own infallibility as that of their sect, few express it so naturally as a certain French lady who, in a dispute with her sister, said, "I don't know how it happens, sister, but I meet with nobody but myself that's always in the right—*Il n'y a que moi qui a toujours raison.*"

In these sentiments, sir, I agree to this Constitution with all its faults, if they are such; because I think a general government necessary for us, and there is no form of government but what may be a blessing to the people if well administered, and believe farther that this is likely to be well administered for a course of years, and can only end in despotism, as other forms have done before it, when the people shall become so corrupted as to need despotic government, being incapable of any other. I doubt, too, whether any other convention we can obtain may be able to make a better Constitution; for when you assemble a number of men to have the advantage of their joint wisdom, you inevitably assemble with those men all their prejudices, their passions, their errors of opinion, their local interests, and their selfish views. From such an assembly can a perfect production be expected?

It therefore astonishes me, sir, to find this system approaching so near to perfection as it does; and I think it will astonish our enemies, who are waiting with confidence to hear that our councils are confounded like those of the builders of Babel; and that our states are on the point of separation, only to meet hereafter for the purpose of cutting one another's throats. Thus I consent, sir, to this Constitution because I expect no better, and because I am not sure that it is not the best. The opinions I have had of its errors I sacrifice to the public good. I have never whispered a syllable of them abroad. Within these walls they were born, and here they shall die. . . .

The members then proceeded to sign the instrument.

While the last members were signing it, Dr. Franklin, looking toward the President's chair, at the back of which a rising sun happened to be painted, observed to a few members near him that painters had found it difficult to distinguish in their art a rising from a setting sun. "I have," said he, "often, and often in the course of the session, and the vicissitudes of my hopes and fears as to its issue, looked at that behind the President without being able to tell whether it was rising or setting. But now at length I have the happiness to know that it is a rising and not a setting sun."

APPENDIX B

The Federalist and Anti-Federalist Papers

FEARS AND HOPES: These were what divided the opponents of ratification of the Constitution from the document's advocates. The opponents used a wide variety of arguments, but essentially they feared a national government that might prove too strong. Having so recently fought a war for independence, they were not about to find themselves once more subject to an overbearing authority that was heedless of their rights and freedoms.

The advocates of the Constitution focused on the weakness of the Articles of Confederation, a document whose provisions could be so easily undercut by any or all of the states. The United States of America, yet to be, needed a frame of government equal to the task of strengthening and perpetuating a vigorous and growing nation.

The proponents of the Constitution were called Federalists and the opponents Anti-Federalists. Within a few years these adversaries would line up in the first political parties under the new government. During the ratification debates, both sides published their arguments in newspapers within each state; and their arguments were widely circulated. Both sets of arguments have since been collected, but it was the work of the Constitution's proponents that has come down to posterity as one of the most notable books on constitutional government: *The Federalist*. This collection of eighty-five essays was written by John Jay, Alexander Hamilton, and James Madison during 1787 and 1788.

The selections printed below are in two parts. The first set consists of statements, some of them anonymous, by Anti-Federalists. The second set comprises statements from *The Federalist*.

ANTI-FEDERALIST PAPERS

Richard Henry Lee:
Letters from the Federal Farmer to the Republican
(October 9, 1787)

. . . If it were possible to consolidate the states and preserve the features of a free government, still it is evident that the middle states, the parts of the Union about the seat of government, would enjoy great advantages, while the remote states would experience the many inconveniences of remote provinces. Wealth, offices, and the benefits of government would collect in the center; and the extreme states and their principal towns become much less important. . . .

There are certain unalienable and fundamental rights, which in forming the social compact ought to be explicitly ascertained and fixed. A free and enlightened people, in forming this compact, will not resign all their rights to those who govern, and they will fix limits to their legislators and rulers, which will soon be plainly seen by those who are governed, as well as by those who govern; and the latter will know they cannot be passed unperceived by the former and without giving a general alarm. These rights should be made the basis of every constitution; and if a people be so situated, or have such different opinions, that they cannot agree in ascertaining and fixing them, it is a very strong argument against their attempting to form one entire society, to live under one system of laws only. . . .

Richard Henry Lee:
Letters from the Federal Farmer to the Republican
(October 10, 1787)

. . . These powers—legislative, executive, and judicial—respect internal as well as external objects. Those respecting external objects, as all foreign concerns, commerce, imposts, all causes arising on the seas, peace and war, and Indian affairs, can be lodged nowhere else, with any propriety, but in this government. Many powers that respect internal objects ought clearly to be lodged in it; as those to regulate trade between the states, weights and measurers, the coin or current monies, post offices, naturalization, etc. These powers may be exercised without essentially affecting the internal police of the respective states.

But powers to lay and collect internal taxes, to form the militia, to make bankrupt laws, and to decide on appeals, questions arising on the internal laws of the respective states, are of a very serious nature, and carry with them almost all other powers. These taken in connection with the others, and powers to raise armies and build navies, proposed to be lodged in this government, appear to me to comprehend all the essential powers in this community, and those which will be left to the states will be of no great importance.

Richard Henry Lee:
Letters from the Federal Farmer to the Republican
(October 12, 1787)

. . . It is to be observed that when the people shall adopt the proposed Constitution it will be their last and supreme act; it will be adopted not by the people of New Hampshire, Massachusetts, etc., but by the people of the United States; and wherever this Constitution, or any part of it, shall be incompatible with the ancient customs, rights, the laws, or the constitutions heretofore established in the United States, it will entirely abolish them and do them away. And not only this, but the laws of the United States which shall be made in pursuance of the federal Constitution will be also supreme laws, and wherever they shall be incompatible with those customs, rights, laws, or constitutions heretofore established, they will also entirely abolish them and do them away. . . .

"Centinel":
Anonymous letters in the *Philadelphia Independent Gazetteer*
(October 5, 1787)

. . . If one general government could be instituted and maintained on principles of freedom, it would not be so competent to attend to the various local concerns and wants, of every particular district, as well as the peculiar governments, who are nearer the scene, and possessed of superior means of information; besides, if the business of the *whole* Union is to be managed by one government, there would not be time. Do we not already see that the inhabitants in a number of larger states, who are remote from the seat of government, are loudly complaining of the inconveniences and disadvantages they are subjected to on this account, and that, to enjoy the comforts of local government, they are separating into smaller divisions? . . .

The Senate, the great efficient body in this plan of government, is constituted on the most unequal principles. The smallest state in the Union has equal weight with the great states of Virginia, Massachusetts, or Pennsylvania. The Senate, besides its legislative functions, has a very considerable share in the executive; none of the principal appointments to office can be made without its advice and consent. The term and mode of its appointment will lead to permanency. The members are chosen for six years, the mode is under the control of Congress, and as there is no exclusion by rotation, they may be continued for life, which, from their extensive means of influence, would follow of course. The President, who would be a mere pageant of state unless he coincides with the views of the Senate, would either become the head of the aristocratic junto in that body, or its minion; besides, their influence being the most predominant could the best secure his reelection to office. And from his power of granting pardons, he might screen from punishment the most treasonable attempts on the liberties of the people when instigated by the Senate. . . .

"A Federalist":
Anonymous essay in the *Boston Gazette* and the *Country Journal*
(November 26, 1787)

. . . If we can confederate upon terms that will secure to us our liberties, it is an object highly desirable because of its additional security to the whole. If the proposed plan proves such a one, I hope it will be adopted; but if it will endanger our liberties as it stands, let it be amended; in order to which it must and ought to be open to inspection and free inquiry. The inundation of abuse that has been thrown out upon the heads of those who have had any doubts of its universal good qualities have been so redundant that it may not be improper to scan the characters of its most strenuous advocates.

It will first be allowed that many undesigning citizens may wish its adoption from the best motives, but these are modest and silent when compared to the greater number who endeavor to suppress all attempts for investigation. These violent partisans are for having the people gulp down the gilded pill blindfolded, whole and without any qualification whatever. These consist generally of the noble order of Cincinnatus, holders of public securities, men of great wealth and expectations of public office, bankers, and lawyers. These, with their train of dependents, form the aristocratic combination. The lawyers in particular keep up an incessant declamation for its adoption; like greedy gudgeons they long to satiate their voracious stomachs with the golden bait. The numerous tribunals to be erected by the new plan of consolidated empire will find employment for ten times their present numbers; these are the loaves and fishes for which they hunger. They will probably find it suited to their habits, if not to the habits of the people. . . .

Luther Martin:
Speech before the Maryland legislature
(November 29, 1787)

. . . It was the states as states, by their representatives in Congress, that formed the Articles of Confederation; it was the states as states, by their legislatures, who ratified those Articles; and it was there established and provided that the states as states (that is, by their legislatures) should agree to any alterations that should hereafter be proposed in the federal government, before they should be binding: and any alterations agreed to in any other manner cannot release the states from the obligation they are under to each other by virtue of the original Articles of Confederation. The people of the different states never made any objection to the manner in which the Articles of Confederation were formed or ratified, or to the mode by which alterations were to be made in that government—with the rights of their respective states they wished not to interfere. Nor do I believe the people, in their individual capacity, would ever have expected or desired to have been appealed to on the present occasion, in violation of the rights of their respective states, if the favorers of the proposed Constitution, imagining they had a better chance of forcing it to be adopted by a hasty appeal to the people at large (who could not be so good judges of the dangerous consequence), had not insisted upon this mode. Nor do these positions in the least interfere with the principle that all power originates from the people; because, when once the people have exercised their power in establishing and forming themselves into a state government, it never devolves back to them; nor have they a right to resume or again to exercise that power until such events take place as will amount to a dissolution of their state government. And it is an established principle that a dissolution or alteration of a federal government does not dissolve the state governments which compose it. . . .

William Findley, Robert Whitehill, and John Smilie: *"The Address and Reasons of Dissent of the Minority of the State of Pennsylvania to the Constituents"* (December 18, 1787)

. . . The powers of Congress under the new Constitution are complete and unlimited over the *purse* and the *sword*, and are perfectly independent of and supreme over the state governments, whose intervention in these great points is entirely destroyed. By virtue of their power of taxation, Congress may command the whole or any part of the property of the people. They may impose what imposts upon commerce, they may impose what land taxes, poll taxes, excises, duties on all written instruments and duties on every other article that they may judge proper; in short, every species of taxation, whether of an external or internal nature, is comprised in Article I, Section 8, viz.:

> The Congress shall have power to lay and collect taxes, duties, imposts, and excises, to pay the debts, and provide for the common defense and general welfare of the United States.

As there is no one article of taxation reserved to the state governments, the Congress may monopolize every source of revenue, and thus indirectly demolish the state governments, for without funds they could not exist. . . .

The judicial powers vested in Congress are also so various and extensive that by legal ingenuity they may be extended to every case, and thus absorb the state judiciaries, and when we consider the decisive influence that a general judiciary would have over the civil polity of the several states, we do not hesitate to pronounce that this power, unaided by the legislative, would effect a consolidation of the states under one government. . . .

The President is to have the control over the enacting of laws, so far as to make the concurrence of two-thirds of the representatives and senators present necessary, if he should object to the laws.

Thus it appears that the liberties, happiness, interests, and great concerns of the whole United States may be dependent upon the integrity, virtue, wisdom, and knowledge of 25 or 26 men. How inadequate and unsafe a representation! Inadequate because the sense and views of 3,000,000 or 4,000,000 people, diffused over so extensive a territory, comprising such various climates, products, habits, interests, and opinions, cannot be collected in so small a body; and, besides, it is not a fair and equal representation of the people even in proportion to its number, for the smallest state has as much weight in the Senate as the largest; and from the smallness of the number to be chosen for both branches of the legislature, and from the mode of election and appointment, which is under the control of Congress, and from the nature of the thing, men of the most elevated rank in life will alone be chosen. The other orders in the society, such as farmers, traders, and mechanics, who all ought to have a competent number of their best-informed men in the legislature, shall be totally unrepresented. . . .

The President General is dangerously connected with the Senate; his coincidence with the views of the ruling junto in that body is made essential to his weight and importance in the government, which will destroy all independency and purity in the executive department; and having the power of pardoning without the concurrence of a council, he may screen from punishment the most treasonable attempts that may be made on the liberties of the people when instigated by his coadjutors in the Senate. Instead of this dangerous and improper mixture of the executive with the legislative and judicial, the supreme executive powers ought to have been placed in the President, with a small independent council made personally responsible for every appointment to office or other act by having their opinions recorded; and that without the concurrence of the majority of the quorum of this council, the President should not be capable of taking any step. . . .

Melancton Smith:
An address to the people of the state of New York showing the necessity of making amendments to the Constitution
(1788)

It is agreed, the plan is defective; that some of the powers granted are dangerous; others not well defined; and amendments are necessary. Why, then, not amend it? Why not remove the cause of danger and, if possible, even the apprehension of it? The instrument is yet in the hands of the people; it is not signed, sealed, and delivered, and they have power to give it any form they please.

But it is contended—adopt it first and then amend it. I ask: Why not amend and then adopt it? Most certainly the latter mode of proceeding is more consistent with our ideas of prudence in the ordinary concerns of life. If men were about entering into a contract respecting their private concerns, it would be highly absurd in them to sign and seal an instrument containing stipulations which are contrary to their interests and wishes, under the expectation that the parties, after its execution, would agree to make alterations agreeable to their desire. . . .

Brutus, No. 11:
Anonymous essay in
the *New-York Journal and Weekly Register*
(January 31, 1788)

. . . The judicial power will operate to effect, in the most certain but yet silent and imperceptible manner, what is evidently the tendency of the Constitution: I mean, an entire subversion of the legislative, executive, and judicial powers of the individual states. Every adjudication of the Supreme Court on any question that may arise upon the nature and extent of the general government will affect the limits of the state jurisdiction. In proportion as the former enlarge the exercise of their powers will that of the latter be restricted.

That the judicial power of the United States will lean strongly in favor of the general government, and will give such an explanation to the Constitution as will favor an extension of its jurisdiction, is very evident from a variety of considerations. . . .

John Mercer:
To the members of the conventions of New York and Virginia
(1788)

. . . We are persuaded that the people of so large a continent, so different in interests, so distinct in habits, cannot in all cases legislate in one body by themselves or their representatives. By themselves, it is obviously impracticable. By their representatives, it will be found, on investigation, equally so; for if these representatives are to pursue the general interest without constitutional checks and restraints, it must be done by a mutual sacrifice of the interests, wishes, and prejudices of the parts they represent—

and then they cannot be said to represent those parts, but to misrepresent them. Besides, as their constituents cannot judge of their conduct by their own sense of what is right and proper, and as a representative can always in this view screen his abuse of trust under the cloak of compromise, we do not see what check can remain in the hands of the constituents—for they cannot know how far the compromise was necessary and the representative wrong. . . .

George Mason:
Speech to the Virginia ratifying convention
(1788)

MR. CHAIRMAN, whether the Constitution be good or bad, the present clause clearly discovers that it is a national government and no longer a confederation. I mean that clause which gives the first hint of the general government laying direct taxes. The assumption of this power of laying direct taxes does, of itself, entirely change the confederation of the states into one consolidated government. This power, being at discretion, unconfined and without any kind of control, must carry everything before it. The very idea of converting what was formerly a confederation to a consolidated government is totally subversive of every principle which has hitherto governed us.

This power is calculated to annihilate totally the state governments. Will the people of this great community submit to be individually taxed by two different and distinct powers? Will they suffer themselves to be doubly harassed? These two concurrent powers cannot exist long together; the one will destroy the other: the general government being paramount to and in every respect more powerful than the state governments, the latter must give way to the former. Is it to be supposed that one national government will suit so extensive a country, embracing so many climates and containing inhabitants so very different in manners, habits, and customs? . . .

Patrick Henry:
Speech to the Virginia ratifying convention
(1788)

. . . And here I would make this inquiry of those worthy characters who composed a part of the late federal Convention. I am sure they were fully impressed with the necessity of forming a great consolidated government instead of a confederation. That this is a consolidated government is demonstrably clear; and the danger of such a government is, to my mind, very striking. I have the highest veneration for those gentlemen; but, sir, give me leave to demand—What right had they to say, "We, the people"? My political curiosity, exclusive of my anxious solicitude for the public welfare, leads me to ask—Who authorized them to speak the language of "We, the people," instead of "We, the states"? States are the characteristics and the soul of a confederation. If the states be not the agents of this compact, it must be one great, consolidated, national government of the people of all the states. . . . Will this new system promote manufactures, industry, and frugality? If, instead of this, your hopes and designs will be disappointed, you relinquish a great deal, and hazard indefinitely more, for nothing. Will it enhance the value of your lands? Will it lessen your burdens? Will your looms and wheels go to work by the act of adoption? If it will, in its consequence, produce these things, it will consequently produce a reform and enable you to pay your debts. Gentlemen must prove it. I am a skeptic, an infidel, on this point. I cannot conceive that it will have these happy consequences. I cannot confide in assertions and allegations. The evils that attend us lie in extravagance and want of industry, and can only be removed by assiduity and economy. Perhaps we shall be told by gentlemen that these things will happen because the administration is to be taken from us and placed in the hands of the few who will pay greater attention, and be more studiously careful than we can be supposed to be.

With respect to the economical operation of the new government, I will only remark that the national expenses will be increased; if not doubled, it will approach it very nearly. I might, without incurring the imputation of illiberality or extravagance, say that the expense will be multiplied tenfold. I might tell you of a numerous standing army, a great, powerful navy, a long and rapacious train of officers and dependents, independent of the President, senators, and representatives, whose compensations are without limitation. How are our debts to be discharged unless the taxes are increased, when the expenses of the government are so greatly augmented? . . .

"Aristocritis":
An anonymous satirical essay published in
The Government of Nature Delineated,
or An Exact Picture of the New Federal Constitution
(1788)

. . . Another privilege which the people possess at present, and which the new Congress will find it their interest to deprive them of, is trial by jury; for, of all the powers which the people have wrested from government, this is the most absurd; it is even a gross violation of common sense and most destructive to energy. In the first place, it is absurd that twelve ignorant plebeians should be constituted judges of a law which passed through so many learned hands—first, a learned legislature, after many learned animadversions and criticisms have enacted it; second, learned writers have explained and commented on it; third, learned lawyers twisted, turned, and new modeled it; and, lastly, a learned judge opened up and explained it. Yet after all these learned discussions, an illiterate jury (who have scarce a right to think for themselves instead of judging for others) must determine whether it applies to the fact or not; and by their verdict the learned judge must be governed in passing sentence; and perhaps a learned gentleman be cast in an action with an insignificant cottager. . . .

William Lenoir:
Speech to the North Carolina ratifying convention
(1788)

. . . The right of representation is not fairly and explicitly preserved to the people, it being easy to evade that privilege as provided in this system, and the terms of election being too long. If our General Assembly be corrupt, at the end of the year we can make new men of them by sending others in their stead. It is not so here. If there be any reason to think that human nature is corrupt, and that there is a disposition in men to aspire to power, they may embrace an opportunity, during their long continuance in office, by means of their powers, to take away the rights of the people. The senators are chosen for six years, and two-thirds of them, with the President, have most extensive powers. They may enter into a dangerous combination. And they may be continually reelected. The President may be as good a man as

any in existence, but he is but a man. He may be corrupt. He has an
opportunity of forming plans dangerous to the community at large. . . .

It was urged here that the President should have power to grant reprieves
and pardons. This power is necessary with proper restrictions. But the
President may be at the head of a combination against the rights of the
people, and may reprieve or pardon the whole. It is answered to this that
he cannot pardon in cases of impeachment. What is the punishment in such
cases? Only removal from office and future disqualification. It does not
touch life or property. He has power to do away punishment in every other
case. It is too unlimited, in my opinion. It may be exercised to the public
good, but may also be perverted to a different purpose. Should we get those
who will attend to our interest, we should be safe under any constitution,
or without any. If we send men of a different disposition, we shall be in
danger. Let us give them only such powers as are necessary for the good
of the community. . . .

Thomas Jefferson (neither Federalist nor Anti-Federalist): *Letter to Francis Hopkinson, March 13, 1789, after the new government had begun to function*

You say that I have been dished up to you as an Anti-Federalist, and ask
me if it be just. My opinion was never worthy enough of notice to merit
citing; but, since you ask it, I will tell it to you. I am not a Federalist,
because I never submitted the whole system of my opinions to the creed of
any party of men whatever, in religion, in philosophy, in politics, or in
anything else, where I was capable of thinking for myself. Such an addiction
is the last degradation of a free and moral agent. If I could not go to heaven
but with a party, I would not go there at all. Therefore, I am not of the
party of Federalists.

But I am much farther from that of the Anti-Federalists. I approved,
from the first moment, of the great mass of what is in the new Constitution:
the consolidation of the government; the organization into executive, legislative, and judiciary; the subdivision of the legislative; the happy compromise of interests between the great and little states by the different
manner of voting in the different houses; the voting by persons instead of
states; the qualified negative on laws given to the executive, which, however,
I should have liked better if associated with the judiciary also, as in New
York; and the power of taxation. I thought at first that the latter might have
been limited. A little reflection soon convinced me it ought not to be.

What I disapproved from the first moment, also, was the want of a bill of rights to guard liberty against the legislative as well as the executive branches of the government; that is to say, to secure freedom in religion, freedom of the press, freedom from monopolies, freedom from unlawful imprisonment, freedom from a permanent military, and a trial by jury, in all cases determinable by the laws of the land. I disapproved, also, the perpetual reeligibility of the President. To these points of disapprobation I adhere. . . .

SELECTIONS FROM *THE FEDERALIST*

Number 2: John Jay

. . . Providence has been pleased to give this one connected country to one united people—a people descended from the same ancestors, speaking the same language, professing the same religion, attached to the same principles of government, very similar in their manners and customs, and who, by their joint counsels, arms, and efforts, fighting side by side throughout a long and bloody war, have nobly established general liberty and independence.

This country and this people seem to have been made for each other, and it appears as if it was the design of Providence, that an inheritance so proper and convenient for a band of brethren, united to each other by the strongest ties, should never be split into a number of unsocial, jealous, and alien sovereignties. . . .

Number 4: John Jay

. . . One government can collect and avail itself of the talents and experience of the ablest men, in whatever part of the Union they may be found. It can move on uniform principles of policy. It can harmonise, assimilate, and protect the several parts and members, and extend the benefit of its foresight and precautions to each. In the formation of treaties, it will regard the interest of the whole, and the particular interests of the parts as connected with that of the whole. It can apply the resources and power of the whole to the defence of any particular part, and that more easily and expeditiously than State governments or separate confederacies can possibly do, for want of concert and unity of system. It can place the militia under one plan of discipline, and, by putting their officers in a proper line of subordination to the Chief Magistrate, will, as it were, consolidate them into one corps, and thereby render them more efficient than if divided into thirteen or into three or four distinct independent companies. . . .

Number 6: Alexander Hamilton

. . . A man must be far gone in Utopian speculations who can seriously doubt that, if these States should either be wholly disunited, or only united in partial confederacies, the subdivisions into which they might be thrown would have frequent and violent contests with each other. To presume a want of motives for such contests as an argument against their existence, would be to forget that men are ambitious, vindictive, and rapacious. To look for a continuation of harmony between a number of independent, unconnected sovereignties in the same neighbourhood, would be to disregard the uniform course of human events, and to set at defiance the accumulated experience of ages. . . .

Number 10: James Madison

[It] may be concluded that a pure democracy, by which I mean a society consisting of a small number of citizens, who assemble and administer the government in person, can admit of no cure for the mischiefs of faction. A common passion or interest will, in almost every case, be felt by a majority of the whole; a communication and concert result from the form of government itself; and there is nothing to check the inducements to sacrifice the weaker party or an obnoxious individual. Hence it is that such democracies have ever been spectacles of turbulence and contention; have ever been found incompatible with personal security or the rights of property; and have in general been as short in their lives as they have been violent in their deaths. Theoretic politicians, who have patronised this species of government, have erroneously supposed that by reducing mankind to a perfect equality in their political rights, they would, at the same time, be perfectly equalised and assimilated in their possessions, their opinions, and their passions.

A republic, by which I mean a government in which the scheme of representation takes place, opens a different prospect, and promises the cure for which we are seeking. Let us examine the points in which it varies from pure democracy, and we shall comprehend both the nature of the cure and the efficacy which it must derive from the Union. . . .

Hence, it clearly appears, that the same advantage which a republic has over a democracy, in controlling the effects of faction, is enjoyed by a large over a small republic—is enjoyed by the Union over the States composing it. Does the advantage consist in the substitution of representatives whose enlightened views and virtuous sentiments render them superior to local prejudices and to schemes of injustice? It will not be denied that the representation of the Union will be most likely to possess these requisite endowments. Does it consist in the greater security afforded by a greater variety of parties, against the event of any one party being able to outnumber and oppress the rest? In an equal degree does the increased variety of parties comprised within the Union increase this security? Does it, in fine, consist in the greater obstacles opposed to the concert and accomplishment of the secret wishes of an unjust and interested majority? Here, again, the extent of the Union gives it the most palpable advantage.

The influence of factious leaders may kindle a flame within their particular States, but will be unable to spread a general conflagration through the other States. A religious sect may degenerate into a political faction in a part of the Confederacy; but the variety of sects dispersed over the entire face of it must secure the national councils against any danger from that source. A rage for paper money, for an abolition of debts, for an equal division of property, or for any other improper or wicked project, will be less apt to pervade the whole body of the Union than a particular member of it; in the same proportion as such a malady is more likely to taint a particular county or district, than an entire State. . . .

Number 11: Alexander Hamilton

. . . Under a vigorous national government, the natural strength and resources of the country, directed to a common interest, would baffle all the combinations of European jealousy to restrain our growth. This situation would even take away the motive to such combinations, by inducing an impracticability of success. An active commerce, an extensive navigation, and a flourishing marine would then be the offspring of moral and physical necessity. We might defy the little arts of the little politicians to control or vary the irresistible and unchangeable course of nature. . . .

Number 14: Alexander Hamilton

. . . In the first place it is to be remembered that the general government is not to be charged with the whole power of making and administering laws. Its jurisdiction is limited to certain enumerated objects, which concern all the members of the republic, but which are not to be attained by the separate provisions of any. The subordinate governments, which can extend their care to all those other objects which can be separately provided for, will retain their due authority and activity. Were it proposed by the plan of the Convention to abolish the governments of the particular States, its adversaries would have some ground for their objection; though it would not be difficult to show that if they were abolished the general government would be compelled, by the principle of self-preservation, to reinstate them in their proper jurisdiction.

A second observation to be made is that the immediate object of the federal Constitution is to secure the union of the thirteen primitive States, which we know to be practicable; and to add to them such other States as may arise in their own bosoms, or in their neighbourhoods, which we cannot doubt to be equally practicable. The arrangements that may be necessary for those angles and fractions of our territory which lie on our north-western frontier must be left to those whom further discoveries and experience will render more equal to the task.

Let it be remarked, in the third place, that the intercourse throughout the Union will be facilitated by new improvements. Roads will everywhere be shortened, and kept in better order; accommodations for travellers will be multiplied and meliorated; an interior navigation on our eastern side will be opened throughout, or nearly throughout, the whole extent of the thirteen States. The communication between the Western and Atlantic districts, and between different parts of each, will be rendered more and more easy by those numerous canals with which the beneficence of nature has intersected our country, and which art finds it so little difficult to connect and complete.

A fourth and still more important consideration is that as almost every State will, on one side or other, be a frontier, and will thus find, in a regard to its safety, an inducement to make some sacrifices for the sake of the general protection; so the States which lie at the greatest distance from the heart of the Union, and which, of course, may partake least of the ordinary circulation of its benefits, will be at the same time immediately contiguous to foreign nations, and will consequently stand, on particular occasions, in greatest need of its strength and resources. . . .

Number 25: Alexander Hamilton

. . . Reasons have been already given to induce a supposition that the State governments will too naturally be prone to a rivalship with that of the Union, the foundation of which will be the love of power; and that in any contest between the federal head and one of its members the people will be most apt to unite with their local government. If, in addition to this immense advantage, the ambition of the members should be stimulated by the separate and independent possession of military forces, it would afford too strong a temptation and too great a facility to them to make enterprises upon, and finally to subvert, the constitutional authority of the Union. On the other hand, the liberty of the people would be less safe in this state of things than in that which left the national forces in the hands of the national government. As far as an army may be considered as a dangerous weapon of power, it had better be in those hands of which the people are most likely to be jealous than in those of which they are least likely to be jealous. For it is a truth, which the experience of ages has attested, that the people are always most in danger when the means of injuring their rights are in the possession of those of whom they entertain the least suspicion. . . .

Number 33: Alexander Hamilton

. . . But it is said that the laws of the Union are to be the *supreme law* of the land. But what inference can be drawn from this, or what would they amount to, if they were not to be supreme? It is evident they would amount to nothing. A LAW, by the very meaning of the term, includes supremacy. It is a rule which those to whom it is prescribed are bound to observe. This results from every political association. If individuals enter into a state of society, the laws of that society must be the supreme regulator of their conduct. If a number of political societies enter into a larger political society, the laws which the latter may enact, pursuant to the powers intrusted to it by its constitution, must necessarily be supreme over those societies, and the individuals of whom they are composed. It would otherwise be a mere treaty, dependent on the good faith of the parties, and not a government, which is only another word for POLITICAL POWER AND SUPREMACY. But it will not follow from this doctrine that acts of the larger society which are *not pursuant* to its constitutional powers, but which are invasions of the residuary authorities of the smaller societies, will become the supreme law

of the land. These will be merely acts of usurpation, and will deserve to
be treated as such. . . .

Number 34: Alexander Hamilton

I flatter myself it has been clearly shown in my last number that the particular States, under the proposed Constitution, would have COEQUAL authority with the Union in the article of revenue, except as to duties on
imports. As this leaves open to the States far the greatest part of the resources
of the community there can be no colour for the assertion that they would
not possess means as abundant as could be desired for the supply of their
own wants, independent of all external control. . . .

Number 39: James Madison

. . . In order to ascertain the real character of the government, it may be
considered in relation to the foundation on which it is to be established; to
the sources from which its ordinary powers are to be drawn; to the operation
of those powers; to the extent of them; and to the authority by which future
changes in the government are to be introduced.

On examining the first relation, it appears, on one hand, that the Constitution is to be founded on the assent and ratification of the people of
America, given by deputies elected for the special purpose; but, on the
other, that this assent and ratification is to be given by the people, not as
individuals composing one entire nation, but as composing the distinct and
independent States to which they respectively belong. It is to be the assent
and ratification of the several States, derived from the supreme authority
in each State,—the authority of the people themselves. The act, therefore,
establishing the Constitution, will not be a *national*, but a *federal* act.

That it will be a federal and not a national act, as these terms are understood by the objectors; the act of the people, as forming so many independent
States, not as forming one aggregate nation, is obvious from this single
consideration, that it is to result neither from the decision of a *majority* of
the people of the Union, nor from that of a *majority* of the States. It must
result from the *unanimous* assent of the several States that are parties to it,
differing no otherwise from their ordinary assent than in its being expressed,
not by the legislative authority, but by that of the people themselves. . . .

Number 45: James Madison

. . . The adversaries to the plan of the Convention, instead of considering in the first place what degree of power was absolutely necessary for the purposes of the federal government, have exhausted themselves in a secondary inquiry into the possible consequences of the proposed degree of power to the government of the particular States. But if the Union, as has been shown, be essential to the security of the people of America against foreign danger; if it be essential to their security against contentions and wars among the different States; if it be essential to guard them against those violent and oppressive factions which embitter the blessings of liberty, and against those military establishments which must gradually poison its very fountain; if, in a word, the Union be essential to the happiness of the people of America, is it not preposterous to urge as an objection to a government, without which the objects of the Union cannot be attained, that such a government may derogate from the importance of the governments of the individual States? Was, then, the American Revolution effected, was the American Confederacy formed, was the precious blood of thousands spilt, and the hard-earned substance of millions lavished, not that the people of America should enjoy peace, liberty, and safety, but that the government of the individual States, that particular municipal establishments, might enjoy a certain extent of power, and be arrayed with certain dignities and attributes of sovereignty? We have heard of the impious doctrine in the Old World, that the people were made for kings, not kings for the people. Is the same doctrine to be revived in the New in another shape—that the solid happiness of the people is to be sacrificed to the views of political institutions of a different form? It is too early for politicians to presume on our forgetting that the public good, the real welfare of the great body of the people, is the supreme object to be pursued; and that no form of government whatever has any other value than as it may be fitted for the attainment of this object. . . .

Number 46: James Madison

. . . Were it admitted that the federal government may feel an equal disposition with the State governments to extend its power beyond the due limits, the latter would still have the advantage in the means of defeating such encroachments. If an act of a particular State, though unfriendly to the national government, be generally popular in that State, and should not too grossly violate the oaths of the state officers, it is executed immediately and, of course, by means on the spot and depending on the State alone. The opposition of the federal government, or the interposition of federal officers, would but inflame the zeal of all parties on the side of the States, and the evil could not be prevented or repaired, if at all, without the employment of means which must always be resorted to with reluctance and difficulty. On the other hand, should an unwarrantable measure of the federal government be unpopular in particular States, which would seldom fail to be the case, or even a warrantable measure be so, which may sometimes be the case, the means of opposition to it are powerful and at hand. The disquietude of the people; their repugnance and, perhaps, refusal to co-operate with the officers of the Union; the frowns of the executive magistracy of the State; the embarrassments created by legislative devices, which would often be added on such occasions, would oppose, in any State, difficulties not to be despised; would form, in a large State, very serious impediments; and where the sentiments of several adjoining States happened to be in unison, would present obstructions which the federal government would hardly be willing to encounter. . . .

Number 51: Alexander Hamilton

. . . But the great security against a gradual concentration of the several powers in the same department consists in giving to those who administer each department the necessary constitutional means and personal motives to resist encroachments of the others. The provision for defence must in this, as in all other cases, be made commensurate to the danger of attack. Ambition must be made to counteract ambition. The interest of the man must be connected with the constitutional rights of the place. It may be a reflection on human nature that such devices should be necessary to control the absues of government. But what is government itself but the greatest of all reflections on human nature? If men were angels, no government would be necessary. If angels were to govern men, neither external nor internal controls on government would be necessary. In framing a government which is to be administered by men over men, the great difficulty lies in this: you must first enable the government to control the governed; and in the next place oblige it to control itself. . . .

Number 64: John Jay

. . . As all the States are equally represented in the Senate, and by men the most able and the most willing to promote the interests of their constituents, they will all have an equal degree of influence in that body, especially while they continue to be careful in appointing proper persons, and to insist on their punctual attendance. In proportion as the United States assume a national form and a national character, so will the good of the whole be more and more an object of attention, and the government must be a weak one indeed if it should forget that the good of the whole can only be promoted by advancing the good of each of the parts or members which compose the whole. It will not be in the power of the President and Senate to make any treaties by which they and their families and estates will not be equally bound and affected with the rest of the community; and, having no private interests distinct from that of the nation, they will be under no temptation to neglect the latter. . . .

Number 68: Alexander Hamilton

. . . Nothing was more to be desired than that every practicable obstacle should be opposed to cabal, intrigue, and corruption. These most deadly adversaries of republican government might naturally have been expected to make their approaches from more than one quarter, but chiefly from the desire in foreign powers to gain an improper ascendant in our councils. How could they better gratify this than by raising a creature of their own to the chief magistracy of the Union? But the Convention have guarded against all danger of this sort with the most provident and judicious attention. They have not made the appointment of the President to depend on any pre-existing bodies of men, who might be tampered with beforehand to prostitute their votes; but they have referred it in the first instance to an immediate act of the people of America, to be exerted in the choice of persons for the temporary and sole purpose of making the appointment. And they have excluded from eligibility to this trust all those who from situation might be suspected of too great devotion to the President in office. No senator, representative, or other person holding a place of trust or profit under the United States can be of the numbers of the electors. Thus without corrupting the body of the people, the immediate agents in the election will at least enter upon the task free from any sinister bias. . . .

Number 78: Alexander Hamilton

. . . If it be said that the legislative body are themselves the constitutional judges of their own powers, and that the construction they put upon them is conclusive upon the other departments, it may be answered that this cannot be the natural presumption where it is not to be collected from any particular provisions in the Constitution. It is not otherwise to be supposed that the Constitution could intend to enable the representatives of the people to substitute their *will* to that of their constituents. It is far more rational to suppose that the courts were designed to be an intermediate body between the people and the legislature, in order, among other things, to keep the latter within the limits assigned to their authority. The interpretation of the laws is the proper and peculiar province of the courts. A constitution is, in fact, and must be regarded by the judges, as a fundamental law. It therefore belongs to them to ascertain its meaning, as well as the meaning of any particular act proceeding from the legislative body. If there should happen to be an irreconcilable variance between the two, that which has the superior obligation and validity ought, of course, to be preferred; or, in other words, the Constitution ought to be preferred to the statute, the intention of the people to the intention of their agents. . . .

Number 84: Alexander Hamilton

. . . I . . . affirm that bills of rights, in the sense and to the extent in which they are contended for, are not only unnecessary in the proposed Constitution, but would even be dangerous. They would contain various exceptions to powers not granted; and, on this very account, would afford a colourable pretext to claim more than were granted. For why declare that things shall not be done which there is no power to do? Why, for instance, should it be said that the liberty of the press shall not be restrained when no power is given by which restrictions may be imposed? I will not contend that such a provision would confer a regulating power; but it is evident that it would furnish, to men disposed to usurp, a plausible pretence for claiming that power. They might urge with a semblance of reason that the Constitution ought not to be charged with the absurdity of providing against the abuse of an authority which was not given, and that the provision against restraining the liberty of the press afforded a clear implication that a power to prescribe proper regulations concerning it was intended to be vested in the national government. . . .

Number 85: Alexander Hamilton

. . . Concessions on the part of the friends of the plan, that it has not a claim to absolute perfection, have afforded matter of no small triumph to its enemies. "Why," say they, "should we adopt an imperfect thing? Why not amend it and make it perfect before it is irrevocably established?" No advocate of the measure can be found who will not declare as his sentiment that the system, though it may not be perfect in every part, is, upon the whole, a good one; is the best that the present views and circumstances of the country will permit; and is such an one as promises every species of security which a reasonable people can desire.

I answer, in the next place, that I should esteem it the extreme of imprudence to prolong the precarious state of our national affairs, and to expose the Union to the jeopardy of successive experiments, in the chimerical pursuit of a perfect plan. I never expect to see a perfect work from imperfect man. The result of the deliberations of all collective bodies must necessarily be a compound, as well of the errors and prejudices as of the good sense and wisdom, of the individuals of whom they are composed. The compacts which are to embrace thirteen distinct States in a common bond of amity and union must as necessarily be a compromise of as many dissimilar interests and inclinations. How can perfection spring from such materials? . . .

Commentaries on the Constitution from 1796 to 1923

FROM THE MOMENT it became public, the merits and defects, the weaknesses and strengths of the Constitution were debated. And the debates did not cease with the inauguration of the new government in 1789. In fact, the whole period until the end of the Civil War in 1865 was one of frequently furious controversy over the Constitution. Differences of opinion were sharp over the existence of slavery, the powers of the three branches of government, fears of too strong a national government, and the rights of the states.

The random comments that follow are from a number of well-known Americans, ranging from George Washington in the eighteenth century to Calvin Coolidge in the twentieth.

Since the Civil War, the Constitution has taken its place in American life as a near-sacred text. The Founding Fathers are revered for having contrived an instrument of government that has proved workable for 200 years with remarkably little tampering. Controversy today is less on the Constitution's merits than on how to make the government it established work for all citizens and interests.

George Washington:
Farewell Address
(1796)

. . . It is important, likewise, that the habits of thinking in a free country should inspire caution in those entrusted with its administration to confine themselves within their respective constitutional spheres, avoiding in the exercise of the powers of one department to encroach upon another. The spirit of encroachment tends to consolidate the powers of all the departments in one and thus to create, whatever the form of government, a real despotism. A just estimate of that love of power and proneness to abuse it which predominates in the human heart is sufficient to satisfy us of the truth of this position.

The necessity of reciprocal checks in the exercise of political power, by dividing and distributing it into different depositories, and constituting each the guardian of the public weal against invasions by the others, has been evinced by experiments ancient and modern, some of them in our country and under our own eyes. To preserve them must be as necessary as to institute them. If, in the opinion of the people, the distribution or modification of the constitutional powers be in any particular wrong, let it be corrected by an amendment in the way which the Constitution designates. . . .

Thomas Jefferson:
Letter to Gideon Granger of Connecticut
(August 13, 1800)

. . . The true theory of our Constitution is surely the wisest and best, that the states are independent as to everything within themselves, and united as to everything respecting foreign nations. Let the general government be reduced to foreign concerns only, and let our affairs be disentangled from those of all other nations, except as to commerce, which the merchants will manage the better the more they are left free to manage for themselves, and our general government may be reduced to a very simple organization, and a very unexpensive one—a few plain duties to be performed by a few servants. But, I repeat that this simple and economical mode of government can never be secured if the New England States continue to support the contrary system. I rejoice, therefore, in every appearance of their returning

to those principles which I had always imagined to be almost innate in
them. . . .

Daniel Webster:
Speech in the United States Senate, a reply to Robert Y. Hayne of South Carolina on the issue of nullification
(January 1830)

. . . The people have preserved this, their own chosen Constitution, for
forty years and have seen their happiness, prosperity, and renown grow
with its growth, and strengthen with its strength. They are now, generally,
strongly attached to it. Overthrown by direct assault, it cannot be; evaded,
undermined, *nullified* it will not be if we, and those who shall succeed us
here, as agents and representatives of the people, shall conscientiously and
vigilantly discharge the two great branches of our public trust, faithfully to
preserve and wisely to administer it. . . .

Zelotes Fuller, Universalist clergyman:
Washington's Birthday Address
(1830)

. . . Wisely did the framers of the Constitution of our government, after
defining with unexampled accuracy the rights of the citizens and limiting
the authority of Congress, expressly prohibit the latter from interfering with
the religious opinions of the people. There has been no change as yet in
this particular, and we most sincerely pray that there never may be. Every
species of creeds and varieties of faith receive equal toleration and protection.
The freedom of inquiry and the right of private judgment, the freedom of
the press and of public speech are still our rich inheritance—they are privileges which the laws of our common country guarantee to every citizen.
This is as it should be. These privileges are just and unalienable; they
originate in perfect equity; they are the birthright of every individual, and
should not be infringed by anyone; nor will they be, willingly or designedly,
by any *real* friend to the peace and happiness of humankind.

No government under heaven affords such encouragement as that of
America to genius and enterprise, or promises such rich rewards to talent
and industry. Here, if a man rise to eminence, he rises by merit and not

by birth, nor yet by mammon. This is as it ought to be—this is perfect justice. By the liberal government of our country, ample provision is made for the encouragement of the honest and ingenious artist, and due support is given to every laudable undertaking. Here, talent is not frowned into silence or trampled in the dust for the want of gold to support its dignity, nor for the want of noble parentage, but commands the respectful attentions of all the truly wise and candid, however obscure the corner from whence it emanates, and receives that encouragement and support from a generous government to which it is justly and lawfully entitled.

Here, every man labors for himself, and not to pamper the pride of royalty, not to support kingly pomp, luxury, and dissipation! Here, no ghostly priest stalks forth, and by virtue of prerogative seizes upon a tenth of the hard earnings of the industrious poor, leaving them in a state of want and wretchedness; but they may apply their little all to the conveniences of themselves and families. He who toils and labors in the field or in the shop or in whatever employment he may engage has the high satisfaction to reflect that it is wholly for the comfort and happiness of himself or family, if he so please, and that he is not bound by law to contribute to the support of an artful, tyrannical, and corrupted priesthood. . . .

John C. Calhoun:
Address to the people of the United States
(1832)

. . . We, then, hold it as unquestionable that on the separation from the Crown of Great Britain, the people of the several colonies became free and independent states, possessed of the full right of self-government; and that no power can be rightfully exercised over them but by the consent and authority of their respective states, expressed or implied. We also hold it as equally unquestionable that the Constitution of the United States is a compact between the people of the several states, constituting free, independent, and sovereign communities; that the government it created was formed and appointed to execute, according to the provisions of the instrument, the powers therein granted as the joint agent of the several states; that all its acts, transcending these powers, are simply and of themselves null and void, and that in case of such infractions, it is the right of the states, in their sovereign capacity, each acting for itself and its citizens, in like manner as they adopted the Constitution to judge thereof in the last resort and to adopt such measures—not inconsistent with the compact—as may be deemed fit to arrest the execution of the act within their respective limits. Such we hold to be the right of the states in reference to an unconstitutional act of the government; nor do we deem their duty to exercise it on proper occasions less certain and imperative than the right itself is clear. . . .

Andrew Jackson:
Protest to the Senate on the occasion of its censure of the President
(April 15, 1834)

. . . Were the Congress to assume, with or without a legislative act, the power of appointing officers, independently of the President, to take the charge and custody of the public property contained in the military and naval arsenals, magazines, and storehouses, it is believed that such an act would be regarded by all as a palpable usurpation of executive power, subversive of the form as well as the fundamental principles of our government. But where is the difference in principle whether the public property be in the form of arms, munitions of war, and supplies, or in gold and silver or banknotes? None can be perceived; none is believed to exist. Congress cannot, therefore, take out of the hands of the Executive Department the custody of the public property or money without an assumption of executive power and a subversion of the first principles of the Constitution. . . .

John Quincy Adams:
Speech on the fiftieth anniversary
of George Washington's first
inauguration
(April 30, 1839)

. . . The Constitution of the United States was republican and democratic; but the experience of all former ages had shown that, of all human governments, democracy was the most unstable, fluctuating, and shortlived; and it was obvious that if virtue—the virtue of the people—was the foundation of republican government, the stability and duration of the government must depend upon the stability and duration of the virtue by which it is sustained.

Now the *virtue* which had been infused into the Constitution of the United States, and was to give to its vital existence the stability and duration to which it was destined, was no other than the concretion of those abstract principles which had been first proclaimed in the Declaration of Independence; namely, the self-evident truths of the natural and unalienable rights of man, of the indefeasible constituent and dissolvent sovereignty of the people, always subordinate to a rule of right and wrong, and always responsible to the Supreme Ruler of the universe for the *rightful* exercise of that sovereign, constituent, and dissolvent power.

This was the platform upon which the Constitution of the United States had been erected. Its VIRTUES, its republican character consisted in its conformity to the principles proclaimed in the Declaration of Independence, and as its administration must necessarily be always pliable to the fluctuating varieties of public opinion; its stability and duration by a like overruling and irresistible necessity was to depend upon the stability and duration in the hearts and minds of the people of that *virtue*, or, in other words, of those principles proclaimed in the Declaration of Independence and embodied in the Constitution of the United States. . . .

William H. Seward:
Speech in the United States Senate during the debate on Henry Clay's Compromise of 1850

. . . The Constitution regulates our stewardship; the Constitution devotes the domain to union, to justice, to defense, to welfare, and to liberty.

But there is a higher law than the Constitution which regulates our authority over the domain and devotes it to the same noble purposes. The territory is a part—no inconsiderable part—of the common heritage of mankind, bestowed upon them by the Creator of the universe. We are His stewards and must so discharge our trust as to secure, in the highest attainable degree, their happiness. . . .

Abraham Lincoln:
A "Fragment on Government"
(July 1854)

The legitimate object of government is to do for a community of people whatever they need to have done, but cannot do at all, or cannot so well do for themselves in their separate and individual capacities. In all that the people can individually do as well for themselves, government ought not to interfere.

The desirable things which the individuals of a people cannot do, or cannot well do, for themselves fall into two classes: those which have relation to wrongs, and those which have not. Each of these branch off into an infinite variety of subdivisions.

The first—that in relation to wrongs—embraces all crimes, misdemeanors, and non-performance of contracts. The other embraces all which, in its nature and without wrong, requires combined action, as public roads and highways, public schools, charities, pauperism, orphanage, estates of the deceased, and the machinery of government itself.

From this it appears that if all men were just, there still would be some, though not so much, need of government.

Wisconsin State Legislature:
Protest resolution against the fugitive slave law
(March 19, 1859)

. . . *Resolved*, that the government formed by the Constitution of the United States was not made the exclusive or final judge of the extent of the powers delegated to itself; but that, as in all other cases of compact among parties having no common judge, each party has an equal right to judge for itself, as well of infractions as of the mode and measure of redress.

Resolved, that the principle and construction contended for by the party which now rules in the councils of the nation, that the general government is the exclusive judge of the extent of the powers delegated to it, stop nothing short of despotism, since the *discretion* of those who administer the government and not the *Constitution* would be the measure of their powers; that the several states which formed that instrument, being sovereign and independent, have the unquestionable right to judge of its infraction; and that a *positive defiance* of those sovereignties, of all unauthorized acts done or attempted to be done under color of that instrument, is the rightful remedy.

James Russell Lowell:
Essay in *The Atlantic Monthly*
(February 1861)

. . . If secession be a right, then the moment of its exercise is wholly optional with those possessing it. . . . Within the limits of the Constitution, two sovereignties cannot coexist; and yet what practical odds does it make if a state becomes sovereign by simply declaring herself so? The legitimate consequence of secession is not that a state becomes sovereign but that, so far as the general government is concerned, she has outlawed herself, nullified her own existence as a state, and become an aggregate of riotous men who resist the execution of the laws. . . .

Abraham Lincoln:
First inaugural address
(March 4, 1861)

. . . I hold that, in contemplation of universal law and of the Constitution, the Union of these states is perpetual. Perpetuity is implied, if not expressed, in the fundamental law of all national governments. It is safe to assert that no government proper ever had a provision in its organic law for its own termination. Continue to execute all the express provisions of our national Constitution, and the Union will endure forever—it being impossible to destroy it except by some action not provided for in the instrument itself.

Again, if the United States be not a government proper, but an association of states in the nature of contract merely, can it, as a contract, be peaceably unmade by less than all the parties who made it? One party to a contract may violate it—break it, so to speak—but does it not require all to lawfully rescind it? Descending from these general principles, we find the proposition that in legal contemplation, the Union is perpetual, confirmed by the history of the Union itself.

The Union is much older than the Constitution. It was formed, in fact, by the Articles of Association in 1774. It was matured and continued by the Declaration of Independence in 1776. It was further matured, and the faith of all the then thirteen states expressedly plighted and engaged, that it should be perpetual by the Articles of Confederation of 1778. And finally, in 1787, one of the declared objects for ordaining and establishing the Constitution, was *"to form a more perfect union."*

But if destruction of the Union by one or by a part only of the states be lawfully possible, the Union is *less* perfect than before the Constitution, having lost the vital element of perpetuity. . . .

Calvin Coolidge:
Memorial Day address
(1923)

. . . The authority of law here is not something which is imposed upon the people; it is the will of the people themselves. The decision of the court here is not something which is apart from the people; it is the judgment of the people themselves. The right of the ownership of property here is not something withheld from the people; it is the privilege of the people themselves. Their sovereignty is absolute and complete. A definition of the relationship between the institutions of our government and the American people entirely justifies the assertion that: "All things were made by *them*; and without *them* was not anything made that was made." It is because the American government is the sole creation and possession of the people that they have always cherished it and defended it, and always will. . . .

APPENDIX D

Judicial Interpretations of the Constitution

THE AUTHORITY of the Supreme Court to review legislative acts of Congress and pronounce on their validity was not spelled out in the Constitution. However, the notion was not without precedent. In 1787, a North Carolina court declared unconstitutional a statute passed by the state legislature concerning property confiscated from Loyalists during the American Revolution. In *Bayard* v. *Singleton* the court disallowed the right of the legislature to take away property (a right embedded in the state constitution) without a jury trial.

In spite of this and other precedents, there was no settled position on the authority of the judiciary to review the acts of Congress or the President. Thomas Jefferson, in a letter of June 11, 1815, commented: "There is not a word in the Constitution which has given that power to them [the courts] more than to the executive or legislative branches." It was Jefferson's opinion that each branch of government must look to its own authority to decide upon the constitutionality of its actions.

Jefferson's view did not prevail. In fact, twelve years before he wrote his letter, Chief Justice John Marshall had handed down a ruling in the most famous of all Supreme Court decisions explicitly stating the doctrine of judicial review. A portion of Marshall's decision in *Marbury* v. *Madison* (1803) is reprinted below.

If Jefferson's opinion did not prevail, it was not without its supporters. The issue of judicial review was one that continued to be debated for some decades. President Andrew Jackson went so far as to ignore the Court entirely when it came to his policy of Indian removal. When Marshall handed down a ruling opposed to the President, Jackson replied, in effect: Mr. Marshall has made his ruling; let him enforce it.

Since the Civil War and the triumph of federalism, however, the challenges to the Court's authority have diminished sharply. Presidents and Congress have bowed to its rulings, although not always happily.

To cover the whole range of issues on which the Court has handed down rulings would be impossible here. The decisions quoted are some of the major judicial statements about the powers of government, citizenship, and individual rights. The first case quoted after *Marbury* v. *Madison* is John Marshall's remarkable and farsighted statement in *Cohens* v. *Virginia* (1821) about the nature of a national government and about the Constitution.

THE POWERS OF GOVERNMENT

These cases make no pretense at being definitive statements on all the powers of the federal government under the Constitution. They are, rather, samples of how the Supreme Court has ruled on a few specific issues under the authority conferred by *Marbury* v. *Madison*, as well as under the sweeping statements on nationalism made by John Marshall in *Cohens* v. *Virginia*.

Marbury v. *Madison* (1803)

President John Adams, on the eve of his leaving office, made a number of judicial appointments in order to pack the judiciary with members of his Federalist party. The Jefferson administration was reluctant to let the appointments be filled. William Marbury, in trying to force Secretary James Madison to give him his commission as justice of the peace, sued in court. When the case came before Chief Justice John Marshall, a Federalist, he was faced with the dilemma of deciding in favor of Marbury only to see his order unenforced by the new Republican officeholders. Marshall's ruling was brilliant. He decided that Marbury had a right to the commission under the provisions of the Judiciary Act of 1789. He then ruled that the act was unconstitutional. In so doing he established the doctrine of judicial review as a prerogative of federal courts. This case, almost as much as the Constitution itself, became the Supreme Court's charter for reviewing acts of Congress.

. . . The question whether an act repugnant to the Constitution can become the law of the land is a question deeply interesting to the United States but, happily, not of an intricacy proportioned to its interest. It seems only necessary to recognize certain principles, supposed to have been long and well established, to decide it.

That the people have an original right to establish, for their future government, such principles as, in their opinion, shall most conduce to their own happiness is the basis on which the whole American fabric has been erected. The exercise of this original right is a very great exertion; nor can it, nor ought it, to be frequently repeated. The principles, therefore, so established are deemed fundamental. And as the authority from which they proceed is supreme and can seldom act, they are designed to be permanent.

This original and supreme will organizes the government and assigns to different departments their respective powers. It may either stop here or establish certain limits not to be transcended by those departments.

The government of the United States is of the latter description. The powers of the legislature are defined and limited; and that those limits may not be mistaken or forgotten, the Constitution is written. To what purpose are powers limited, and to what purpose is that limitation committed to writing, if these limits may, at any time, be passed by those intended to be restrained? The distinction between a government with limited and unlimited powers is abolished if those limits do not confine the persons on whom they are imposed, and if acts prohibited and acts allowed are of equal obligation. It is a proposition too plain to be contested that the Constitution controls any legislative act repugnant to it or that the legislature may alter the Constitution by an ordinary act. . . .

If an act of the legislature repugnant to the Constitution is void, does it, notwithstanding its invalidity, bind the courts and oblige them to give it effect? Or, in other words, though it be not law, does it constitute a rule as operative as if it was a law? This would be to overthrow in fact what was established in theory and would seem, at first view, an absurdity too gross to be insisted on. It shall, however, receive a more attentive consideration.

It is, emphatically, the province and duty of the Judicial Department to say what the law is. Those who apply the rule to particular cases must of necessity expound and interpret that rule. If two laws conflict with each other, the courts must decide on the operation of each. So if a law be in opposition to the Constitution, if both the law and the Constitution apply to a particular case, so that the court must either decide that case conformably to the law, disregarding the Constitution, or conformably to the Constitution, disregarding the law, the court must determine which of these conflicting rules governs the case. This is of the very essence of judicial duty. If, then, the courts are to regard the Constitution, and the Constitution is superior to any ordinary act of the legislature, the Constitution, and not such ordinary act, must govern the case to which they both apply.

Those, then, who controvert the principle that the Constitution is to be considered in court as a paramount law are reduced to the necessity of maintaining that courts must close their eyes on the Constitution and see only the law.

This doctrine would subvert the very foundation of all written constitutions. It would declare that an act which, according to the principles and theory of our government, is entirely void, is yet, in practice, completely obligatory. It would declare that if the legislature shall do what is expressly forbidden, such act, notwithstanding the express prohibition, is in reality effectual. It would be giving to the legislature a practical and real omnipotence, with the same breath which professes to restrict their powers within narrow limits. It is prescribing limits and declaring that those limits may be passed at pleasure.

That it thus reduces to nothing what we have deemed the greatest improvement on political institutions, a written constitution, would of itself be sufficient in America, where written constitutions have been viewed with so much reverence, for rejecting the construction. But the peculiar expressions of the Constitution of the United States furnish additional arguments in favor of its rejection.

The judicial power of the United States is extended to all cases arising under the Constitution. Could it be the intention of those who gave this power to say that, in using it, the Constitution should not be looked into?

That a case arising under the Constitution should be decided without examining the instrument under which it arises?

This is too extravagant to be maintained. In some cases, then, the Constitution must be looked into by the judges. And if they can open it at all, what part of it are they forbidden to read or to obey? . . .

Cohens v. *Virginia* (1821)

This case arose when two men were arrested and convicted under state law for selling tickets in a national lottery that was permitted under federal law. At issue before Chief Justice John Marshall was: (1) the supremacy of federal over state law, and (2) the appellate jurisdiction of the Supreme Court in a case where the parties were a state and citizens of that state. The ruling was one of Marshall's landmark opinions in establishing the authority of the federal government over the states.

The general government, though limited as to its objects, is supreme with respect to those objects. This principle is a part of the Constitution; and if there be any who deny its necessity, none can deny its authority.

To this supreme government, ample powers are confided; and if it were possible to doubt the great purposes for which they were so confided, the people of the United States have declared that they are given "in order to form a more perfect union, establish justice, insure domestic tranquillity, provide for the common defense, promote the general welfare, and secure the blessings of liberty to themselves and their posterity." With the ample powers confided to this supreme government, for these interesting purposes, are connected many express and important limitations on the sovereignty of the states which are made for the same purposes. The powers of the Union, on the great subjects of war, peace, and commerce, and on many others, are in themselves limitations of the sovereignty of the states; but, in addition to these, the sovereignty of the states is surrendered, in many instances, where the surrender can only operate to the benefit of the people, and where, perhaps, no other power is conferred on Congress than a conservative power to maintain the principles established in the Constitution.

The maintenance of these principles in their purity is certainly among the great duties of the government. . . .

The Constitution gave to every person having a claim upon a state a right to submit his case to the Court of the nation. However unimportant his claim might be, however little the community might be interested in its decision, the framers of our Constitution thought it necessary, for the purposes of justice, to provide a tribunal as superior to influence as possible in which that claim might be decided. . . . The judicial power of every well-constituted government must be coextensive with the legislative, and must be capable of deciding every judicial question which grows out of the Constitution and laws. . . .

A constitution is framed for ages to come, and is designed to approach immortality as nearly as human institutions can approach it. Its course cannot always be tranquil. It is exposed to storms and tempests, and its framers must be unwise statesmen indeed if they have not provided it, so far as its nature will permit, with the means of self-preservation from the perils it may be destined to encounter. No government ought to be so defective in its organization as not to contain within itself the means of securing the execution of its own laws against other dangers than those which occur every day. Courts of justice are the means most usually employed; and it is reasonable to expect that a government should repose on its own courts rather than on others. . . .

It is very true that whenever hostility to the existing system shall become universal, it will be also irresistible. The people made the Constitution, and the people can unmake it. It is the creature of their will, and lives only by their will. But this supreme and irresistible power to make or to unmake resides only in the whole body of the people, not in any subdivision of them. The attempt of any of the parts to exercise it is usurpation and ought to be repelled by those to whom the people have delegated their power of repelling it. . . .

In a government so constituted, is it unreasonable that the judicial power should be competent to give efficacy to the constitutional laws of the legislature? That department can decide on the validity of the Constitution or law of a state if it be repugnant to the Constitution or to a law of the United States. Is it unreasonable that it should also be empowered to decide on the judgment of a state tribunal enforcing such unconstitutional law? Is it so very unreasonable as to furnish a justification for controlling the words of the Constitution?

We think it is not. We think that in a government, acknowledgedly supreme, with respect to objects of vital interest to the nation, there is nothing inconsistent with sound reason, nothing incompatible with the nature of government, in making all its departments supreme, so far as respects those objects and so far as is necessary to their attainment. The exercise of the appellate power over those judgments of the state tribunals which may contravene the Constitution or laws of the United States is, we believe, essential to the attainment of those objects.

McCulloch v. Maryland (1819)

From its incorporation the states had been hostile to the Bank of the United States. During the depression of 1818–1819 several state legislatures laid taxes on bank branches within their jurisdiction, with the intent of destroying the institution. James McCulloch, cashier of the Baltimore branch, refused to pay the tax and was sued by the state of Maryland. The Maryland court upheld the tax, so McCulloch took the case to the Supreme Court. The issues were: Does Congress have the authority to charter a national bank; and, Can the states tax branches of the bank. Chief Justice John Marshall upheld the right of Congress in his interpretation of the "necessary and proper" clause of the Constitution.

. . . We admit, as all must admit, that the powers of the government are limited, and that its limits are not to be transcended. But we think the sound construction of the Constitution must allow to the national legislature that discretion, with respect to the means by which the powers it confers are to be carried into execution, which will enable that body to perform the high duties assigned to it, in the manner most beneficial to the people. Let the end be legitimate, let it be within the scope of the Constitution, and all means which are appropriate, which are plainly adapted to that end, which are not prohibited, but consist with the letter and spirit of the Constitution, are constitutional. . . .

The power of Congress to create, and of course to continue, the bank, was the subject of the preceding part of this opinion; and is no longer to be considered as questionable.

That the power of taxing it by the states may be exercised so as to destroy it is too obvious to be denied. But taxation is said to be an absolute power which acknowledges no other limits than those expressly prescribed in the Constitution, and like sovereign power of every other description, is trusted to the discretion of those who use it. . . .

The argument on the part of the State of Maryland is, not that the states may directly resist a law of Congress but that they may exercise their acknowledged powers upon it, and that the Constitution leaves them this right in the confidence that they will not abuse it. . . .

If we apply the principle for which the State of Maryland contends to the Constitution generally, we shall find it capable of changing totally the character of that instrument. We shall find it capable of arresting all the measures of the government, and of prostrating it at the foot of the states. The American people have declared their Constitution, and the laws made in pursuance thereof, to be supreme; but this principle would transfer the supremacy, in fact, to the states. . . .

The question is, in truth, a question of supremacy; and if the right of the states to tax the means employed by the general government be conceded, the declaration that the Constitution, and the laws made in pursuance thereof, shall be the supreme law of the land is empty and unmeaning declamation. . . .

The Court has bestowed on this subject its most deliberate consideration. The result is a conviction that the states have no power, by taxation or otherwise, to retard, impede, burden, or in any manner control the operations of the constitutional laws enacted by Congress to carry into execution the powers vested in the general government. This is, we think, the unavoidable consequence of that supremacy which the Constitution has declared.

We are unanimously of opinion that the law passed by the legislature of Maryland, imposing a tax on the Bank of the United States, is unconstitutional and void. . . .

Dartmouth College v. Woodward (1819)

New Hampshire had, in 1815, altered the terms of Dartmouth College's charter of 1769 and changed the school into a university. The college sued William H. Woodward, former secretary-treasurer of the school, to recover its original charter. The state court found for Woodward. When the case came before the Supreme Court, however, the decision was reversed. Chief Justice Marshall ruled that corporation charters were contracts protected by the contract clause of the Constitution.

. . . The founders of the college contracted, not merely for the perpetual application of the funds which they gave to the objects for which those funds were given; they contracted, also, to secure that application by the constitution of the corporation. They contracted for a system, which should, as far as human foresight can provide, retain forever the government of the literary institution they had formed in the hands of persons approved by themselves.

This system is totally changed. The charter of 1769 exists no longer. It is reorganized; and reorganized in such a manner as to convert a literary institution, molded according to the will of its founders and placed under the control of private literary men, into a machine entirely subservient to the will of government. This may be for the advantage of this college in particular, and may be for the advantage of literature in general, but it is not according to the will of the donors, and is subversive of that contract, on the faith of which their property was given. . . .

Gibbons v. *Ogden* (1824)

The significance of this case lies in Chief Justice Marshall's broad interpretation of the commerce clause of the Constitution, giving Congress the right to regulate commerce with foreign nations and among the states. The case arose over the right of New York to issue a license conferring a monopoly on boat transportation between New York and New Jersey. Aaron Ogden had such a monopoly, but Thomas Gibbons had a license from the federal government to operate over the same route.

. . . The genius and character of the whole government seem to be that its action is to be applied to all the external concerns of the nation and to those internal concerns which affect the states generally; but not to those which are completely within a particular state, which do not affect other states, and with which it is not necessary to interfere for the purpose of executing some of the general powers of the government. The completely internal commerce of a state, then, may be considered as reserved for the state itself.

But, in regulating commerce with foreign nations, the power of Congress does not stop at the jurisdictional lines of the several states. It would be a very useless power if it could not pass those lines. The commerce of the United States with foreign nations is that of the whole United States. Every district has a right to participate in it. The deep streams which penetrate our country in every direction pass through the interior of almost every state in the Union, and furnish the means of exercising this right. If Congress has the power to regulate it, that power must be exercised whenever the subject exists. If it exists within the states, if a foreign voyage may commence or terminate at a port within a state, then the power of Congress may be exercised within a state. . . .

A.L.A. Schechter Poultry Corporation et al. v. United States (1935)

This was one of several cases concerning New Deal legislation that came before the Court in the mid-1930s. The Schechter company sued the government, claiming that controls over its operations within New York State by the National Recovery Administration were illegal. The Court, with Chief Justice Charles Evans Hughes rendering the opinion, found in favor of Schechter and declared the NRA unconstitutional. One of his reasons was that the NRA Act had delegated legislative powers to the executive branch.

. . . If the federal government may determine the wages and hours of employees in the internal commerce of a state because of their relation to cost and prices and their indirect effect upon interstate commerce, it would seem that a similar control might be exerted over other elements of cost also affecting prices, such as the number of employees, rents, advertising, methods of doing business, etc. All the processes of production and distribution that enter into cost would likewise be controlled. If the cost of doing an intrastate business is in itself the permitted object of federal control, the extent of the regulation of cost would be a question of discretion and not of power.

The government also makes the point that efforts to enact state legislation establishing high labor standards have been impeded by the belief that unless similar action is taken generally, commerce will be diverted from the states adopting such standards, and that this fear of diversion has led to demands for federal legislation on the subject of wages and hours. The apparent implication is that the federal authority under the commerce clause should be deemed to extend to the establishment of rules to govern wages and hours in intrastate trade and industry generally throughout the country, thus overriding the authority of the states to deal with domestic problems arising from labor conditions in their internal commerce.

It is not the province of the Court to consider the economic advantages or disadvantages of such a centralized system. It is sufficient to say that the federal Constitution does not provide for it. Our growth and development have called for wide use of the commerce power of the federal government in its control over the expanded activities of interstate commerce and in protecting that commerce from burdens, interferences, and conspiracies to restrain and monopolize it. But the authority of the federal government may not be pushed to such an extreme as to destroy the distinction, which the commerce clause itself establishes, between commerce "among the several states" and the internal concerns of a state. . . .

The Ashwander Rules (1936)

In 1936, the case of *Ashwander* v. *TVA* came before the Court. The Court upheld the right of the federal government to build dams over rivers that flow through more than one state. But more interesting than the decision itself was the concurring opinion of Associate Justice Louis B. Brandeis. In it, Brandeis contended that the case should never have come before the Court in the first place. Then he proceeded to set forth the rules by which the Court selects cases for review.

The Court has frequently called attention to the "great gravity and delicacy" of its function in passing upon the validity of an act of Congress, and has restricted exercise of this function by rigid insistence that the jurisdiction of federal courts is limited to actual cases and controversies, and that they have no power to give advisory opinions. On this ground it has in recent years ordered the dismissal of several suits challenging the constitutionality of important acts of Congress. . . .

The Court developed, for its own governance in the cases confessedly within its jurisdiction, a series of rules under which it has avoided passing upon a large part of all the constitutional questions pressed upon it for decision. They are:

1. The Court will not pass upon the constitutionality of legislation in a friendly, nonadversary proceeding, declining because to decide such questions "is legitimate only in the last resort, and as a necessity in the determination of real, earnest, and vital controversy between individuals. It never was the thought that, by means of a friendly suit, a party beaten in the legislature could transfer to the courts an inquiry as to the constitutionality of the legislative act." . . .

2. The Court will not "anticipate a question of constitutional law in advance of the necessity of deciding it." . . .

3. The Court will not "formulate a rule of constitutional law broader than is required by the precise facts to which it is to be applied." . . .

4. The Court will not pass upon a constitutional question, although properly presented by the record, if there is also present some other ground upon which the case may be disposed of. This rule has found most varied application. Thus, if a case can be decided on either of two grounds—one involving a constitutional question, the other a question of statutory construction or general law—the Court will decide only the latter. . . .

5. The Court will not pass upon the validity of a statute upon complaint of one who fails to show that he is injured by its operation. . . .

6. The Court will not pass upon the constitutionality of a statute at the instance of one who has availed himself of its benefits. . . .

7. "When the validity of an act of the Congress is drawn in question, and even if a serious doubt of constitutionality is raised, it is a cardinal principle that this Court will first ascertain whether a construction of the statute is fairly possible by which the question may be avoided." . . .

United States v. Curtiss-Wright Export Corporation (1934)

The defendants in this case, officers in the Curtiss-Wright Export Corporation, were indicted for selling machine guns to Bolivia during its war with Paraguay in 1934. At issue in the case was the President's right to sole conduct of foreign policy and his right to forbid interference in it by independent individuals and organizations. The corporation had acted in contravention of a Joint Resolution of Congress of May 28, 1934, and presidential proclamation of the same day, pursuant to the resolution. Associate Justice George Sutherland delivered the opinion of the Court, finding in favor of the President.

. . . It is important to bear in mind that we are here dealing not alone with an authority vested in the President by an exertion of legislative power, but with such an authority plus the very delicate, plenary and exclusive power of the President as the sole organ of the federal government in the field of international relations—a power which does not require as a basis for its exercise an act of Congress, but which, of course, like every other governmental power, must be exercised in subordination to the applicable provisions of the Constitution. It is quite apparent that if, in the maintenance of our international relations, embarrassment—perhaps serious embarrassment—is to be avoided and success for our aims achieved, congressional legislation which is to be made effective through negotiation and inquiry within the international field must often accord to the President a degree of discretion and freedom from statutory restriction which would not be admissible were domestic affairs alone involved. Moreover, he, not Congress, has the better opportunity of knowing the conditions which prevail in foreign countries, and especially is this true in time of war. He has his confidential sources of information. He has his agents in the form of diplomatic, consular and other officials. Secrecy in respect of information gathered by them may be highly necessary, and the premature disclosure of it productive of harmful results. . . .

In the light of the foregoing observations, it is evident that this Court should not be in haste to apply a general rule which will have the effect of condemning legislation like that under review as constituting an unlawful delegation of legislative power. The principles which justify such legislation find overwhelming support in the unbroken legislative practice which has prevailed almost from the inception of the national government to the present day. . . .

Youngstown Sheet and Tube Company v. *Sawyer* (1952)

During the Korean War, American steelworkers threatened to go on strike. When the labor dispute continued unresolved, President

Harry Truman ordered the Secretary of Commerce to seize the steel companies to keep them operating. The companies sued, and when the case came before the Supreme Court the ruling invalidated the President's order. The Court reasoned that Congress had given no prior authorization for nationalizing the steel industry. Associate Justice Hugo Black delivered the decision.

. . . The President's power, if any, to issue the order must stem either from an act of Congress or from the Constitution itself. There is no statute that expressly authorizes the President to take possession of property as he did here. Nor is there any act of Congress to which our attention has been directed from which such a power can fairly be implied. Indeed, we do not understand the Government to rely on statutory authorization for this seizure. There are two statutes which do authorize the President to take both personal and real property under certain conditions. However, the Government admits that these conditions were not met and that the President's order was not rooted in either of the statutes. . . .

The President's order does not direct that a congressional policy be executed in a manner prescribed by Congress—it directs that a presidential policy be executed in a manner prescribed by the President. The preamble of the order itself, like that of many statutes, sets out reasons why the President believes certain policies should be adopted, proclaims these policies as rules of conduct to be followed, and again, like a statute, authorizes a government official to promulgate additional rules and regulations consistent with the policy proclaimed and needed to carry that policy into execution. The power of Congress to adopt such public policies as those proclaimed by the order is beyond question. It can authorize the taking of private property for public use. It can make laws regulating the relationships between employers and employees, prescribing rules designed to settle labor disputes, and fixing wages and working conditions in certain fields of our economy. The Constitution does not subject this law-making power of Congress to residential or military supervision or control.

It is said that other Presidents without congressional authority have taken possession of private business enterprises in order to settle labor disputes. But even if this be true, Congress has not thereby lost its exclusive constitutional authority to make laws necessary and proper to carry out the powers vested by the Constitution "in the Government of the United States, or any Department or Officer thereof."

The Founders of this Nation entrusted the law-making power to the Congress alone in both good and bad times. It would do no good to recall the historical events, the fears of power and the hopes for freedom that lay behind their choice. Such a review would but confirm our holding that this seizure order cannot stand. . . .

Watkins v. United States (1957)

This case arose during the heyday of congressional investigations into Communist subversion in the United States, commonly known as the McCarthy Era. The defendant had been convicted of contempt of Congress for refusing to answer some questions about persons of his acquaintance and their past activities. He said to the House Committee on Un-American Activities that "I do not believe that any law in this country requires me to testify about persons who may in the past have been Communist party members . . . but who . . . have long since removed themselves from the Communist movement." At issue in the case was the extent of congressional investigative power. Chief Justice Earl Warren found for the defendant in his ruling.

. . . We start with several basic premises on which there is general agreement. The power of the Congress to conduct investigations is inherent in the legislative process. That power is broad. It encompasses inquiries concerning the administration of existing laws as well as proposed or possibly needed statutes. It includes surveys of defects in our social, economic or political system for the purpose of enabling the Congress to remedy them. It comprehends probes into departments of the Federal Government to expose corruption, inefficiency or waste. But broad as is this power of inquiry, it is not unlimited. There is no general authority to expose the private affairs of individuals without justification in terms of the functions of the Congress. This was freely conceded by the Solicitor General in his argument of this case. Nor is the Congress a law enforcement or trial agency. These are functions of the executive and judicial departments of government. No inquiry is an end in itself; it must be related to and in furtherance of a legitimate task of the Congress. Investigations conducted solely for the personal aggrandizement of the investigators or to "punish" those investigated are indefensible.

Baker v. Carr (1962)

Rulings prior to this case had effectively removed the Supreme Court from any decisions on legislative apportionment within the states. For this reason several states had managed to keep their legislatures in the control of rural districts, regardless of massive shifts of population to the cities. Some states had refused to reapportion their districts at all, as was the case with Tennessee in this situation. The ruling in *Baker v. Carr* overturned previous decisions, citing the constitutional mandate that "the judicial power shall extend to all cases in law and equity arising under the Constitution, the laws of the United States, and treaties made under their authority." The ruling also cited the equal protection clause of the Fourteenth Amendment. Associate Justice William Brennan delivered the opinion of the Court.

. . . These appellants seek relief in order to protect or vindicate an interest of their own, and of those similarly situated. Their constitutional claim is, in substance, that the 1901 statute constitutes arbitrary and capricious state action, offensive to the Fourteenth Amendment in its irrational disregard of the standard of apportionment prescribed by the state's constitution or of any standard, effecting a gross disproportion of representation to voting population. The injury which appellants assert is that this classification disfavors the voters in the counties in which they reside, placing them in a position of constitutionally unjustifiable inequality *vis-à-vis* voters in irrationally favored counties. A citizen's right to a vote free of arbitrary impairment by state action has been judicially recognized as a right secured by the Constitution, when such impairment resulted from dilution by a false tally . . . or by a refusal to count votes from arbitrarily selected precincts . . . or by a stuffing of the ballot box. . . .

We hold that the claim pleaded here neither rests upon nor implicates the Guaranty Clause and that its justiciability is therefore not foreclosed by our decisions of cases involving that clause. The District Court misinterpreted *Colegrove v. Green* and other decisions of this Court on which it relied.

Appellants' claim that they are being denied equal protection is justiciable, and if "discrimination is sufficiently shown, the right to relief under the equal protection clause is not diminished by the fact that the discrimination relates to political rights." . . .

CITIZENSHIP

The Supreme Court has ruled upon the nature and rights of citizenship in a number of cases. Two of the better known instances were the *Slaughterhouse* cases of 1873 and *Perez v. Brownell* in 1958. The issues in each case are quite different. The cases of 1873 relate to the definition of citizenship as it was spelled out in the Fourteenth Amendment. The *Perez* case deals with the loss of citizenship. This latter issue has never been resolved.

The Slaughterhouse Cases (1873)

In 1869 the Louisiana legislature granted a monopoly of the slaughterhouse business to one firm in New Orleans. Competitors sued, challenging the monopoly, on the grounds that the Fourteenth Amendment protected them. The state had denied them the equal protection of the laws and deprived them of their property (their businesses) without due process of law. Due process had been defined in the Fifth Amendment and had been inserted into the Fourteenth as well. Its purpose was to set up procedural safeguards for individuals and others in maintaining their rights. When the Fourteenth Amendment was drawn up, the Radical Republicans in Congress intended that the due process clause should protect corporations from state legislation, as well as protecting newly freed blacks in their rights. The Court's ruling here denied the first intended purpose and focused solely on the second and on the nature of citizenship. Associate Justice Samuel F. Miller delivered the ruling, one which was not to stand very long as it related to businesses.

[I]t had been held by this Court, in the celebrated Dred Scott case, only a few years before the outbreak of the Civil War, that a man of African descent, whether a slave or not, was not and could not be a citizen of a state or of the United States. This decision, while it met the condemnation of some of the ablest statesmen and constitutional lawyers of the country, had never been overruled; and, if it was to be accepted as a constitutional limitation of the right of citizenship, then all the negro race who had recently been made freemen were still not only not citizens, but were incapable of becoming so by anything short of an amendment to the Constitution.

To remove this difficulty primarily, and to establish a clear and comprehensive definition of citizenship which should declare what should constitute citizenship of the United States and also citizenship of a state, the 1st clause of the 1st section was framed:

"All persons born or naturalized in the United States and subject to the jurisdiction thereof are citizens of the United States and of the state wherein they reside."

The first observation we have to make on this clause is that it puts at rest both the questions which we stated to have been the subject of differences of opinion. It declares that persons may be citizens of the United States without regard to their citizenship of a particular state, and it overturns the Dred Scott decision by making all persons born within the United States and subject to its jurisdiction citizens of the United States. That its main purpose was to establish the citizenship of the negro can admit of no doubt. The phrase "subject to its jurisdiction" was intended to exclude from its operation children of ministers, consuls and citizens or subjects of foreign states born within the United States.

The next observation is more important in view of the arguments of counsel in the present case. It is that the distinction between citizenship of the United States and citizenship of a state is clearly recognized and established.

Not only may a man be a citizen of the United States without being a citizen of a state, but an important element is necessary to convert the former into the latter. He must reside within the state to make him a citizen of it, but it is only necessary that he should be born or naturalized in the United States to be a citizen of the Union.

It is quite clear, then, that there is a citizenship of the United States and a citizenship of a state, which are distinct from each other and which depend upon different characteristics or circumstances in the individual. . . .

Perez v. Brownell (1958)

Can Congress take away anyone's citizenship for any reason? Congress has legislated that it can do so in certain instances. Voting in a foreign election or holding office under another government are among the reasons Americans have, on rare occasion, lost their citizenship. In this case, the petitioner, Perez, had voted in another country and had been deprived of his citizenship under the terms of the Nationality Act of 1940. The Court agreed with Congress. Chief Justice Earl Warren, however, dissented. Although the law still stands, enforcement of it has become less stringent. An excerpt of Warren's dissent follows.

. . . Citizenship *is* man's basic right for it is nothing less than the right to have rights. Remove this priceless possession and there remains a stateless person, disgraced and degraded in the eyes of his countrymen. He has no lawful claim to protection from any nation, and no nation may assert rights on his behalf. His very existence is at the sufferance of the state within whose borders he happens to be. In this country the expatriate would presumably enjoy, at most, only the limited rights and privileges of aliens, and like the alien he might even be subject to deportation and thereby deprived of the right to assert any rights. This government was not established with power to decree this fate.

The people who created this government endowed it with broad powers. They created a sovereign state with power to function as a sovereignty. But the citizens themselves are sovereign, and their citizenship is not subject to the general powers of their government. Whatever may be the scope of its powers to regulate the conduct and affairs of all persons within its jurisdiction, a government *of* the people cannot take away their citizenship simply because one branch of that government can be said to have a conceivably rational basis for wanting to do so. . . .

The government is without power to take citizenship away from a native-born or lawfully naturalized American. The Fourteenth Amendment recognizes that this priceless right is immune from the exercise of governmental powers. If the Government determines that certain conduct by United States citizens should be prohibited because of anticipated injurious consequences to the conduct of foreign affairs or to some other legitimate governmental interest, it may within the limits of the Constitution proscribe such activity and assess appropriate punishment. But every exercise of governmental power must find its source in the Constitution. The power to denationalize is not within the letter or the spirit of the powers with which our Government was endowed. The citizen may elect to renounce his citizenship, and under some circumstances he may be found to have abandoned his status by voluntarily performing acts that compromise his undivided allegiance to his country. The mere act of voting in a foreign election, however, without regard to the circumstances attending the participation, is not sufficient to show a voluntary abandonment of citizenship. . . .

THE DESEGREGATION CASES

After the Civil War, the white citizens of the South reimposed upon blacks many of the elements of discrimination that had existed under slavery. These Black Codes and Jim Crow laws severely restricted the rights of blacks and officially segregated them from whites in schools, public accommodations, and other instances.

In 1896, the Supreme Court ruled in favor of "separate but equal" facilities. In 1954, the Court overturned that ruling in the famous *Brown* v. *Board of Education of Topeka* decision.

Plessy v. *Ferguson* (1896)

A Louisiana law of 1890 stipulated that railroads must provide equal but separate accommodations for white and black passengers. Homer A. Plessy, a mulatto, challenged the law by riding in a whites-only car. He was arrested, tried, and convicted. On appeal, the case went to the Supreme Court. Associate Justice Henry B. Brown delivered the majority opinion, which held the Louisiana segregation law constitutional. Associate Justice John Marshall Harlan was the lone dissenter. Ironically, his dissent would become the majority fifty-eight years later in the Brown case.

. . . So far, then, as a conflict with the Fourteenth Amendment is concerned, the case reduces itself to the question whether the statute of Louisiana is a reasonable regulation, and with respect to this there must necessarily be a large discretion on the part of the legislature. In determining the question of reasonableness it is at liberty to act with reference to the established usages, customs and traditions of the people, and with a view to the promotion of their comfort, and the preservation of the public peace and good order. Gauged by this standard, we cannot say that a law which authorizes or even requires the separation of the two races in public conveyances is unreasonable, or more obnoxious to the Fourteenth Amendment than the acts of Congress requiring separate schools for colored children in the District of Columbia, the constitutionality of which does not seem to have been questioned, or the corresponding acts of state legislatures. . . .

Legislation is powerless to eradicate racial instincts or to abolish distinctions based upon physical differences, and the attempt to do so can only result in accentuating the difficulties of the present situation. If the civil and political rights of both races be equal, one cannot be inferior to the other civilly or politically. If one race be inferior to the other socially, the Constitution of the United States cannot put them upon the same plane. . . .

Brown v. Board of Education of Topeka (1954)

This Court decision reversed the *Plessy* doctrine on "separate but equal" facilities as it related to education. Coming a few years before the Civil Rights movement got under way, it lent great support to efforts by blacks to regain the rights they had enjoyed so briefly after the Civil War. Chief Justice Earl Warren delivered the opinion for a unanimous Court.

[T]here are findings below that the Negro and white schools involved have been equalized, or are being equalized, with respect to buildings, curricula, qualifications and salaries of teachers, and other "tangible" factors. Our decision, therefore, cannot turn on merely a comparison of these tangible factors in the Negro and white schools involved in each of the cases. We must look instead to the effect of segregation itself on public education.

In approaching this problem, we cannot turn the clock back to 1868 when the Amendment was adopted, or even to 1896 when *Plessy v. Ferguson* was written. We must consider public education in the light of its full development and its present place in American life throughout the Nation. Only in this way can it be determined if segregation in public schools deprives these plaintiffs of the equal protection of the laws.

Today, education is perhaps the most important function of state and local governments. Compulsory school attendance laws and the great expenditures for education both demonstrate our recognition of the importance of education to our democratic society. It is required in the performance of our most basic public responsibilities, even service in the armed forces. It is the very foundation of good citizenship. Today it is a principal instrument in awakening the child to cultural values, in preparing him for later professional training, and in helping him to adjust normally to his environment. In these days, it is doubtful that any child may reasonably be expected to succeed in life if he is denied the opportunity of an education. Such an opportunity, where the state has undertaken to provide it, is a right which must be made available to all on equal terms.

We come then to the question presented: Does segregation of children in public schools solely on the basis of race, even though the physical facilities and other "tangible" factors may be equal, deprive the children of the minority group of equal educational opportunities? We believe that it does. . . . The effect of this separation on their educational opportunities was well stated by a finding in the Kansas case by a court which nevertheless felt compelled to rule against the Negro plaintiffs.

"Segregation of white and colored children in public schools has a detrimental effect upon the colored children. The impact is greater when it has the sanction of the law; for the policy of separating the races is usually interpreted as denoting the inferiority of the Negro group. A sense of inferiority affects the motivation of a child to learn. Segregation with the sanction of law, therefore, has a tendency to retard the educational and mental development of Negro children and to deprive them of some of the benefits they would receive in a racially integrated school system."

Whatever may have been the extent of psychological knowledge at the time of *Plessy* v. *Ferguson*, this finding is amply supported by modern authority. Any language in *Plessy* v. *Ferguson* contrary to this finding is rejected.

We conclude that in the field of public education the doctrine of "separate but equal" has no place. Separate educational facilities are inherently unequal. Therefore, we hold that the plaintiffs and others similarly situated for whom the actions have been brought are, by reason of the segregation complained of, deprived of the equal protection of the laws guaranteed by the Fourteenth Amendment. This disposition makes unnecessary any discussion whether such segregation also violates the Due Process Clause of the Fourteenth Amendment. . . .

AN ASSORTMENT OF RIGHTS CASES

The Supreme Court decisions and dissents that follow range from statements on the rights of corporations (as in the well-known Northern Securities case of 1904) to the rights of individuals. Two cases deal with freedom of expression: *Gitlow* v. *New York* and *Near* v. *Minnesota*. *Engel* v. *Vitale* is the still-controversial school prayer decision. *Gideon* v. *Wainwright* deals with the right of an individual accused of a crime to have a lawyer. *Miranda* v. *Arizona* covers another aspect of criminal law: the right of an accused person to remain silent. *Roe* v. *Wade* is the abortion decision that has aroused so much controversy since it was handed down in 1973. *University of California* v. *Bakke* deals with affirmative action programs as they relate to higher education—another issue that has not been resolved. *Bowers* v. *Hardwick* is an example of Oliver Wendell Holmes's dictum that: "Great cases like hard cases make bad law." It is the 1986 sodomy ruling that immediately calls forth strong differences of opinion on the matter of an individual's right to privacy.

Northern Securities Company v. *United States* (1904)

Northern Securities had been formed as a holding company in 1901 to control three railroads: the Northern Pacific, the Burlington, and the Great Northern. Under the terms of the Sherman Antitrust Act, President Theodore Roosevelt ordered his Attorney General, Philander Knox, to file suit to break up this apparent monopoly. The suit was successful. John Marshall Harlan's majority opinion ruled in favor of the Justice Department. Associate Justice Oliver Wendell Holmes dissented. His dissent was somewhat prophetic: The three railroads have since been merged into one again. Portions of the Holmes dissent follow.

. . . Great cases like hard cases make bad law. For great cases are called great not by reason of their real importance in shaping the law of the future, but because of some accident of immediate, overwhelming interest which appeals to the feelings and distorts the judgment. These immediate interests exercise a kind of hydraulic pressure which makes what previously was clear seem doubtful, and before which even well-settled principles of law will bend. . . .

In the first place, size in the case of railroads is an inevitable incident and if it were an objection under the act, the Great Northern and the Northern Pacific already were too great and encountered the law. In the next place, in the case of railroads it is evident that the size of the combination is reached for other ends than those which would make them monopolies. The combinations are not formed for the purpose of excluding others from the field. Finally, even a small railroad will have the same tendency to exclude others from its narrow area that great ones have to exclude others from a greater one, and the statute attacks the small monopolies as well as the great. The very words of the act make such a distinction impossible in this case, and it has not been attempted in express terms.

If the charter which I have imagined above would have been good notwithstanding the monopoly, in a popular sense, which it created, one next is led to ask whether and why a combination or consolidation of existing roads, although in actual competition, into one company of exactly the same powers and extent, would be any more obnoxious to the law. . . . The monopoly would be the same as if the roads were consolidated after they had begun to compete—and it is on the footing of monopoly that I now am supposing the objection made.

But to meet the objection to the prevention of competition at the same time, I will suppose that three parties apply to a state for charters; one for each of two new and possibly competing lines respectively, and one for both of these lines, and that the charter is granted to the last. I think that charter would be good, and I think the whole argument to the contrary rests on a popular instead of an accurate and legal conception of what the word "monopolize" in the statute means. I repeat, that in my opinion there is no attempt to monopolize, and what, as I have said, in my judgment amounts to the same thing, that there is no combination in restraint of trade, until something is done with the intent to exclude strangers to the combination from competing with it in some part of the business which it carries on. . . .

Gitlow v. *New York* (1925)

After World War II, an anti-Communist hysteria overtook the United States. During this "Red Scare," Benjamin Gitlow was convicted, under New York's Criminal Anarchy statute, of publishing an inflammatory political pamphlet. The Supreme Court upheld the conviction. Associate Justice Edward T. Sanford believed that incendiary publications such as Gitlow's were beyond the protection of the First Amendment on freedom of speech. Oliver Wendell Holmes dissented, and it is his view that has since prevailed. A small section of his dissent follows.

. . . It is said that this Manifesto was more than a theory, that it was an incitement. Every idea is an incitement. It offers itself for belief, and, if believed, it is acted on unless some other belief outweighs it or some failure of energy stifles the movement at its birth. The only difference between the expression of an opinion and an incitement in the narrower sense is the speaker's enthusiasm for the result. Eloquence may set fire to reason. But whatever may be thought of the redundant discourse before us, it had no chance of starting a present conflagration. If in the long run the beliefs expressed in proletarian dictatorship are destined to be accepted by the dominant forces of the community, the only meaning of free speech is that they should be given their chance and have their way.

If the publication of this document had been laid as an attempt to induce an uprising against government at once and not at some indefinite time in the future, it would have presented a different question. The object would have been one with which the law might deal, subject to the doubt whether there was any danger that the publication could produce any result, or in other words, whether it was not futile and too remote from possible consequences. But the indictment alleges the publication and nothing more.

Near v. Minnesota (1931)

A Minnesota statute of 1925 outlawed any "malicious, scandalous and defamatory newspaper, magazine, or other periodical." The *Saturday Press* of Minneapolis had been forbidden to publish on account of this law. The Supreme Court found the statute an unconstitutional restriction on freedom of the press. It also held that the publisher had the right to criticize public officials, even in the strongest terms, without having to prove in advance the truth of everything published. Chief Justice Charles Evans Hughes delivered the opinion.

. . . The statute in question cannot be justified by reason of the fact that the publisher is permitted to show, before injunction issues, that the matter published is true and is published with good motives and for justifiable ends. If such a statute, authorizing suppression and injunction on such a basis, is constitutionally valid, it would be equally permissible for the legislature to provide that at any time the publisher of any newspaper could be brought before a court, or even an administrative officer (as the constitutional protection may not be regarded as resting on mere procedural details) and required to produce proof of the truth of his publication, or of what he intended to publish, and of his motives, or stand enjoined. If this can be done, the legislature may provide machinery for determining in the complete exercise of its discretion what are justifiable ends and restrain publication accordingly. And it would be but a step to a complete system of censorship. The recognition of authority to impose previous restraint upon publication in order to protect the community against the circulation of charges of misconduct, and especially of official misconduct, necessarily would carry with it the admission of the authority of the censor against which the constitutional barrier was erected. The preliminary freedom, by virtue of the very reason for its existence, does not depend, as this Court has said, on proof of truth. . . .

Engel v. Vitale (1962)

Religion has always played a significant role in American public life as well as private. For generations the notion that Bible reading and prayer in public schools were a violation of the First Amendment was not even considered. Only gradually did the religious (and often nonreligious) diversity of the United States emerge as a legal force. This case arose over a school prayer that had been prescribed by the Board of Education of Union Free School District No. 9 in New Hyde Park, New York. Associate Judge Hugo Black delivered the majority opinion.

. . . Under [the First] Amendment's prohibition against governmental establishment of religion, as reinforced by the provisions of the Fourteenth

Amendment, government in this country, be it state or federal, is without power to prescribe by law any particular form of prayer which is to be used as an official prayer in carrying on any program of governmentally sponsored religious activity.

There can be no doubt that New York's state prayer program officially establishes the religious beliefs embodied in the Regents' prayer. . . . Neither the fact that the prayer may be denominationally neutral nor the fact that its observance on the part of the students is voluntary can serve to free it from the limitations of the Establishment Clause, as it might from the Free Exercise Clause, of the First Amendment. . . . Although these two clauses may in certain instances overlap, they forbid two quite different kinds of governmental encroachment upon religious freedom. The Establishment Clause, unlike the Free Exercise Clause, does not depend upon any showing of direct governmental compulsion and is violated by the enactment of laws which establish an official religion whether those laws operate directly to coerce nonobserving individuals or not. This is not to say, of course, that laws officially prescribing a particular form of religious worship do not involve coercion of such individuals. When the power, prestige and financial support of government is placed behind a particular religious belief, the indirect coercive pressure upon religious minorities to conform to the prevailing officially approved religion is plain. But the purposes underlying the Establishment Clause go much further than that. Its first and most immediate purpose rested on the belief that a union of government and religion tends to destroy government and to degrade religion. The history of governmentally established religion, both in England and in this country, showed that whenever government had allied itself with one particular form of religion, the inevitable result had been that it had incurred the hatred, disrespect and even contempt of those who held contrary beliefs. . . . The Establishment Clause thus stands as an expression of principle on the part of the Founders of our Constitution that religion is too personal, too sacred, too holy, to permit its "unhallowed perversion" by a civil magistrate. Another purpose of the Establishment Clause rested upon an awareness of the historical fact that governmentally established religions and religious persecutions go hand in hand. . . .

Gideon v. *Wainwright* (1963)

The Sixth Amendment guarantees the accused in a criminal proceeding the right to counsel. This case arose after the petitioner, Gideon, had been arrested for a felony in Florida. He could not afford a lawyer, and the court refused to appoint one for him. Gideon was forced to conduct his own defense. When an appeal on these proceedings reached the Supreme Court, Associate Justice Hugo Black delivered the unanimous decision in Gideon's favor.

. . . Not only these precedents but also reason and reflection require us to recognize that in our adversary system of criminal justice, any person haled into court who is too poor to hire a lawyer cannot be assured a fair trial unless counsel is provided for him. This seems to us to be an obvious truth. Governments, both state and federal, quite properly spend vast sums of money to establish machinery to try defendants accused of crime. Lawyers to prosecute are everywhere deemed essential to protect the public's interest in an orderly society. Similarly, there are few defendants charged with crime, few indeed, who fail to hire the best lawyers they can get to prepare and present their defense. That government hires lawyers to prosecute and defendants who have the money hire lawyers to defend are the strongest indications of the widespread belief that lawyers in criminal courts are necessities, not luxuries. The right of one charged with crime to counsel may not be deemed fundamental and essential to fair trials in some countries, but it is in ours. From the very beginning, our state and national constitutions and laws have laid great emphasis on procedural and substantive safeguards designed to assure fair trials before impartial tribunals in which every defendant stands equal before the law. This noble ideal cannot be realized if the poor man charged with crime has to face his accusers without a lawyer to assist him. . . .

Miranda v. *Arizona* (1966)

The Fifth Amendment in the Bill of Rights provides a guarantee against self-incrimination. Ernesto Miranda was arrested in Phoenix, Arizona, on charges of rape and robbery. Under intense police questioning he made a signed confession that was admitted as evidence in his trial, and he was convicted. When this case came before the Supreme Court, Chief Justice Earl Warren delivered the majority opinion disavowing such police interrogatory procedures.

The cases before us raise questions which go to the roots of our concepts of American criminal jurisprudence: the restraints society must observe consistent with the federal Constitution in prosecuting individuals for crime. More specifically, we deal with the admissibility of statements obtained from an individual who is subjected to custodial police interrogation and the necessity for procedures which assure that the individual is accorded his privilege under the Fifth Amendment to the Constitution not to be compelled to incriminate himself. . . . Our holding . . . briefly stated . . . is this: the prosecution may not use statements, whether exculpatory or inculpatory, stemming from custodial interrogation of the defendant unless it demonstrates the use of procedural safeguards effective to secure the privilege against self-incrimination.

By custodial interrogation, we mean questioning initiated by law-enforcement officers after a person has been taken into custody or otherwise deprived of his freedom of action in any significant way. As for the procedural safeguards to be employed, unless other fully effective means are devised to inform accused persons of their right of silence and to assure a continuous opportunity to exercise it, the following measures are required:

Prior to any questioning, the person must be warned that he has a right to remain silent, that any statement he does make may be used as evidence against him, and that he has a right to the presence of an attorney, either retained or appointed. The defendant may waive effectuation of these rights, provided the waiver is made voluntarily, knowingly, and intelligently. If, however, he indicates in any manner and at any stage of the process that he wishes to consult with an attorney before speaking, there can be no questioning. Likewise, if the individual is alone and indicates in any manner that he does not wish to be interrogated, the police may not question him. The mere fact that he may have answered some questions or volunteered some statements on his own does not deprive him of the right to refrain from answering any further inquiries until he has consulted with an attorney and thereafter consents to be questioned. . . .

Roe v. Wade (1973)

During the late 1960s, when the Women's Liberation movement was gaining strength, a concerted effort was made to eliminate restrictions on the performance of abortions. Liberal laws were passed in several states. When a Texas statute challenged the liberal view, an appeal eventually reached the Supreme Court. The Court pronounced in favor of liberal abortion laws, with some restrictions. Few decisions have resulted in so much social and religious conflict in this century. Associate Justice Harry A. Blackmun read the majority opinion.

. . . This right of privacy, whether it be founded in the Fourteenth Amendment's concept of personal liberty and restrictions upon state action, as we feel it is, or, as the District Court determined, in the Ninth Amendment's reservation of rights to the people, is broad enough to encompass a woman's decision whether or not to terminate her pregnancy. The detriment that the State would impose upon the pregnant woman by denying this choice altogether is apparent. Specific and direct harm medically diagnosable even in early pregnancy may be involved. Maternity, or additional offspring, may force upon the woman a distressful life and future. Psychological harm may be imminent. Mental and physical health may be taxed by child care. There is also the distress, for all concerned, associated with the unwanted child, and there is the problem of bringing a child into a family already unable, psychologically and otherwise, to care for it. In other cases, as in this one, the additional difficulties and continuing stigma of unwed motherhood may be involved. All these are factors the woman and her responsible physician necessarily will consider in consultation. . . .

With respect to the State's important and legitimate interest in the health of the mother, the "compelling" point, in the light of present medical knowledge, is at approximately the end of the first trimester. This is so because of the now established medical fact, referred to above . . . that until the end of the first trimester mortality in abortion may be less than mortality in normal childbirth. It follows that, from and after this point, a State may regulate the abortion procedure to the extent that the regulation reasonably relates to the preservation and protection of maternal health. Examples of permissible state regulation in this area are requirements as to the qualifications of the person who is to perform the abortion; as to the licensure of that person; as to the facility in which the procedure is to be performed, that is, whether it must be a hospital or may be a clinic or some other place of less-than-hospital status; as to the licensing of the facility; and the like.

This means, on the other hand, that, for the period of pregnancy prior to this "compelling" point, the attending physician, in consultation with his patient, is free to determine, without regulation by the State, that in his medical judgment the patient's pregnancy should be terminated. If that decision is reached, the judgment may be effectuated by an abortion free of interference by the State. . . .

University of California v. *Bakke* (1978)

Affirmative action is the attempt to remedy past racial, sex, and ethnic discrimination in education and the work force. Under provisions of the 1964 Civil Rights Act, as well as executive orders and court rulings, the federal government requires certain businesses and educational institutions receiving federal money to implement affirmative action programs. Often this has been done on a quota basis, leading to charges of reverse discrimination. Under the Bakke ruling the Court held that fixed quotas may not be set aside for minority medical school applicants if white applicants are denied a chance to compete for those places. Associate Justice Lewis F. Powell, Jr., read the majority opinion.

. . . The State certainly has a legitimate and substantial interest in ameliorating, or eliminating where feasible, the disabling effects of identified discrimination. The line of school desegregation cases, commencing with Brown, attests to the importance of this state goal and the commitment of the judiciary to affirm all lawful means towards its attainment. In the school cases, the States were required by court order to redress the wrongs worked by specific instances of racial discrimination. That goal was far more focused than the remedying of the effects of "societal discrimination," an amorphous concept of injury that may be ageless in its reach into the past.

We have never approved a classification that aids persons perceived as members of relatively victimized groups at the expense of other innocent individuals in the absence of judicial, legislative, or administrative findings of constitutional or statutory violations. . . . After such findings have been made, the governmental interest in preferring members of the injured groups at the expense of others is substantial, since the legal rights of the victims must be vindicated. In such a case, the extent of the injury and the consequent remedy will have been judicially, legislatively, or administratively defined. Also, the remedial action usually remains subject to continuing oversight to assure that it will work the least harm possible to other innocent persons competing for the benefit. Without such findings of constitutional or statutory violations, it cannot be said that the government has any greater interest in helping one individual than in refraining from harming another. Thus, the government has no compelling justification for inflicting such harm.

Petitioner does not purport to have made, and is in no position to make, such findings. Its broad mission is education, not the formulation of any legislative policy or the adjudication of particular claims of illegality. . . .

Hence, the purpose of helping certain groups whom the faculty of the Davis Medical School perceived as victims of "societal discrimination" does not justify a classification that imposes disadvantages upon persons like respondent, who bear no responsibility for whatever harm the beneficiaries of the special admissions program are thought to have suffered. To hold otherwise would be to convert a remedy heretofore reserved for violations of legal rights into a privilege that all institutions throughout the Nation could grant at their pleasure to whatever groups are perceived as victims of societal discrimination. That is a step we have never approved. . . .

In summary, it is evident that the Davis special admission program involves the use of an explicit racial classification never before countenanced by this Court. It tells applicants who are not Negro, Asian, or Chicano that they are totally excluded from a specific percentage of the seats in an entering class. No matter how strong their qualifications, quantitative and extracurricular, including their own potential for contribution to educational diversity, they are never afforded the chance to compete with applicants from the preferred groups for the special admissions seats. At the same time, the preferred applicants have the opportunity to compete for every seat in the class.

The fatal flaw in petitioner's preferential program is its disregard of individual rights as guaranteed by the Fourteenth Amendment. . . . Such rights are not absolute. But when a State's distribution of benefits or imposition of burdens hinges on the color of a person's skin or ancestry, that individual is entitled to a demonstration that the challenged classification is necessary to promote a substantial state interest. Petitioner has failed to carry this burden. For this reason, that portion of the California court's judgment holding petitioner's special admissions program invalid under the Fourteenth Amendment must be affirmed. . . .

Bowers v. Hardwick (1986)

For several decades the Supreme Court had been expanding the individual's right to privacy in a variety of cases. The abortion decision of 1973 was one instance. In this 1986 case that trend was suddenly halted. The case arose from prosecution under a 1984 Georgia statute criminalizing sodomy. Associate Justice Byron R. White delivered the majority opinion. Following that is a dissent by Associate Justice Harry A. Blackmun.

JUSTICE WHITE: . . . This case does not require a judgment on whether laws against sodomy between consenting adults in general, or between homosexuals in particular, are wise or desirable. It raises no question about the right or propriety of state legislative decisions to repeal their laws that criminalize homosexual sodomy, or of state court decisions invalidating those laws on state constitutional grounds. The issue presented is whether the Federal Constitution confers a fundamental right upon homosexuals to engage in sodomy and hence invalidates the laws of the many States that still make such conduct illegal and have done so for a very long time. The case also calls for some judgment about the limits of the Court's role in carrying out its constitutional mandate. . . .

Striving to assure itself and the public that announcing rights not readily identifiable in the Constitution's text involves much more than the imposition of the Justices' own choice of values on the States and the Federal Government, the Court has sought to identify the nature of the rights qualifying for heightened judicial protection. . . .

It is obvious to us that neither of these formulations would extend a fundamental right to homosexuals to engage in acts of consensual sodomy. Proscriptions against that conduct have ancient roots. . . .

Nor are we inclined to take a more expansive view of our authority to discover new fundamental rights imbedded in the Due Process Clause. The Court is most vulnerable and comes nearest to illegitimacy when it deals with judge-made constitutional law having little or no cognizable roots in the language or design of the Constitution. . . . Plainly enough, otherwise illegal conduct is not always immunized whenever it occurs in the home. Victimless crimes, such as the possession and use of illegal drugs do not escape the law where they are committed at home. . . . And if respondent's submission is limited to the voluntary sexual conduct between consenting adults, it would be difficult, except by fiat, to limit the claimed right to homosexual conduct while leaving exposed to prosecution adultery, incest, and other sexual crimes even though they are committed in the home. We are unwilling to start down that road.

Even if the conduct at issue here is not a fundamental right, respondent asserts that there must be a rational basis for the law and that there is none in this case other than the presumed belief of a majority of the electorate in Georgia that homosexual sodomy is immoral and unacceptable. This is said to be an inadequate rationale to support the law. The law, however, is constantly based on notions of morality, and if all laws representing essentially moral choices are to be invalidated under the Due Process Clause, the courts will be very busy indeed. Even respondent makes no such claim, but insists that majority sentiments about the morality of homosexuality should be declared inadequate. We do not agree, and are unpersuaded that the sodomy laws of some 25 States should be invalidated on this basis. . . .

JUSTICE BLACKMUN: This case is no more about "a fundamental right to engage in homosexual sodomy," as the Court purports to declare. . . . Rather, this case is about "the most comprehensive of rights and the right most valued by civilized men," namely, "the right to be let alone." . . .

Like Justice Holmes, I believe that "[i]t is revolting to have no better reason for a rule of law than that so it was laid down in the time of Henry IV. It is still more revolting if the grounds upon which it was laid down have vanished long since, and the rule simply persists from blind imitation of the past." . . . I believe we must analyze respondent's claim in the light of the values that underlie the constitutional right to privacy. If that right means anything, it means that before Georgia can prosecute its citizens for making choices about the most intimate aspects of their lives, it must do more than assert that the choice they have made is an " 'abominable crime not fit to be named among Christians.' " . . .

First, the Court's almost obsessive focus on homosexual activity is particularly hard to justify in light of the broad language Georgia has used. Unlike the Court, the Georgia Legislature has not proceeded on the assumption that homosexuals are so different from other citizens that their lives may be controlled in a way that would not be tolerated if it limited the choices of those other citizens. . . . Only the most willful blindness could obscure the fact that sexual intimacy is "a sensitive, key relationship of human existence, central to family life, community welfare, and the development of human personality." . . . In a variety of circumstances we have recognized that a necessary corollary of giving individuals freedom to choose how to conduct their lives is acceptance of the fact that different individuals will make different choices. For example, in holding that the clearly important state interest in public education should give way to a competing claim by the Amish to the effect that extended formal schooling threatened their way of life, the Court declared: "There can be no assumption that today's majority is 'right' and the Amish and others like them are 'wrong.' A way of life that is odd or even erratic but interferes with no rights or interests of others is not to be condemned because it is different." . . . The Court claims that its decision today merely refuses to recognize a fundamental right to engage in homosexual sodomy; what the Court really has refused to recognize is the fundamental interest all individuals have in controlling the nature of their intimate associations with others.

The behavior for which Hardwick faces prosecution occurred in his own home, a place to which the Fourth Amendment attaches special significance. The Court's treatment of this aspect of the case is symptomatic of its overall refusal to consider the broad principles that have informed our treatment of privacy in specific cases. . . .

This case involves no real interference with the rights of others, for the mere knowledge that other individuals do not adhere to one's value system cannot be a legally cognizable interest . . . let alone an interest that can justify invading the houses, hearts, and minds of citizens who choose to live their lives differently.

It took but three years for the Court to see the error in its analysis in *Minersville School District* v. *Gobitis*, 310 U.S. 586 (1940), and to recognize that the threat to national cohesion posed by a refusal to salute the flag was vastly outweighed by the threat to those same values posed by compelling such a salute. . . . I can only hope that here, too, the Court soon will reconsider its analysis and conclude that depriving individuals of the right to choose for themselves how to conduct their intimate relationships poses a far greater threat to the values most deeply rooted in our Nation's history than tolerance of nonconformity could ever do. Because I think the Court today betrays those values, I dissent.

Index